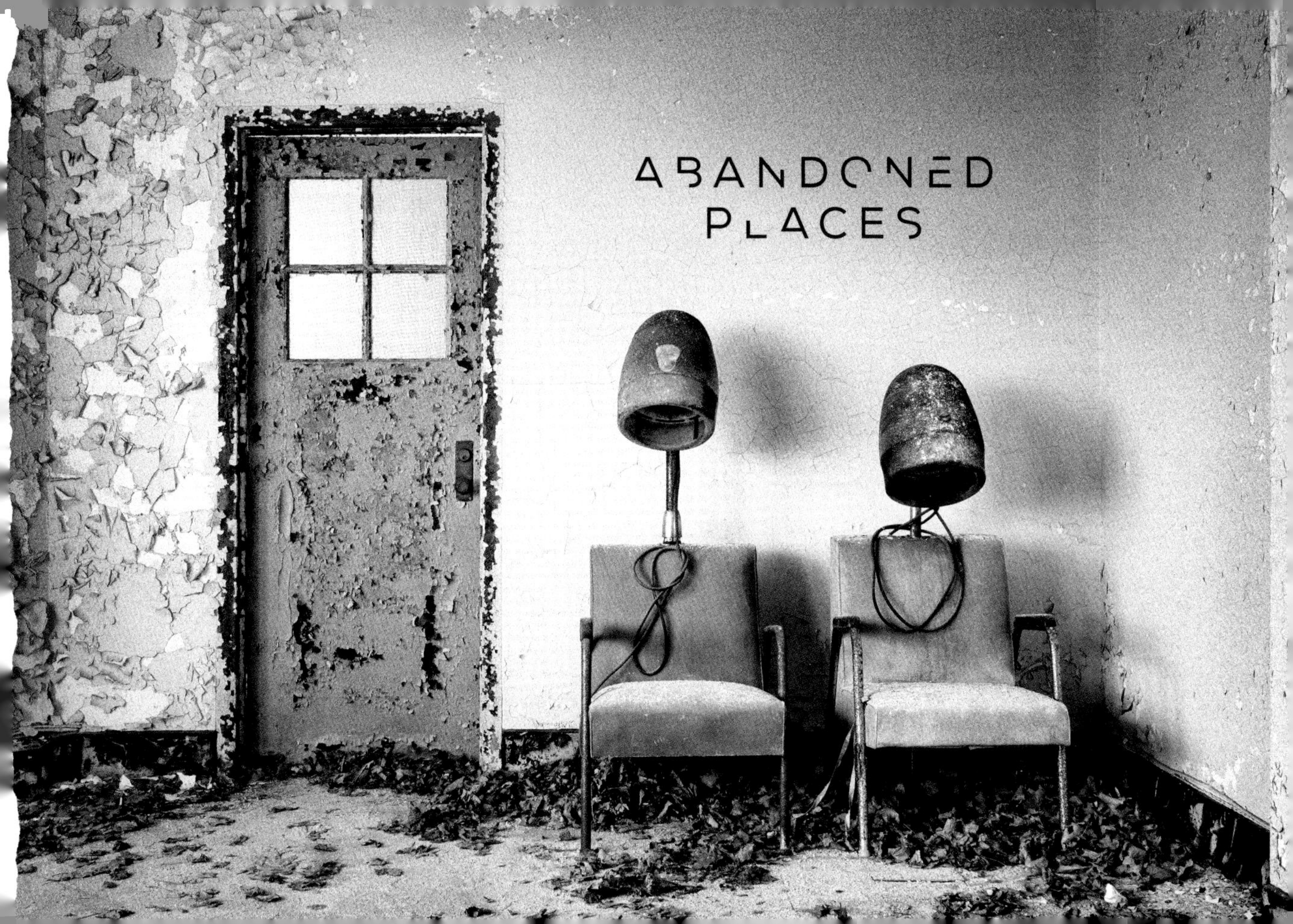
ABANDONED
PLACES

HENK VAN RENSBERGEN

ABANDONED PLACES

LANNOO

P1: New Jersey State Lunatic Asylum, USA, 2004

PREFACE

For days we had been sneaking around the villa in the dunes. Was anyone still living there? Some of the windows had been broken and the front door was wide open, but when we peered inside we could see that there was still furniture there, crockery in the cupboards and the remains of food on the table. Taking that step through the front door seemed like the most challenging feat, but our excitement only increased as we ventured further in. We walked past the coats on the coat stand and into the living room.

The stairs creaked as we climbed them. Suddenly we heard stumbling; there were other people on the stairs. In the half-darkness there was total panic, as everyone tried to run for the front door at the same time, and there, in the daylight, we recognized the boys we had been playing with the previous day on the beach.

It felt as though the summer holidays would never end. We got to know every nook and cranny of the ghost villa. There was an ancient black and white TV, which exploded with a loud bang, sending a cloud of dust into the room. We played hide and seek in the upstairs bedrooms and came upon an old clock that still worked. A year later, the villa had disappeared and the year after that, new apartments had risen up in its place.

I bought my first camera in 1984, when I was 16. I experimented endlessly with things like lighting, night photography and double exposures, and I would increasingly take my camera with me when I had discovered a new abandoned building. In those early years, I mainly had a fascination with all things industrial. Once I got my driving license, I was able to travel further afield towards Charleroi, Anderlues, Tertre, Ghent or Zeebrugge, and of course, to the Buda Marly factory by the canal in Brussels.

In the early 1990s, I built a website (which at that time was still fairly unique) and called it 'Industrial Art'. It was a rather silly name and I replaced it when I had my own domain name with 'abandoned-places.com'. For the first time, I made contact with a number of other photographers who shared my enthusiasm. The press heard about me and the number of 'hits' grew.

Slowly, a network of urban explorers began to develop. We came into contact via our websites, exchanged information and occasionally met up. These early friendships are still alive today, and they have left me with many fond and often exciting memories. Photography became more and more important to me. The challenge was not to strictly record what was there to see, but to reproduce the atmosphere: the tension, the complexity, the emotion, the surprise and the feeling. I went back to the same places regularly, 'befriended' the local iron thieves, and saw how factories were slowly looted and finally razed to the ground.

My flying career enabled me to explore abandoned places abroad. I visited most European countries, went three times to Japan, to Sri Lanka, Mexico, Brazil, Africa, the United States and many more places. I met some fantastic people whom I teamed up with to explore. I was lucky enough to discover New Jersey with John and Nick, Detroit with Brett, Florida and Alabama with Ryan.

When safe to do so, I like to venture out on my own.

In 2007, Lannoo published my first book. The book was reprinted twice, and it has now acquired cult status. In the years that followed, I staged a number of exhibitions and my photos were shown at art fairs in Belgium and the Netherlands. Various magazines, newspapers, websites, TV shows and musicians used my work. In 2010, *Abandoned Places 2* came out, in 2012 *Abandoned Places 3* and in 2014 *The Photographer's Selection*.

With the explosive interest in urban exploration, many new locations were discovered. Explorers jointly hit the road and traveled in groups from factory to castle looking for the ultimate photo, only to find out that their creation appeared in nearly the same way on Facebook or Flickr. For most of them this won't spoil the fun, but for me it was a sign that I had to look for a new idea, a new story that I could perhaps tell in my next book. The book that you are now reading is a collection of my best work, the peaks of my many journeys, from my very first industrial photos, often in black & white, to inaccessible places on the other side of the world.

Enjoy this adventure, and should you ever want to start one yourself, think about the following: 'Take nothing but photos, leave nothing but footsteps.' In any case, it's never the intention to force open windows or doors and thus to literally break in. It is equally important not to invade the privacy of the former residents. Call it urban exploration ethics. ◆

8 Triage Lavoir du Roton, Belgium, 1996

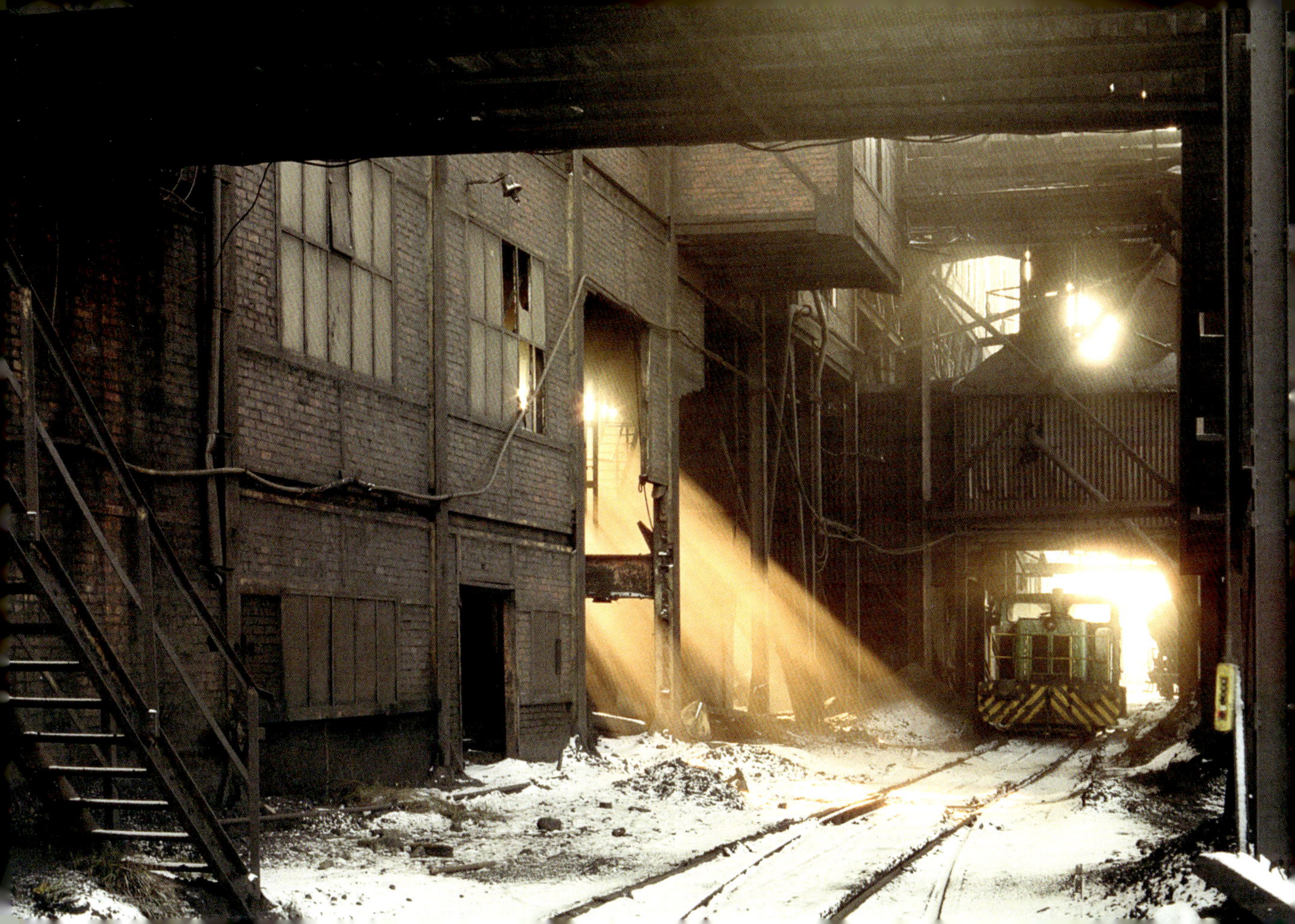

The Electric Company, Philadelphia, USA, 2008

 Tertre, Belgium, 2001–2003

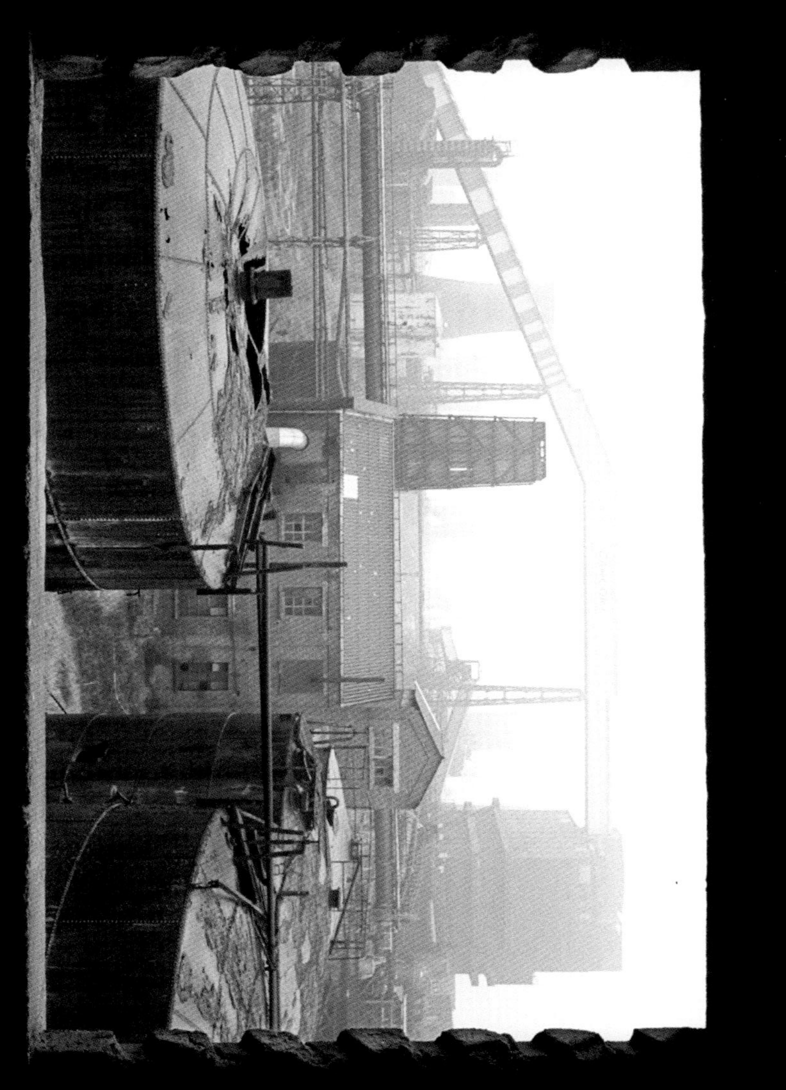

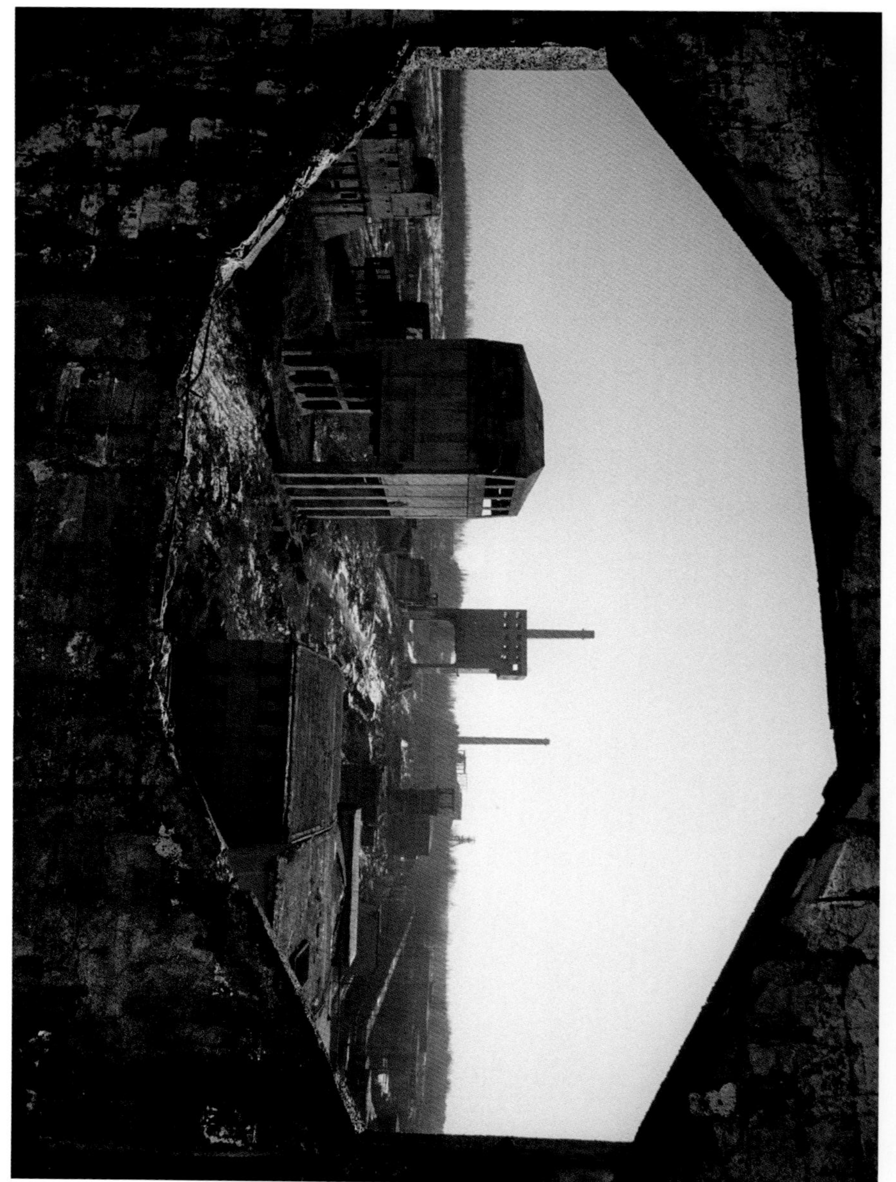

 Ruda Slaska, Poland, 2001

Carsid Marsinelle, Belgium, 2010

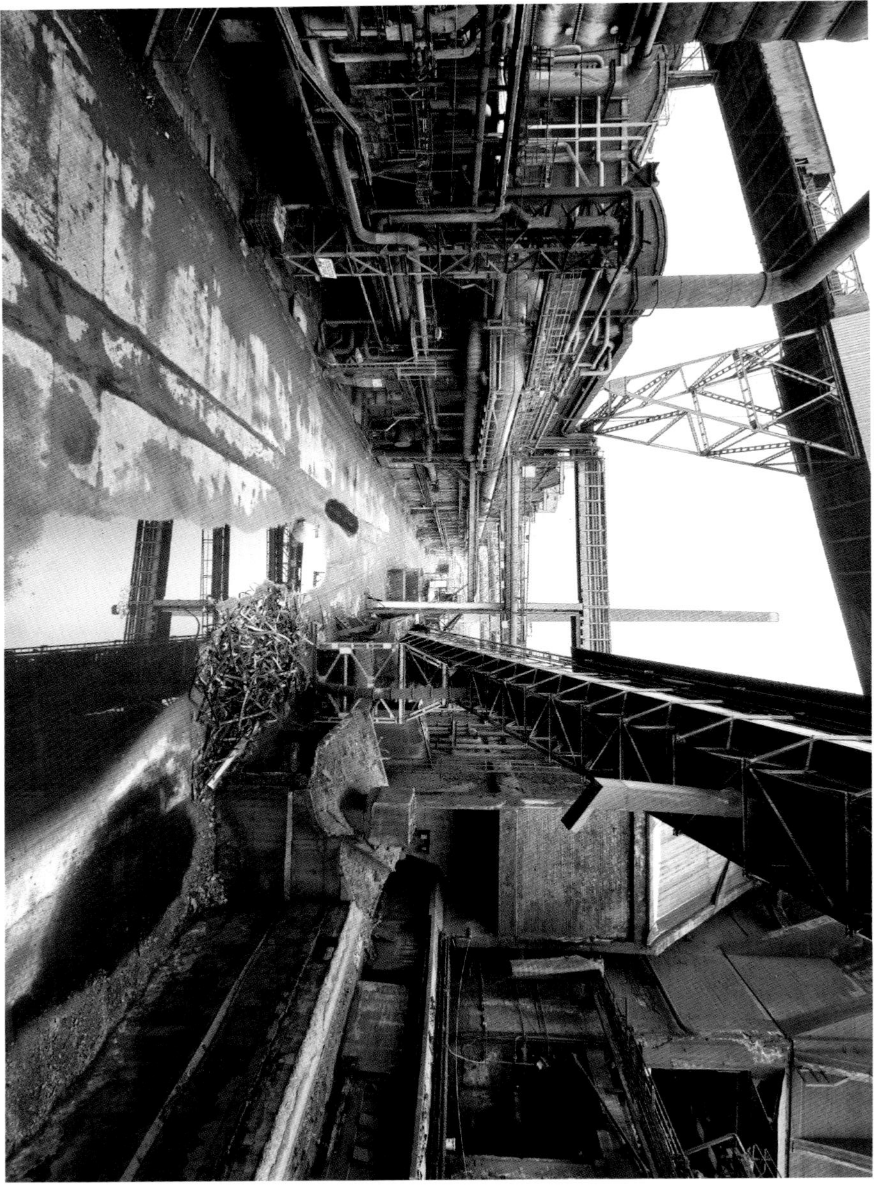

SAFEA ▹

AMMONIA FACTORY, BELGIUM
2003–2006

When I 'discovered' this abandoned factory, it was still completely intact, yet it was virtually impossible to gain entry. Behind the gate lived Georges, the dog and his wife (in ascending order of danger). Nature had completely taken over and all kinds of wild creatures inhabited the place, obviously unaffected by the large-scale pollution. Walking around was like discovering a deserted Maya city, with incomprehensible switchboards and monstrous machines, pipes, meters, taps and knobs, dark corridors, staircases and ladders. In musty offices I found punch cards, lists of names, fossilized plants and a 1970s calendar.

When Georges' wife died, he stopped taking care of himself and moved into a home.

Demolition started right after that. ◆

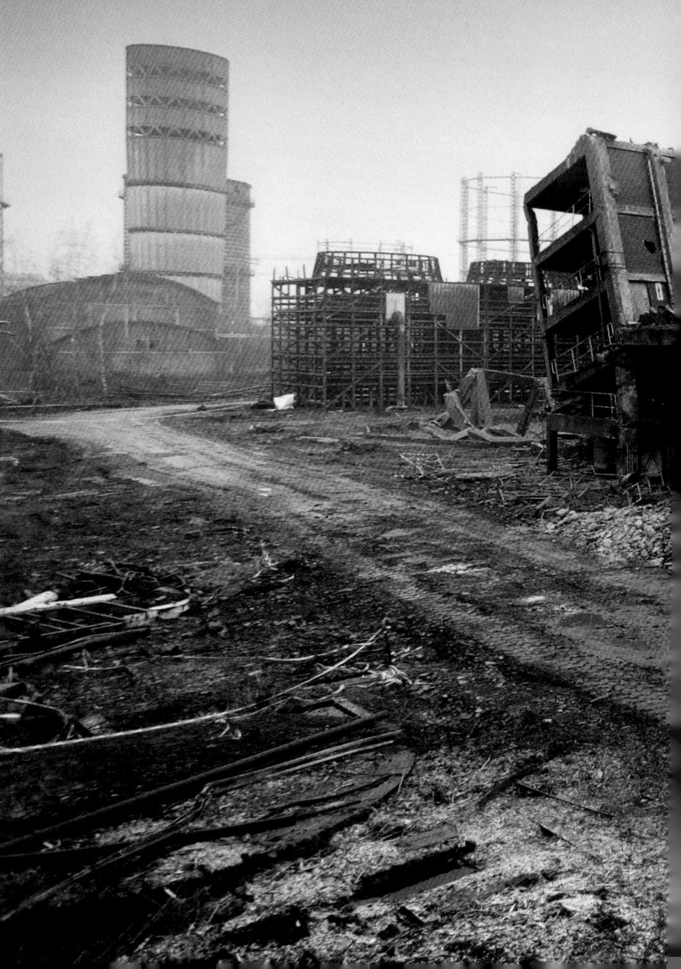

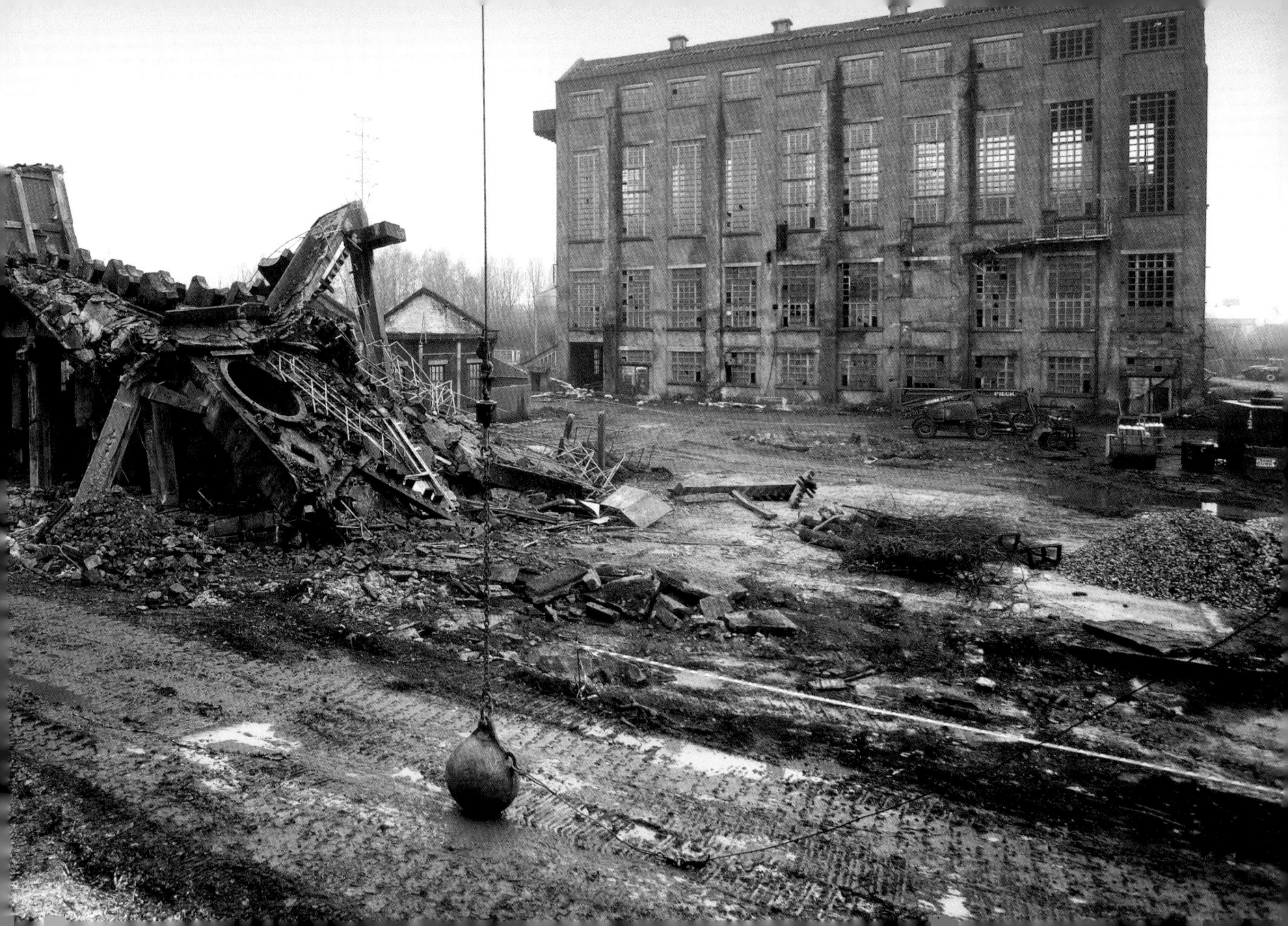
PIECK

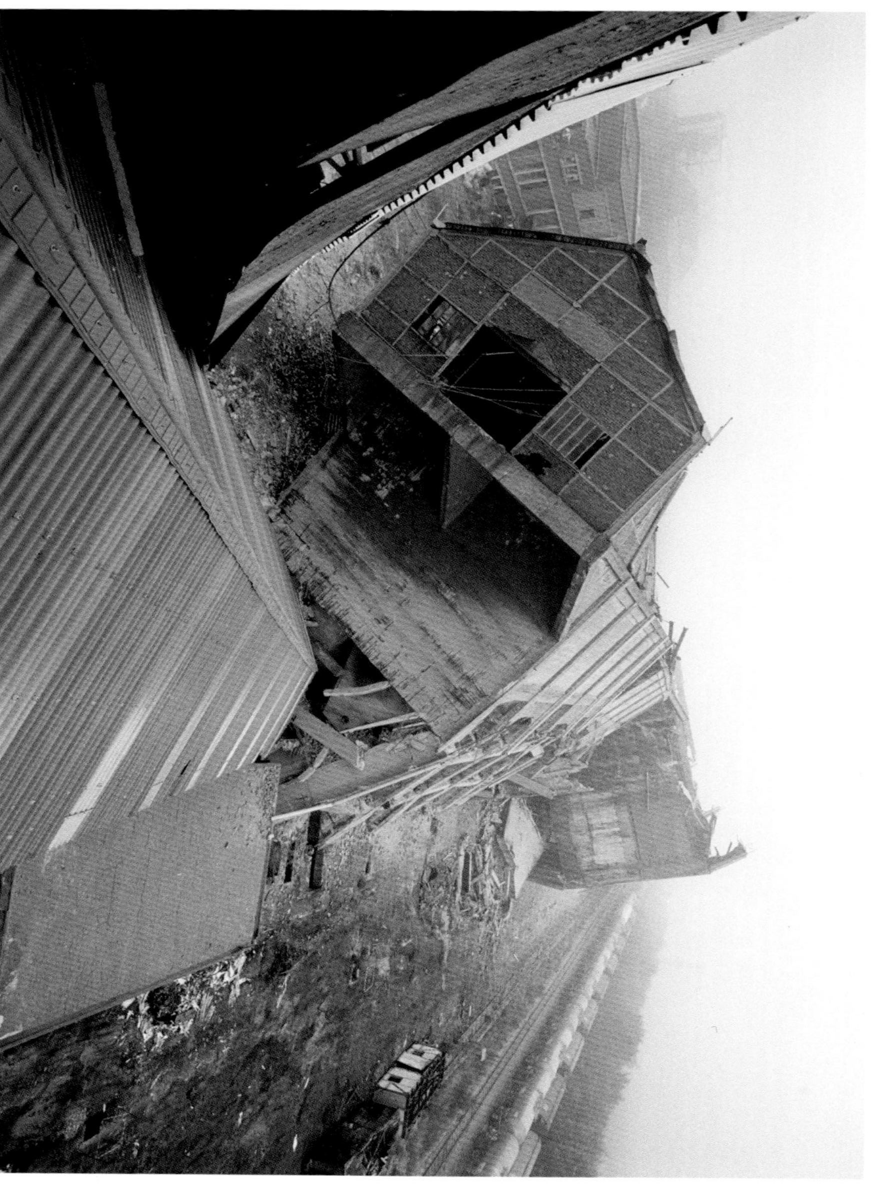

 Tertre, Belgium, 2001–2003

Tertre, Belgium, 2001–2003

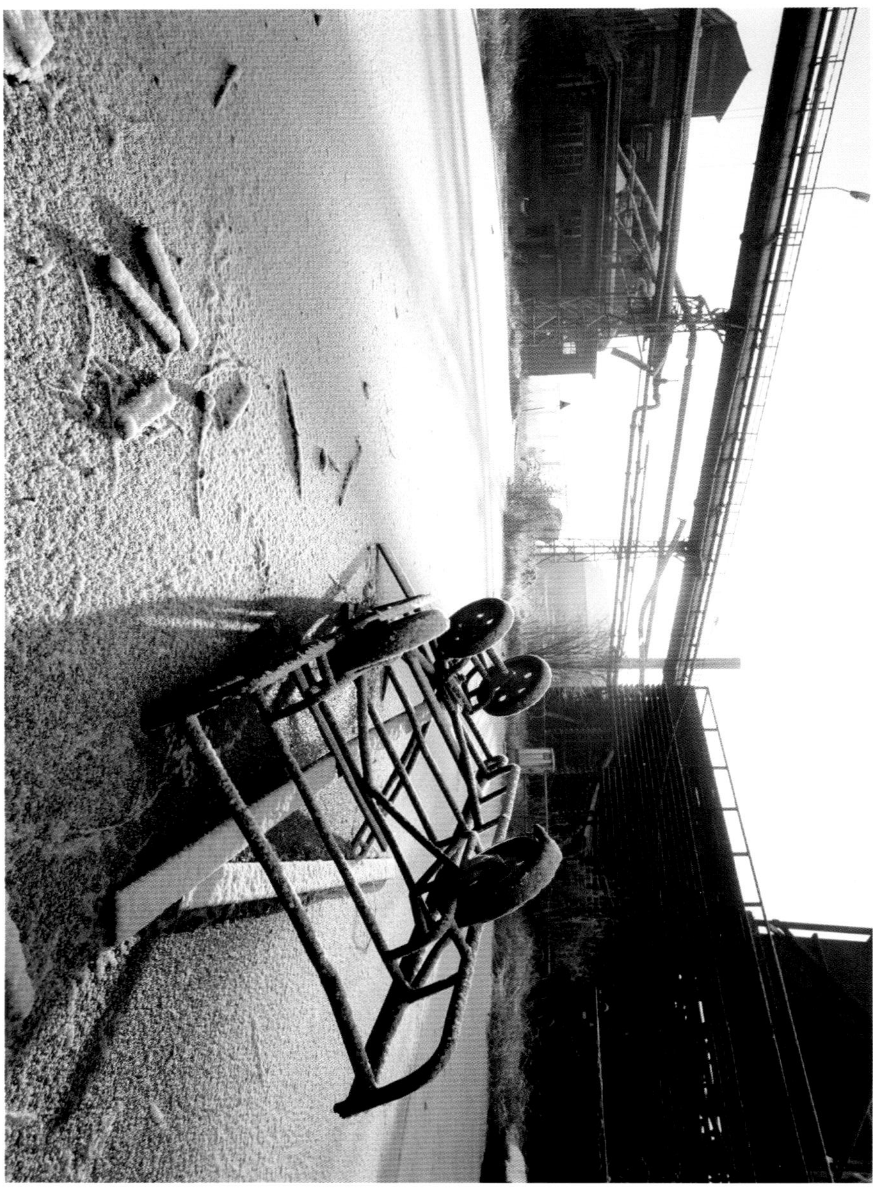

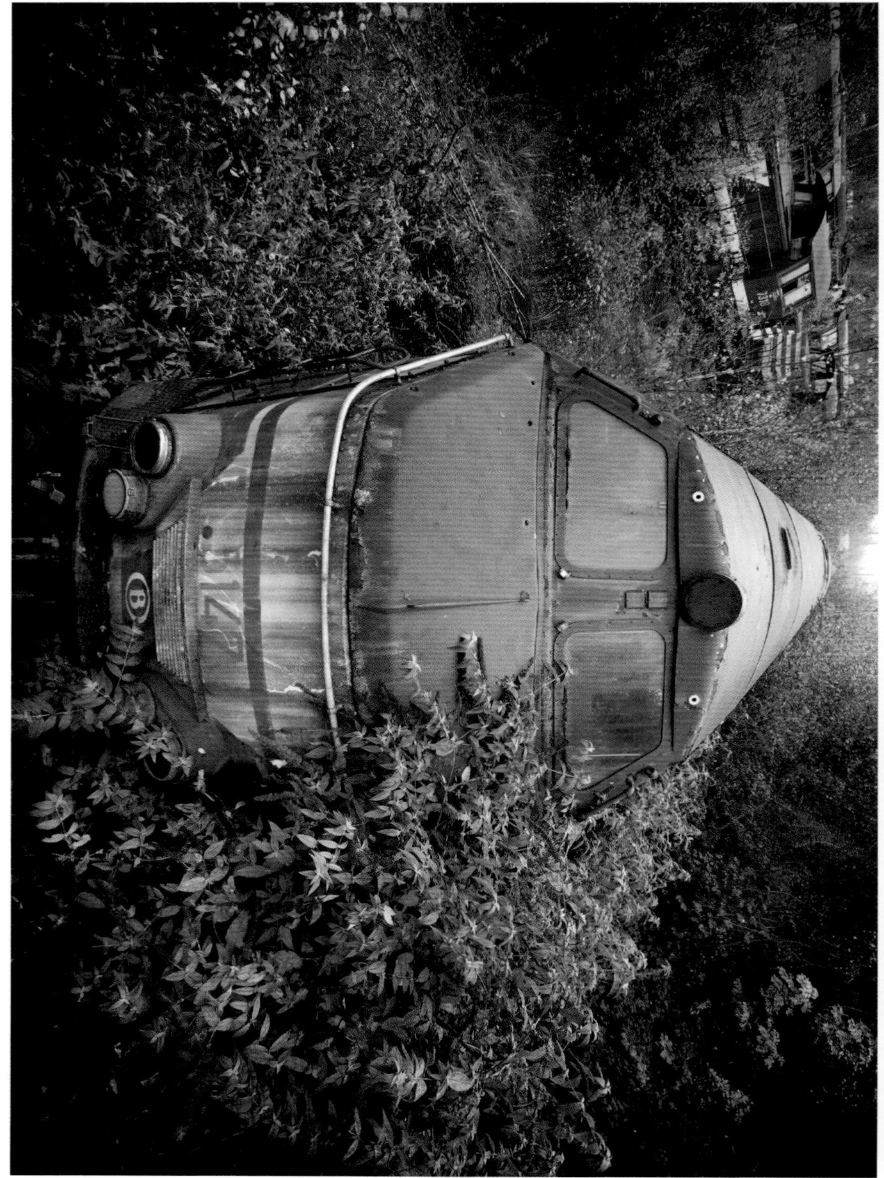

 Marshalling yard, Belgium, 2006

19 Airplane used for fire fighting training, Curaçao, 2006

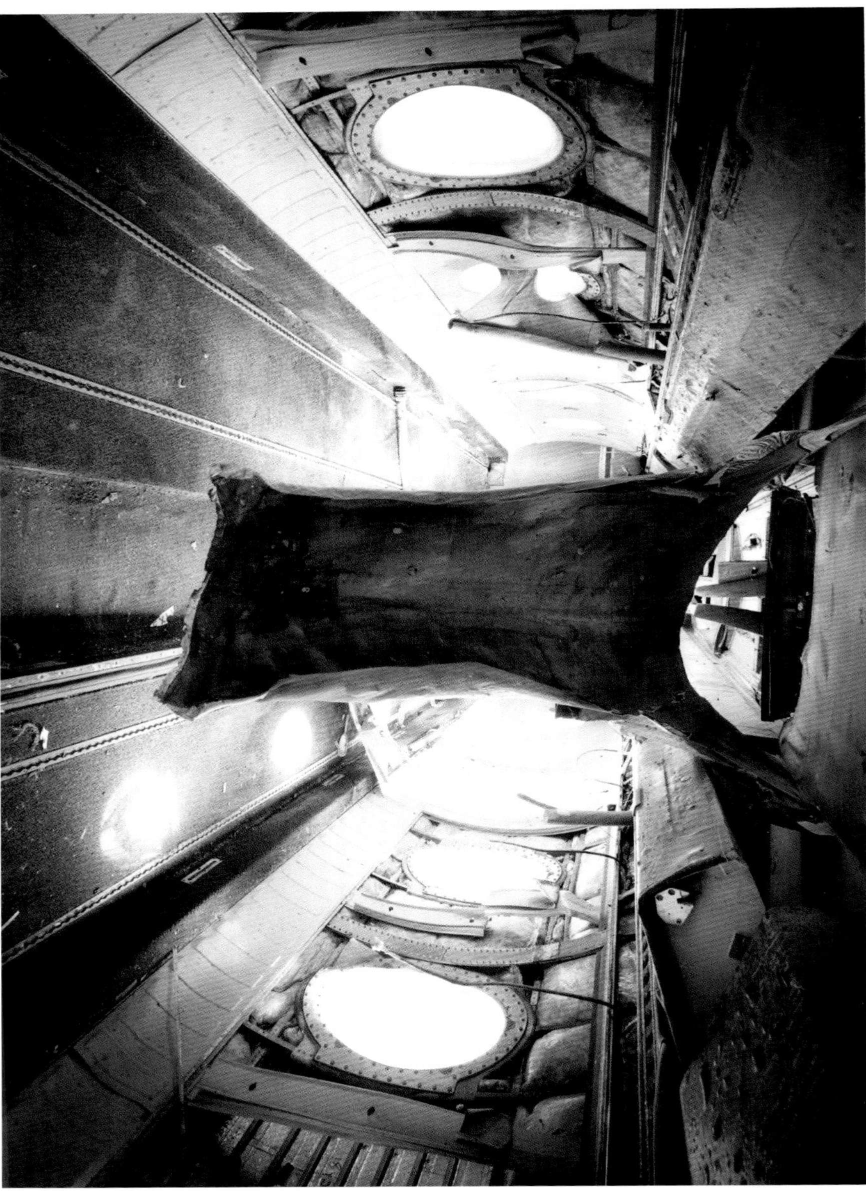

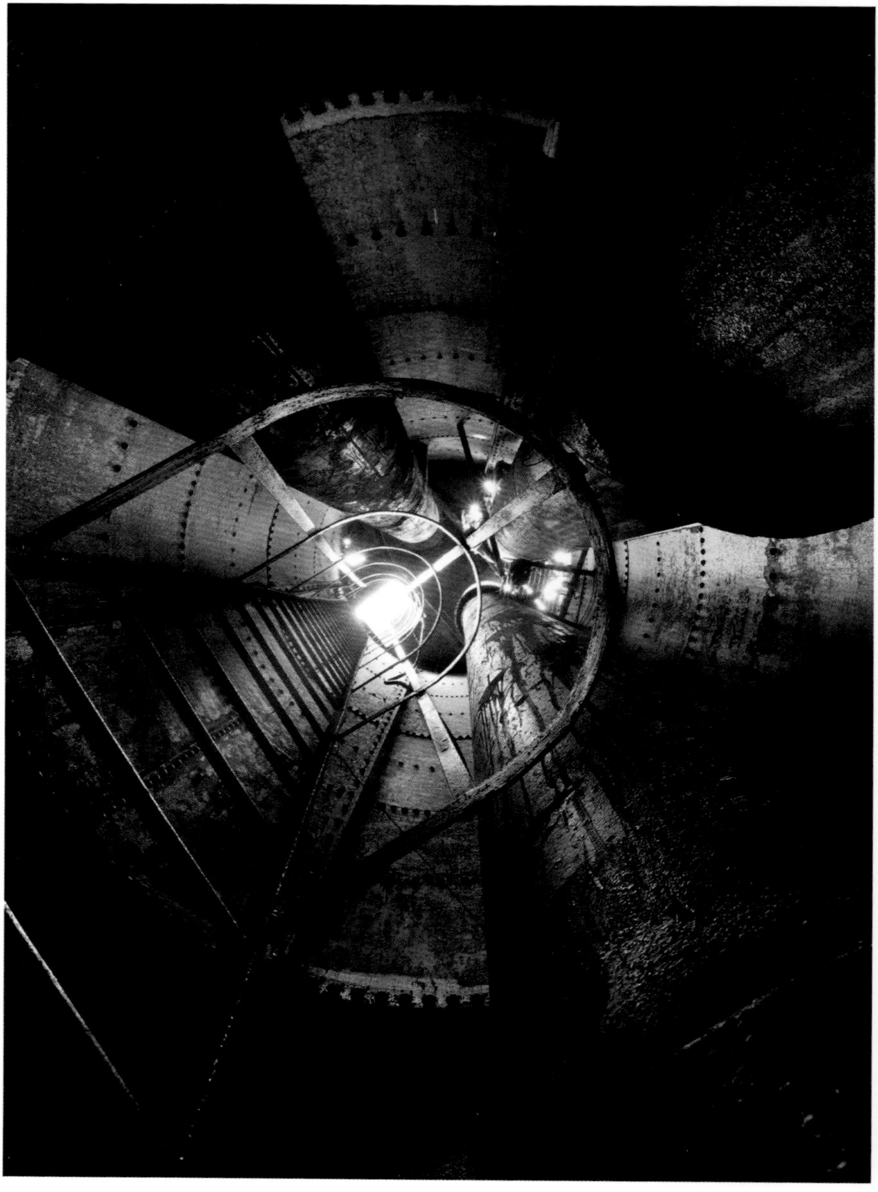

Forges de Clabecq, Belgium, 2007

 Carcoke Zeebrugge, Belgium, 2001

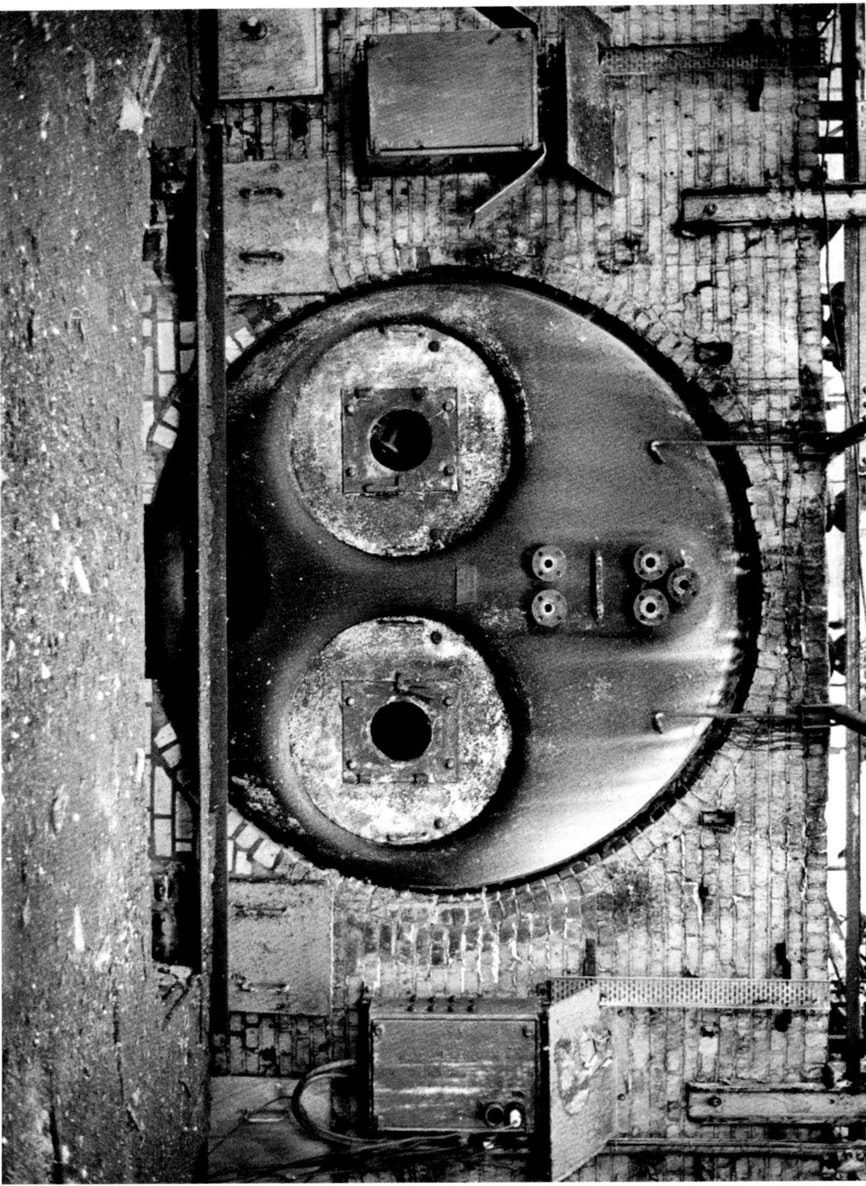

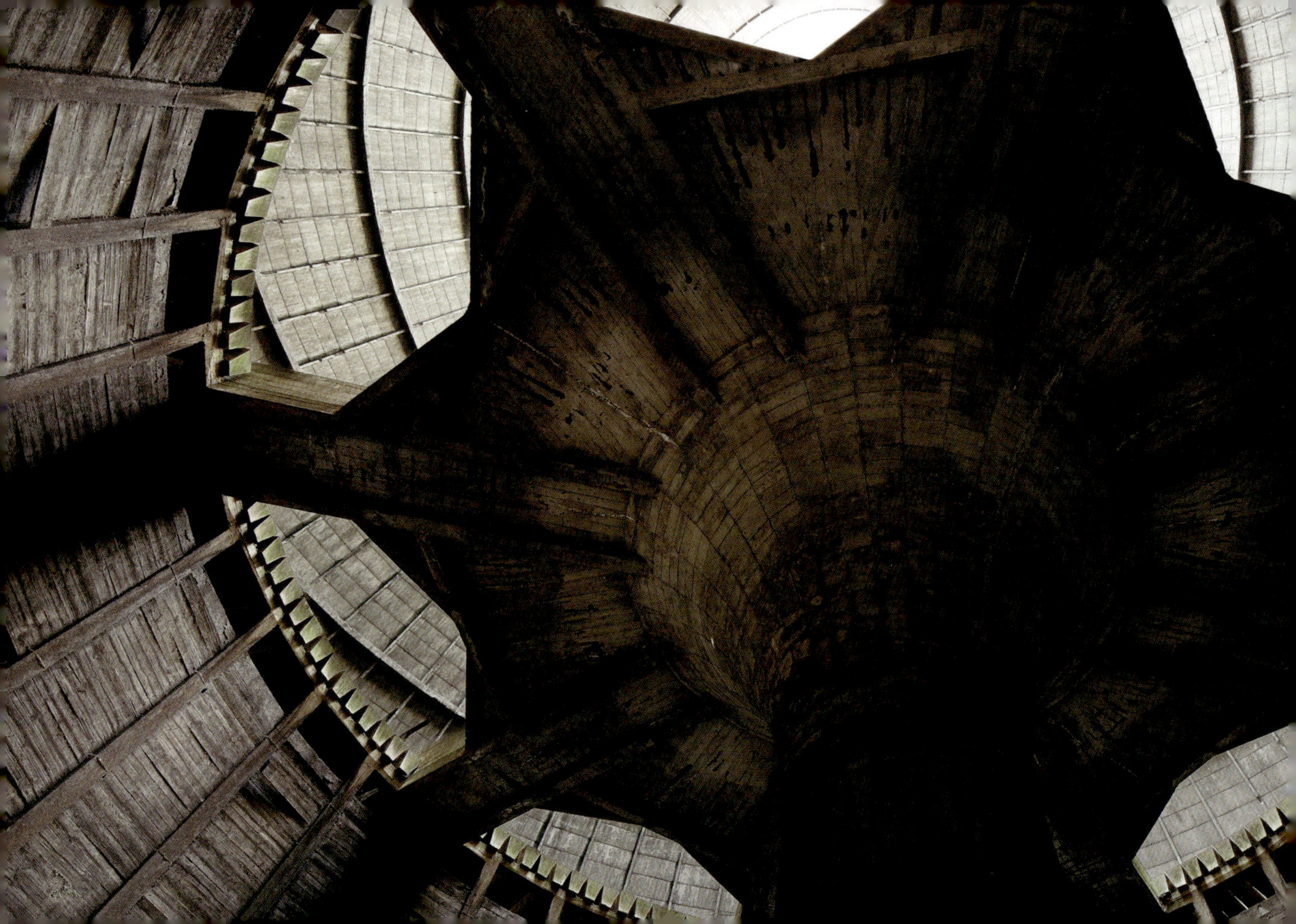

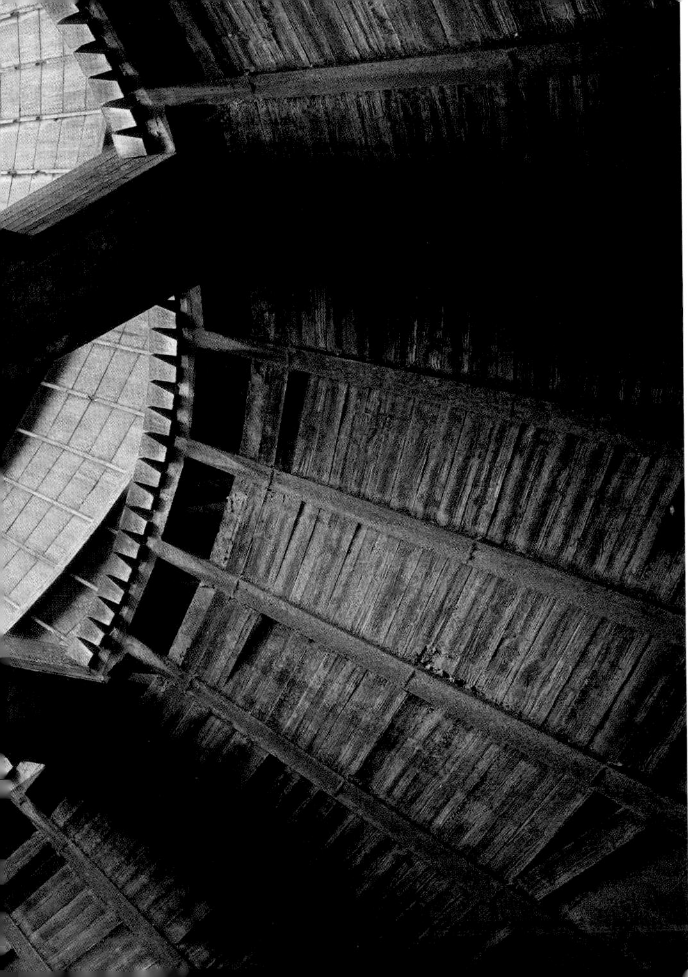

◁ POWERPLANT IM
BELGIUM, 2014

Pays Noir, Black Country, is the region around Charleroi, named so for the presence of coal-mines and heavy steel industry. Even though most of the factories have been closed since the 1950s, the landscape remains dotted with spoil tips and old industrial buildings.

This gigantic cooling tower is just one of many abandoned buildings that dot the gloomy skyline of Charleroi.

Built in 1921 and shut down in 2007, this coal-burning electric power station was responsible for 10% of the CO_2 produced throughout the entire country.

The interior never was and never is completely silent. Even when the building is properly sealed off, East European copper thieves always find ways to get in. ◆

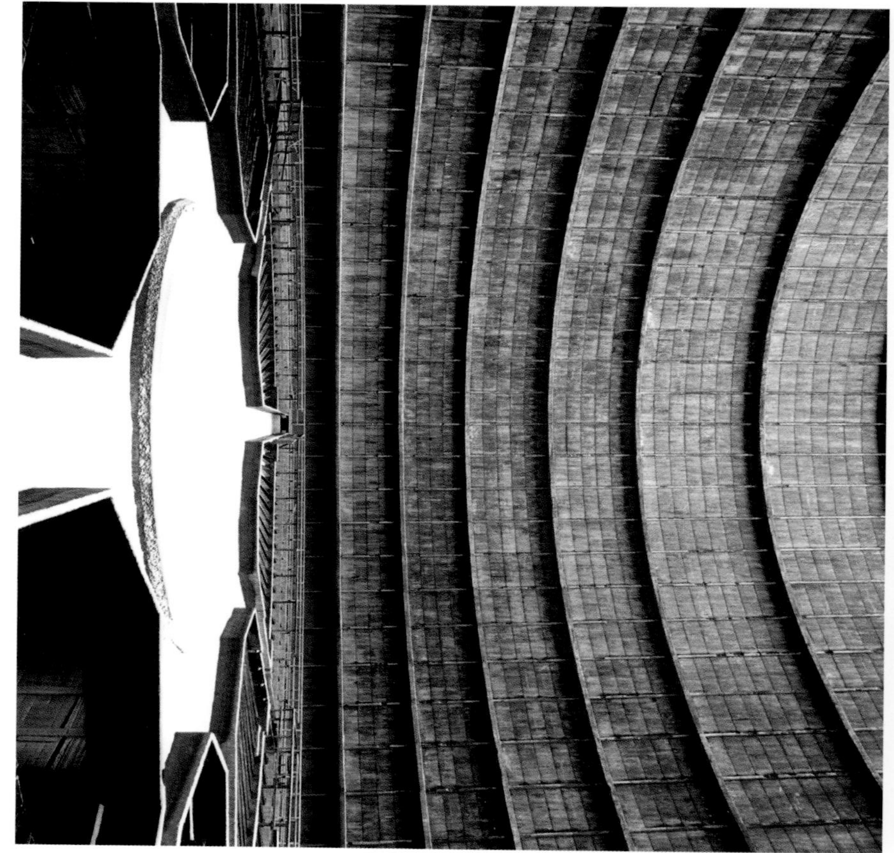

 Powerplant IM, Belgium, 2013

Powerplant IM, Belgium, 2012

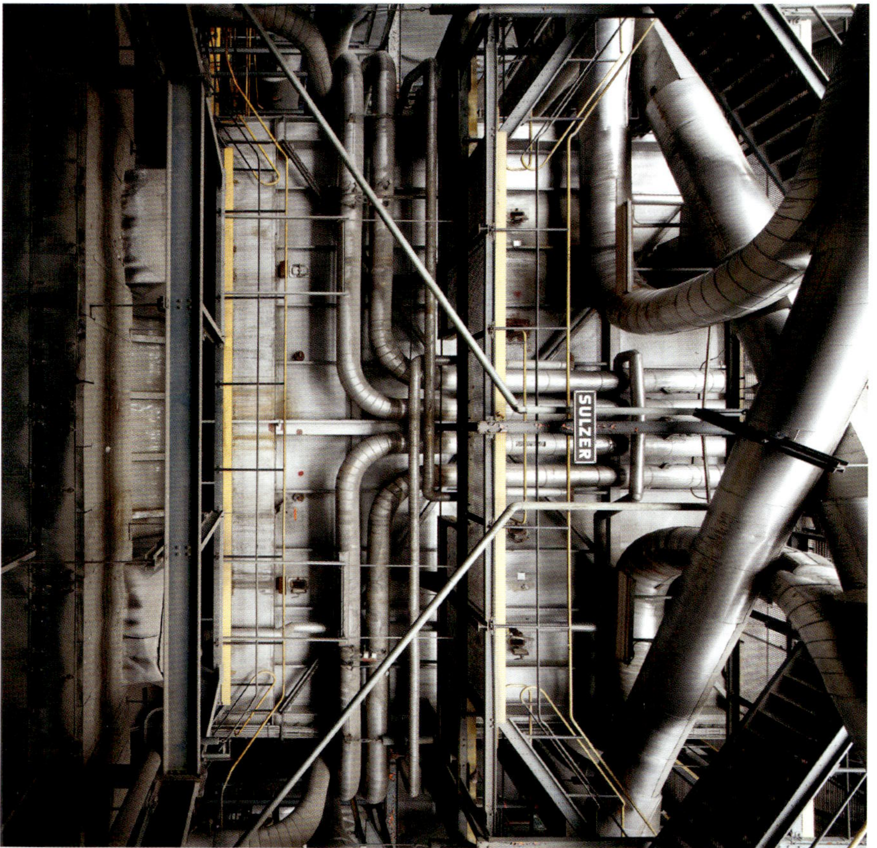

WARSHIP CEMETERY ▹

FRANCE, 2012

This was a risky expedition. In a wide river that flows into the Atlantic Ocean, there are some ten warships waiting to be dismantled. Chains and gangplanks hold them together. Strong currents follow the rhythms of the tides, and military speedboats carry out regular patrols.

When we began to pump up our rubber boats, we found a hole, bigger than the one that sank the Titanic. Plan C was for me to take all the baggage and for my friend to swim over on an airbed. With four bags, my boat was overloaded, and the lack of space made it hard to row. After pausing at the buoys halfway, we set off on the second stage of our journey. The current was much stronger in the middle of the river. The bags in my boat began to slide and I temporarily lost one of the oars. I started drifting off course and saw the boats disappearing in the darkness. There was one last chance of success, and that was the buoy that held the boats in position. I rowed like a madman and was just able to catch hold of the cable...

Once on board, with knocking knees, we exchanged our trademark grin and cracked open a well-earned can of beer!

That night on the boat was magical. It was raining, and the boats were slippery with oil. The deck was full of young gulls that had never seen human beings before. At daybreak, the entire colony of gulls took off and flew over the boats, calling loudly, their droppings raining down on us. ◆

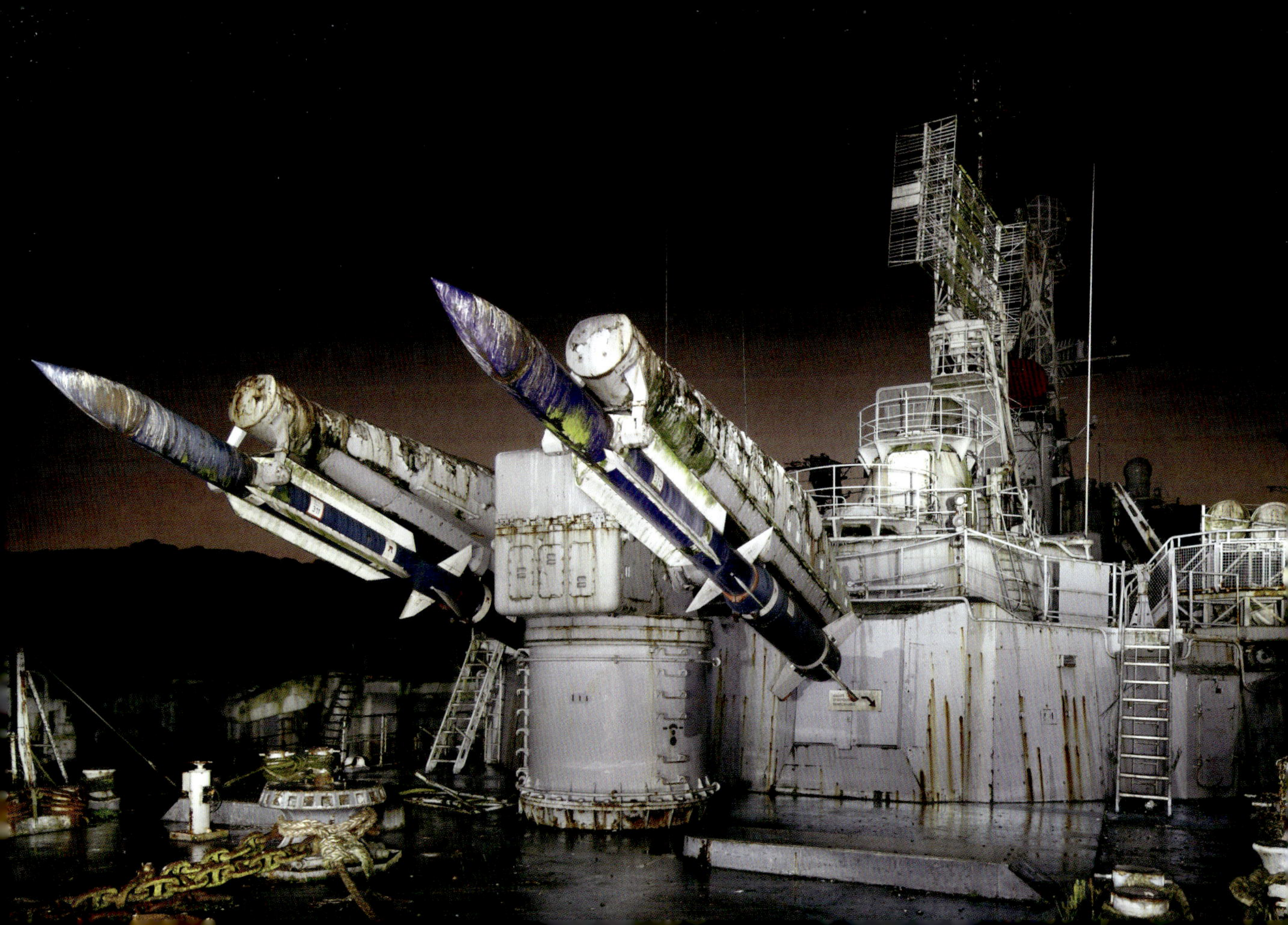

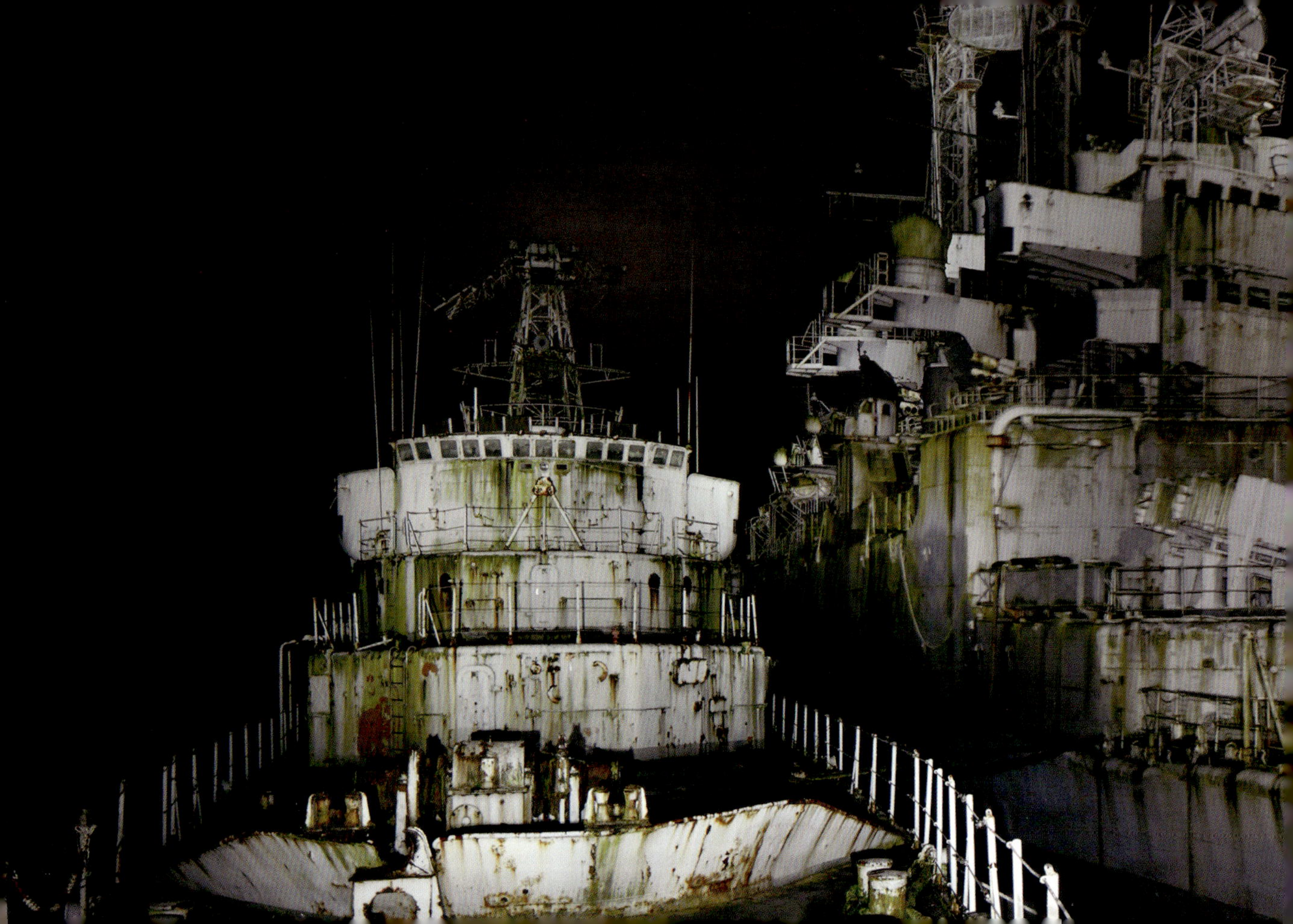

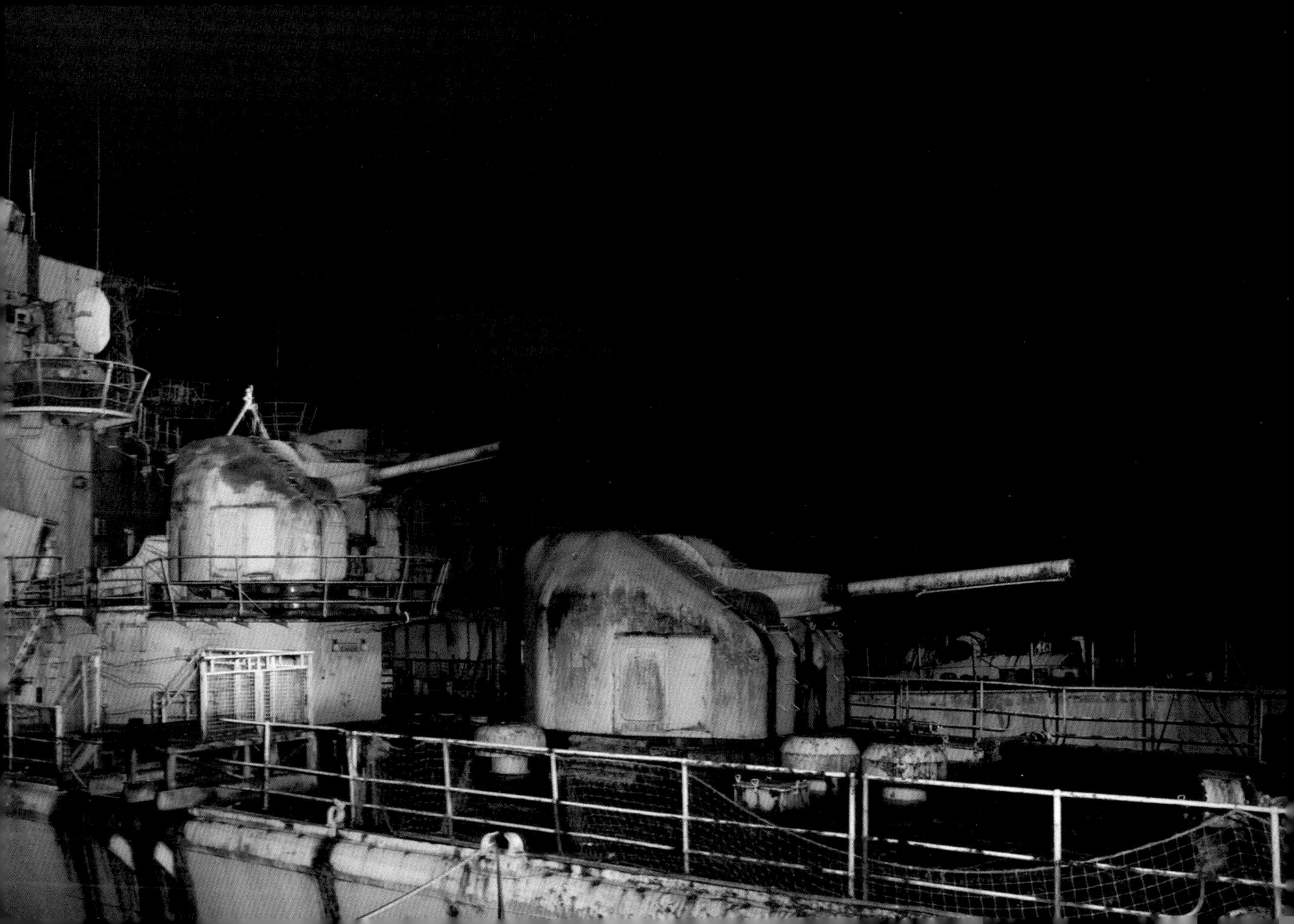

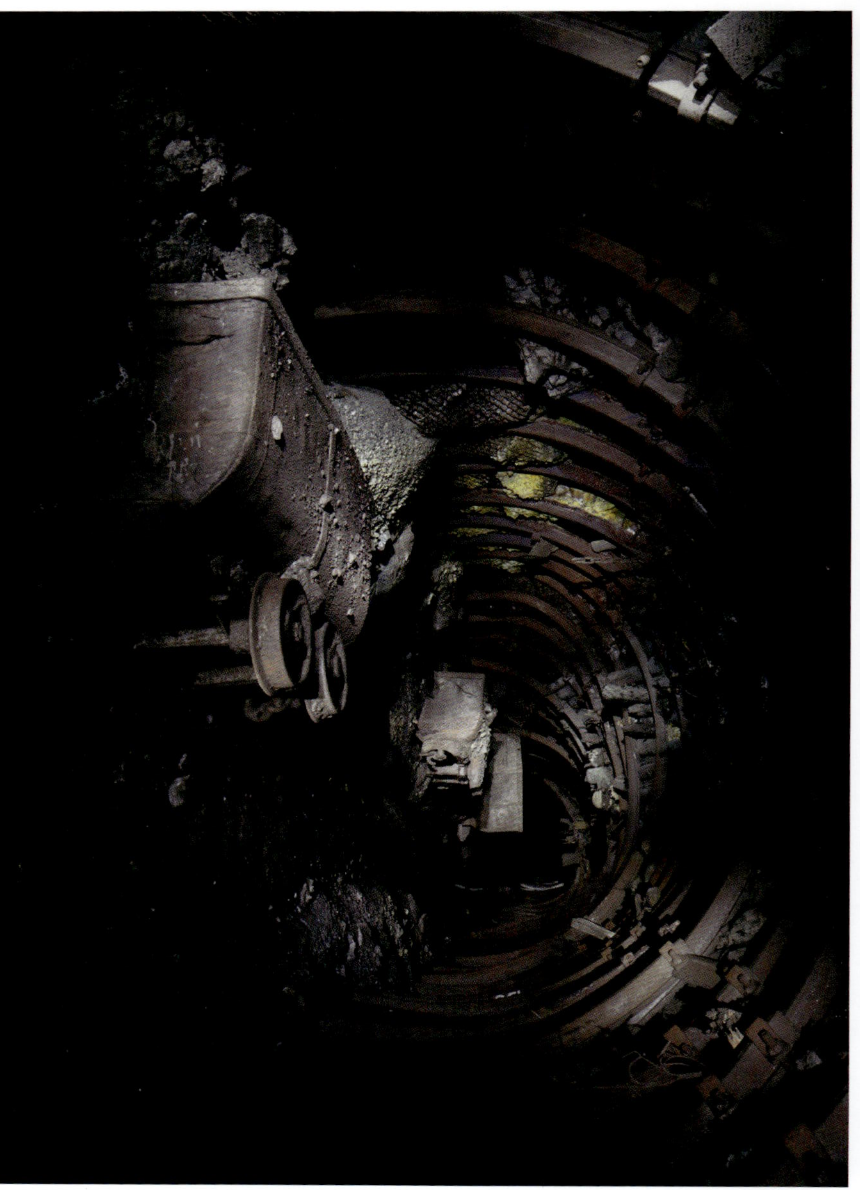

 Abandoned mine corridor, Romania, 2015

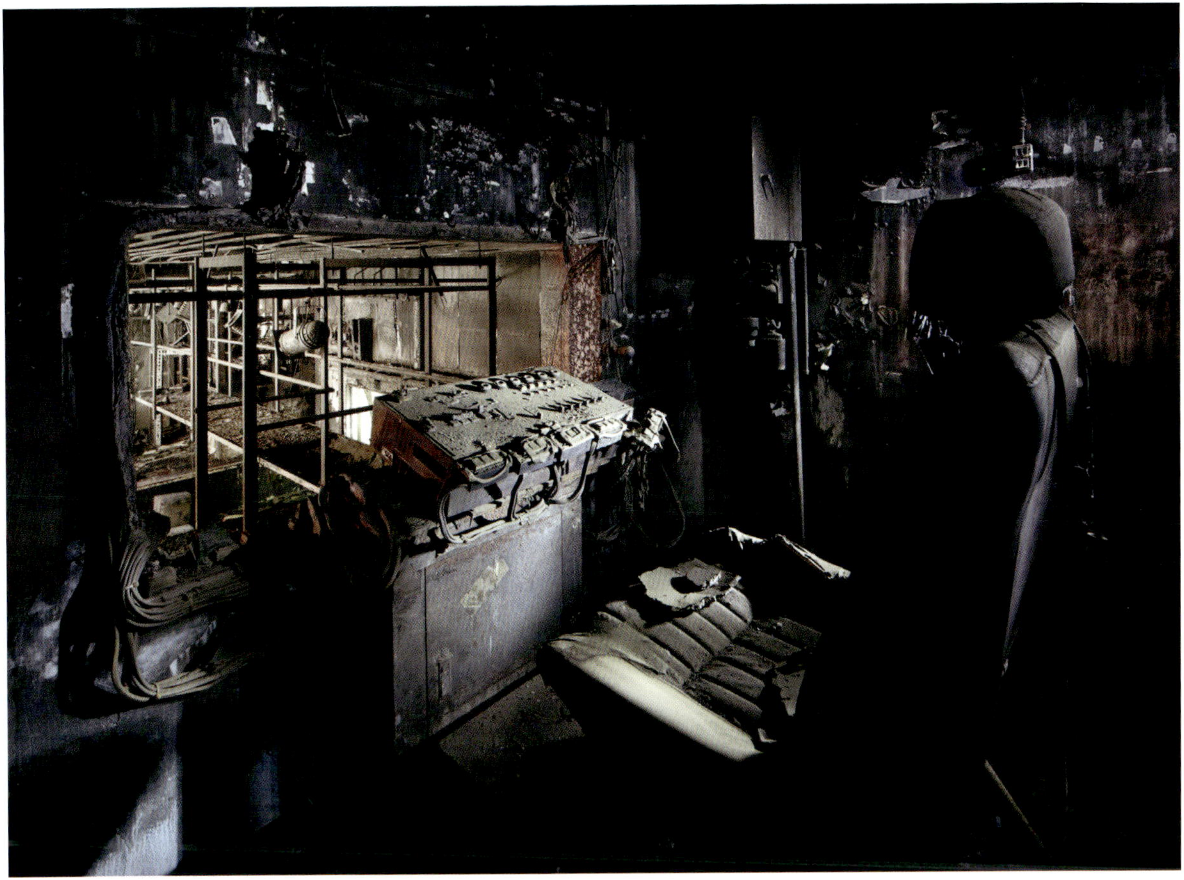

31 Akeno Strip Club, Japan, 2013

BUZLUDZHA ▹

BULGARIA, 2013

In 1981, the Bulgarian communist regime built a monument on 'Mount Buzludzha', a historic but virtually inaccessible place.

Since 1989, Bulgaria's largest ideological building has stood empty. After the villagers stole the copper roofing, the building decayed even faster.

In the winter, access is restricted to 4 wheel drive vehicles or snow scooters, and for the final kilometer, you need snow shoes. 'Buzludzha' literally means 'icy', and for good reason: it is incredibly cold up there; the icy wind blows right through you. At night, temperatures plummet to way below freezing.

The monument stands inviolable on the barren mountaintop like an alien spaceship. I slipped inside through a crack in the concrete. This was where real challenge greeted me: due to a cycle of thawing and freezing, the floors were like a vast ice rink. Even the stairways were covered with a thick layer of slippery ice, making it literally impossible to climb even a few steps. The worse thing is that there are holes in the concrete everywhere, and if you start to slip, it may be impossible to stop...

The reward for all these risks is the beautiful arena with its mosaics and UFO-like roof.

The missing face on the mosaics-covered wall is that of Todor Zhivkov, Bulgaria's last communist leader who reigned from 1954 until 1989. It's unclear whether unhappy people removed his face, or if he ordered its removal so as to distance himself from the collapsing Soviet regime. ◆

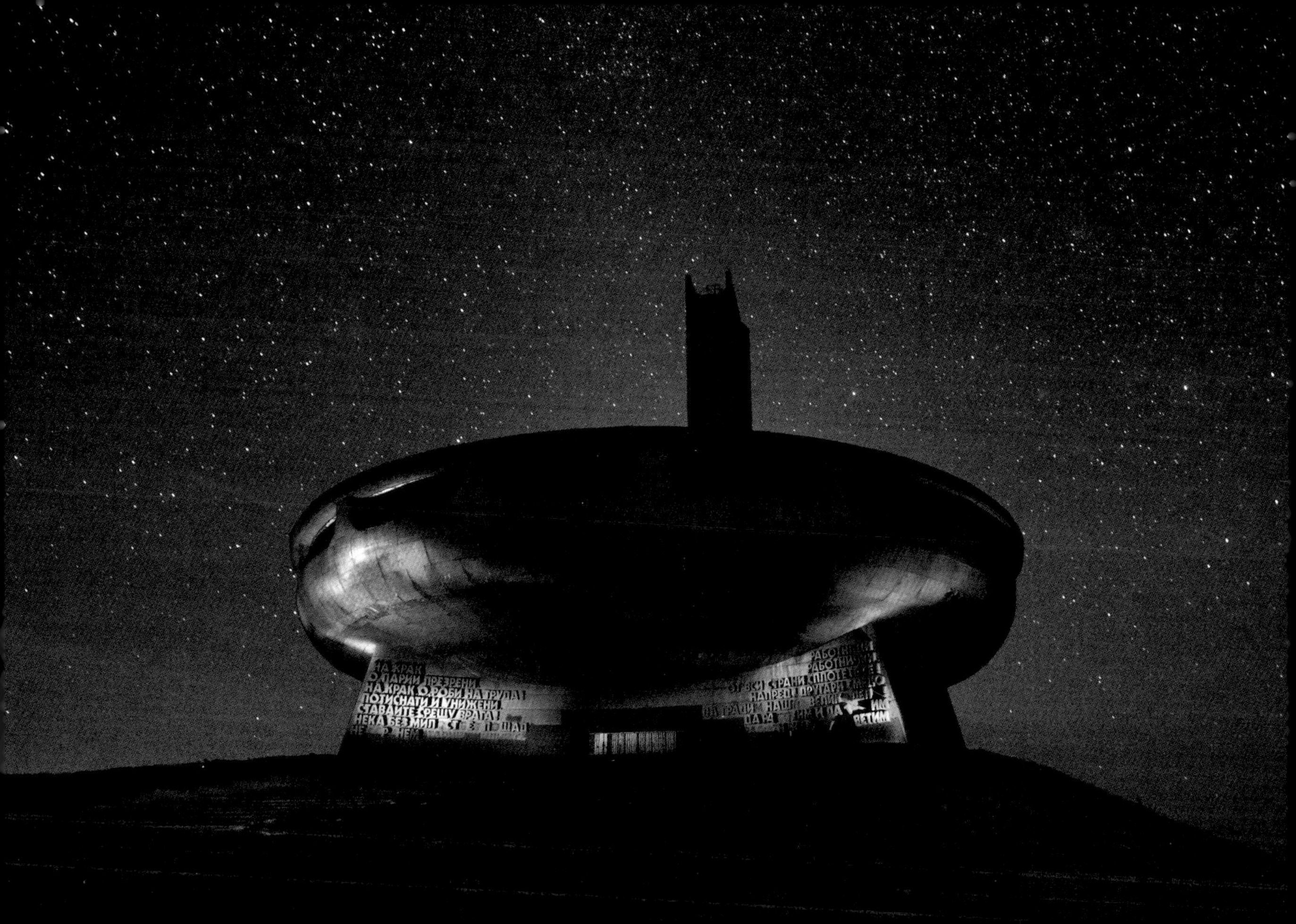
НА КРАК
О ПАРИИ ПРЕЗРЕНИ
НА КРАК О РОБИ НА ТРУДА!
ПОТИСНАТИ И УНИЖЕНИ
СТАВАЙТЕ СРЕЩУ ВРАГА!
НАПРЕД! ДРУГАРИ

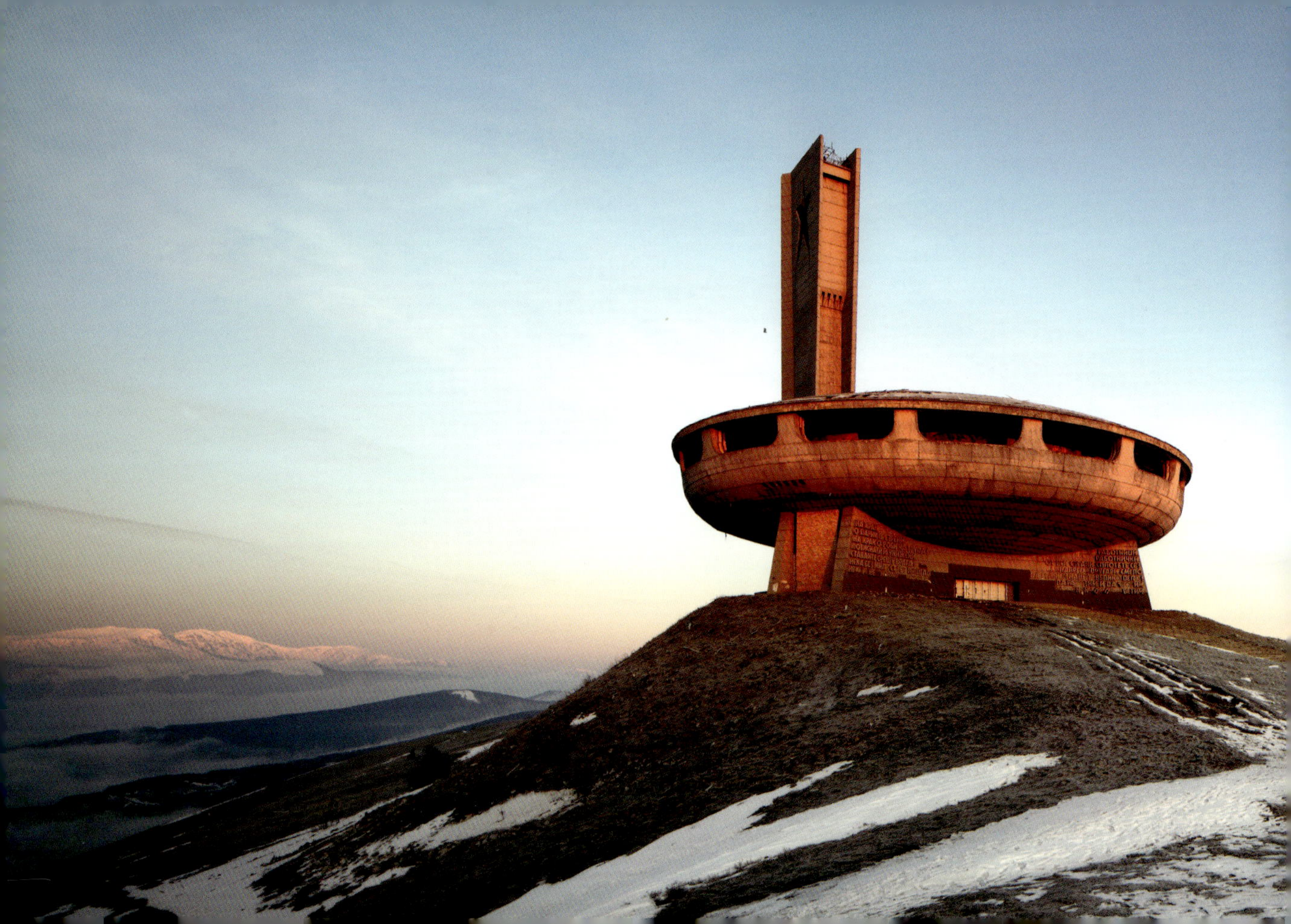

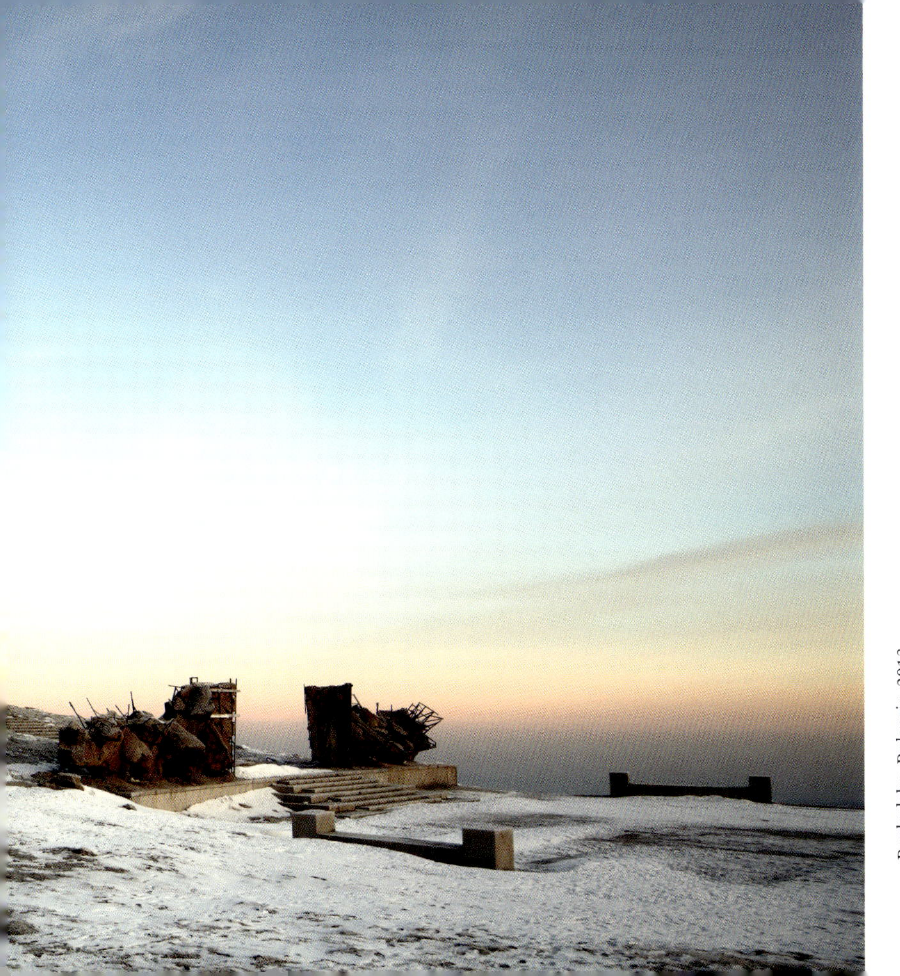

Buzludzha, Bulgaria, 2013

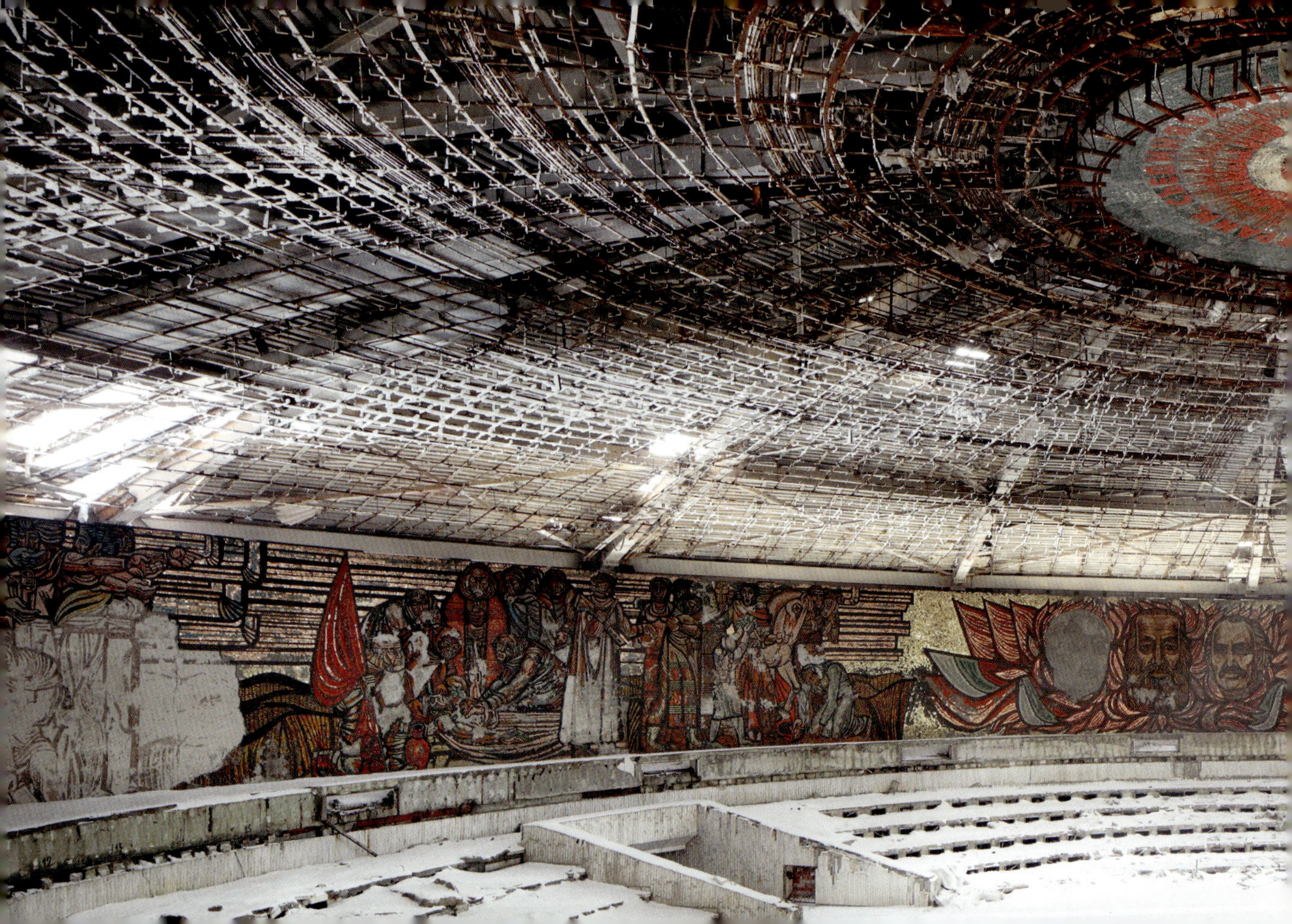

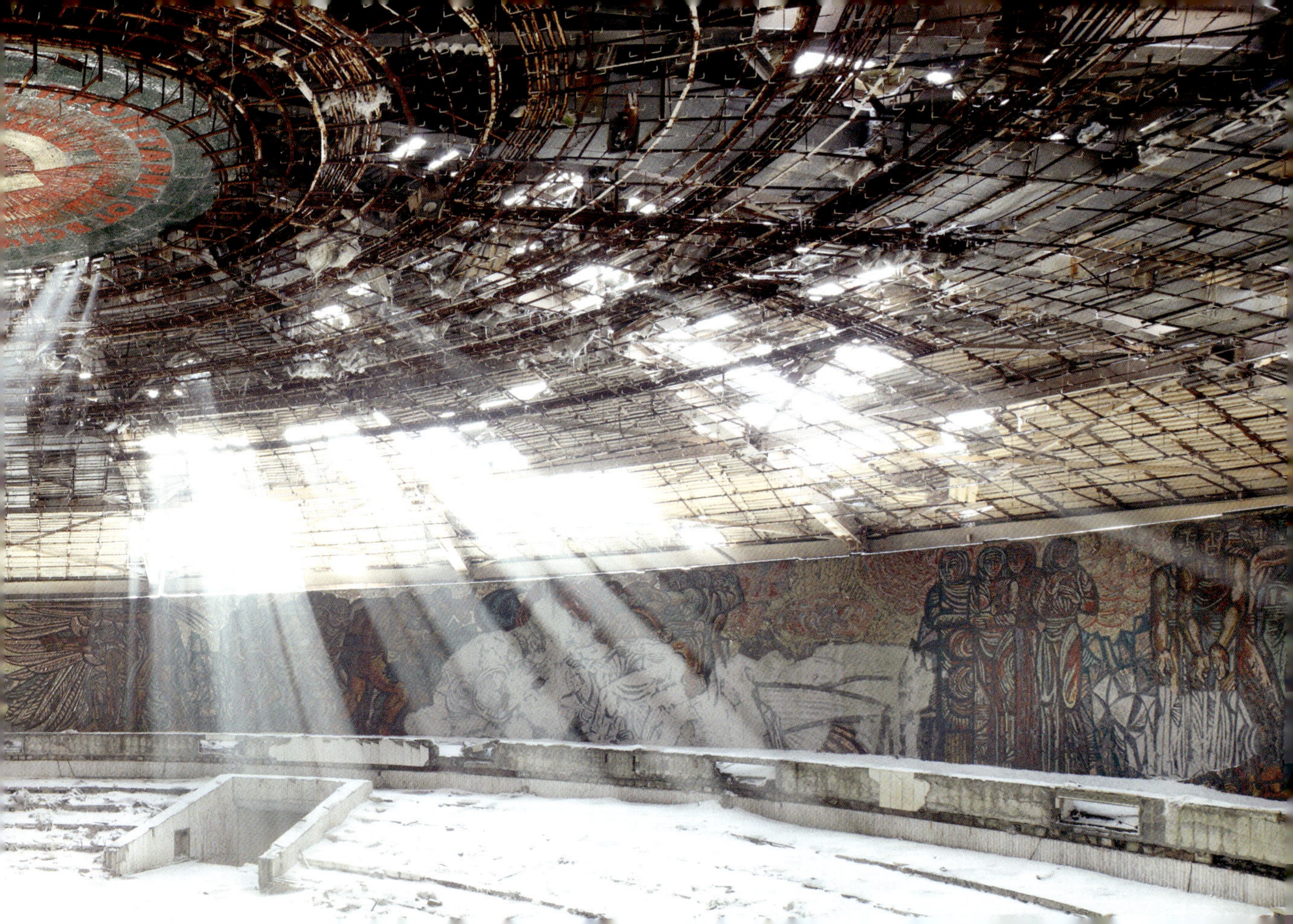

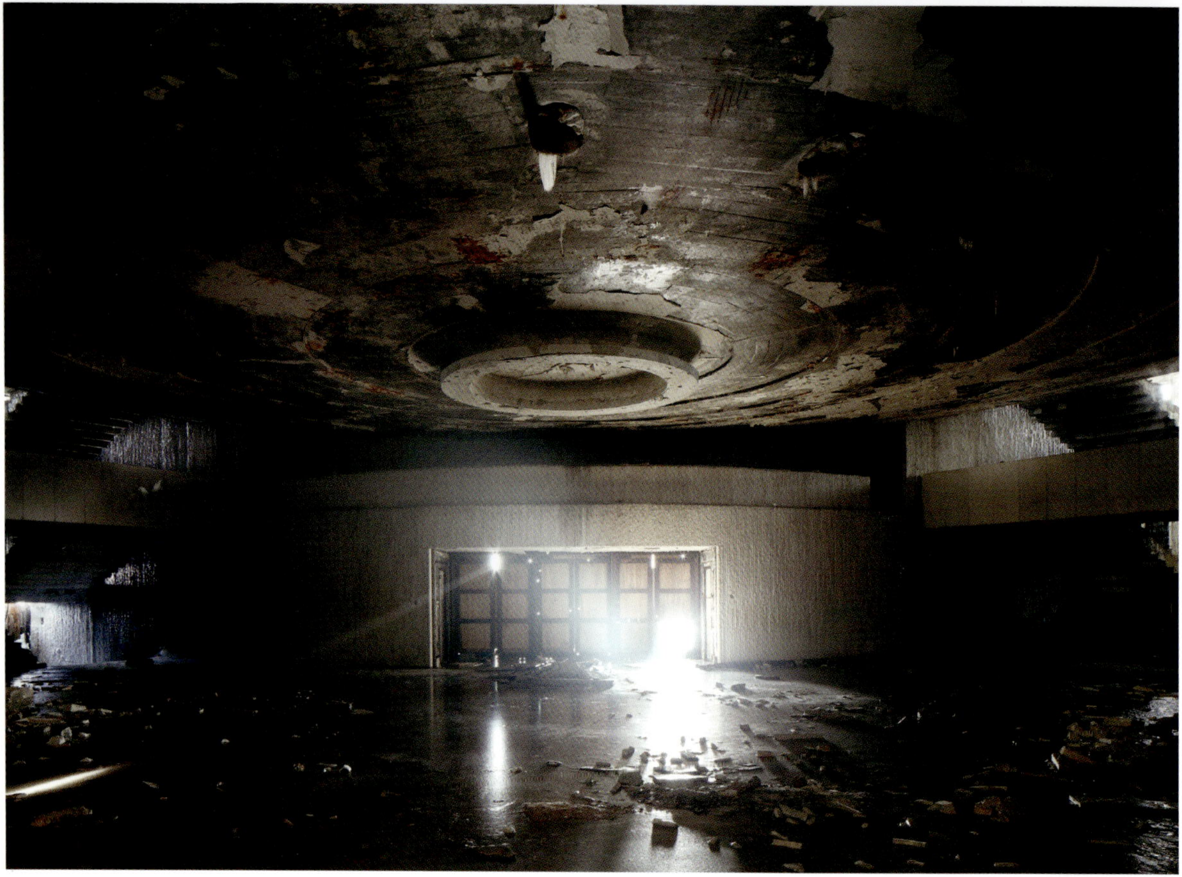

 Buzludzha, Bulgaria, 2013

 Silent Listeners, Italy, 2013

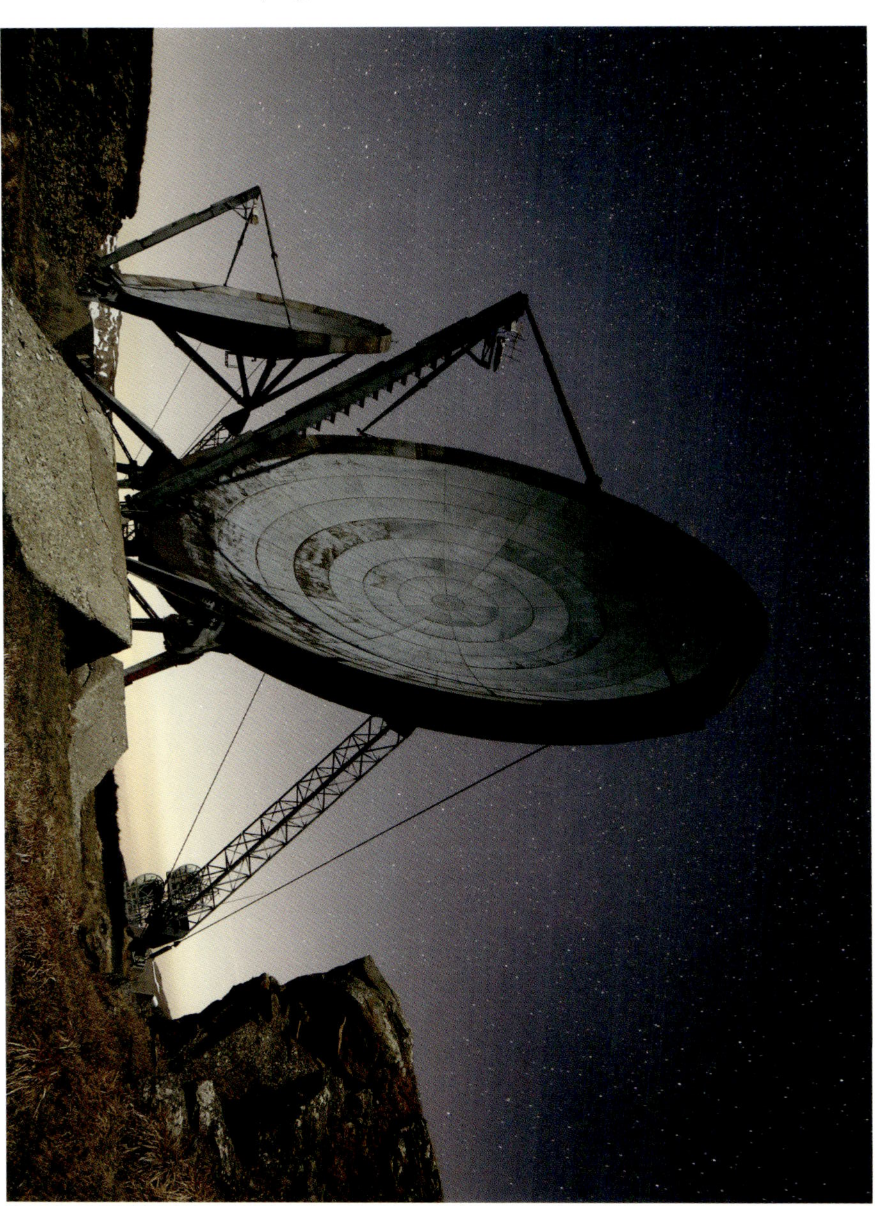

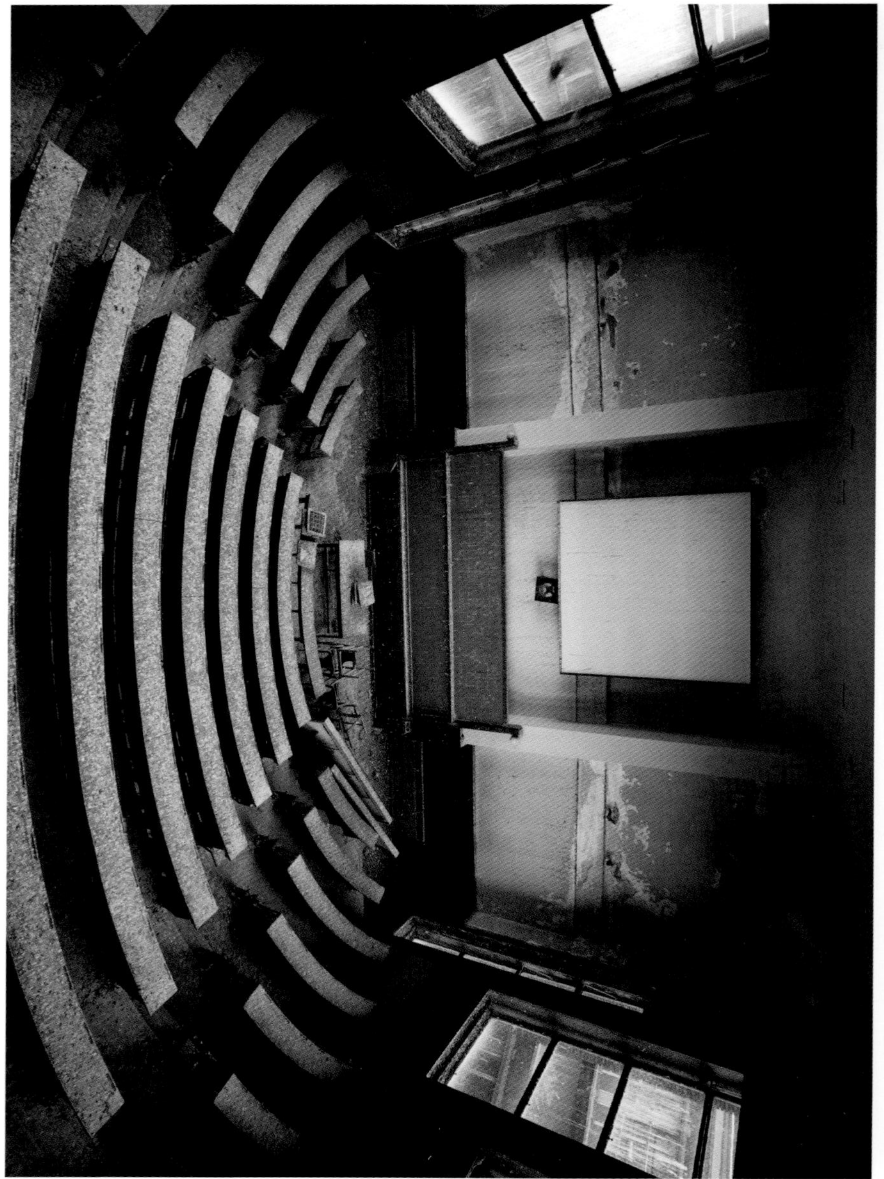

Val Benoit, Belgium, 2010

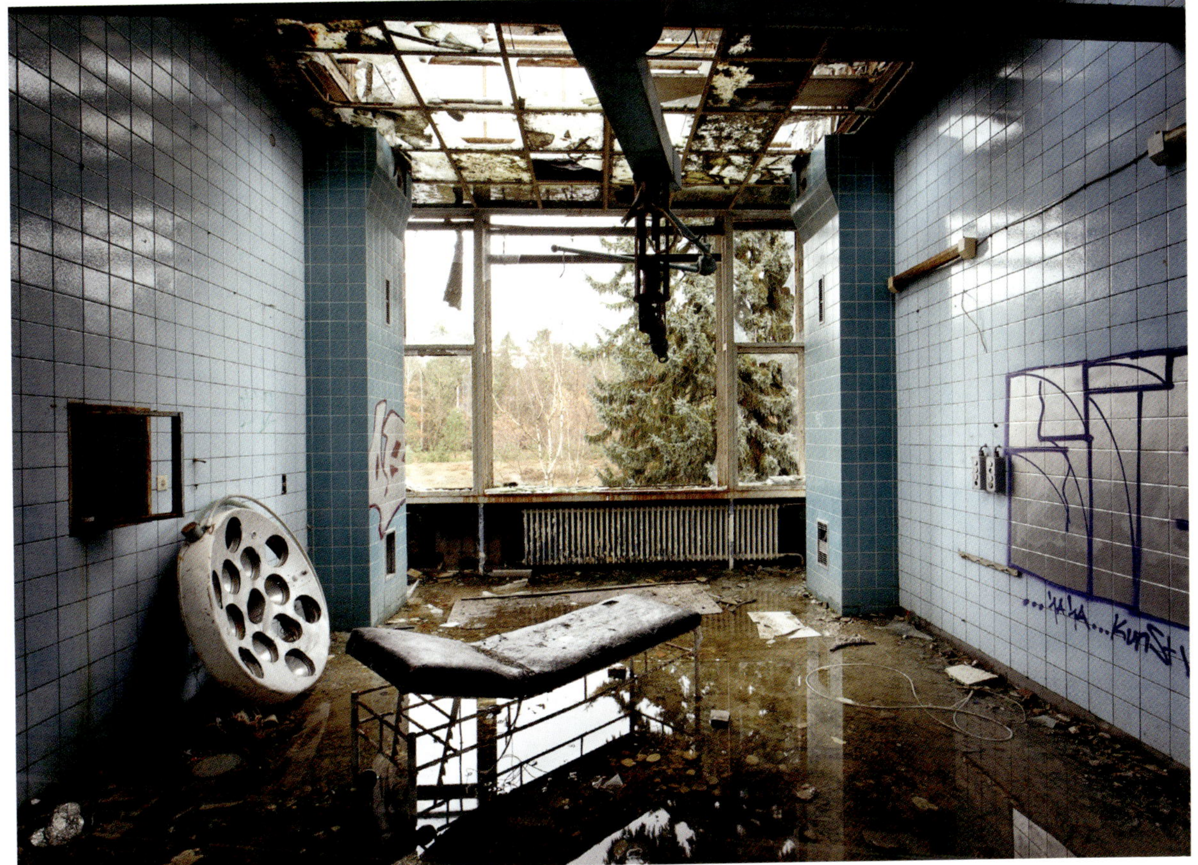

Beelitz Heilstätten, Germany, 2007

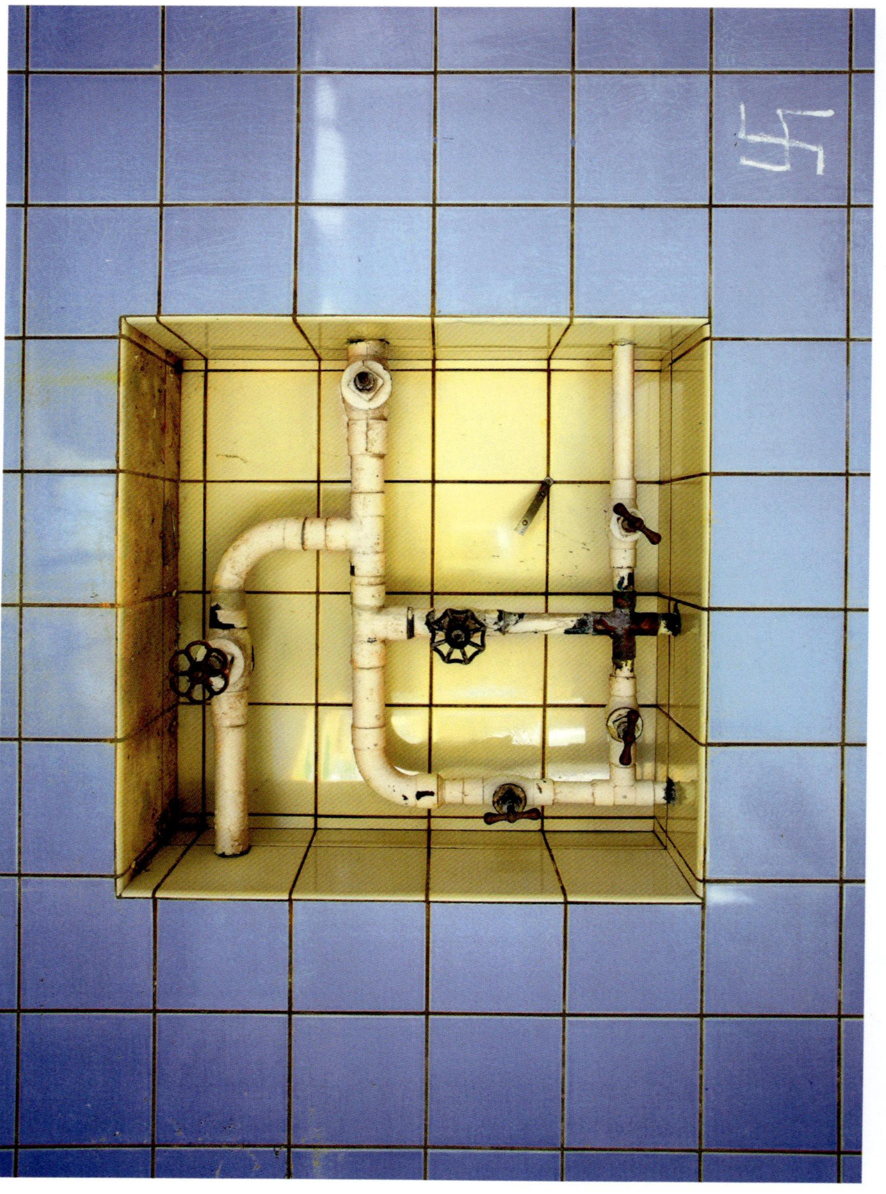

 Swastika plumbing, Château Noisy, Belgium, 2007

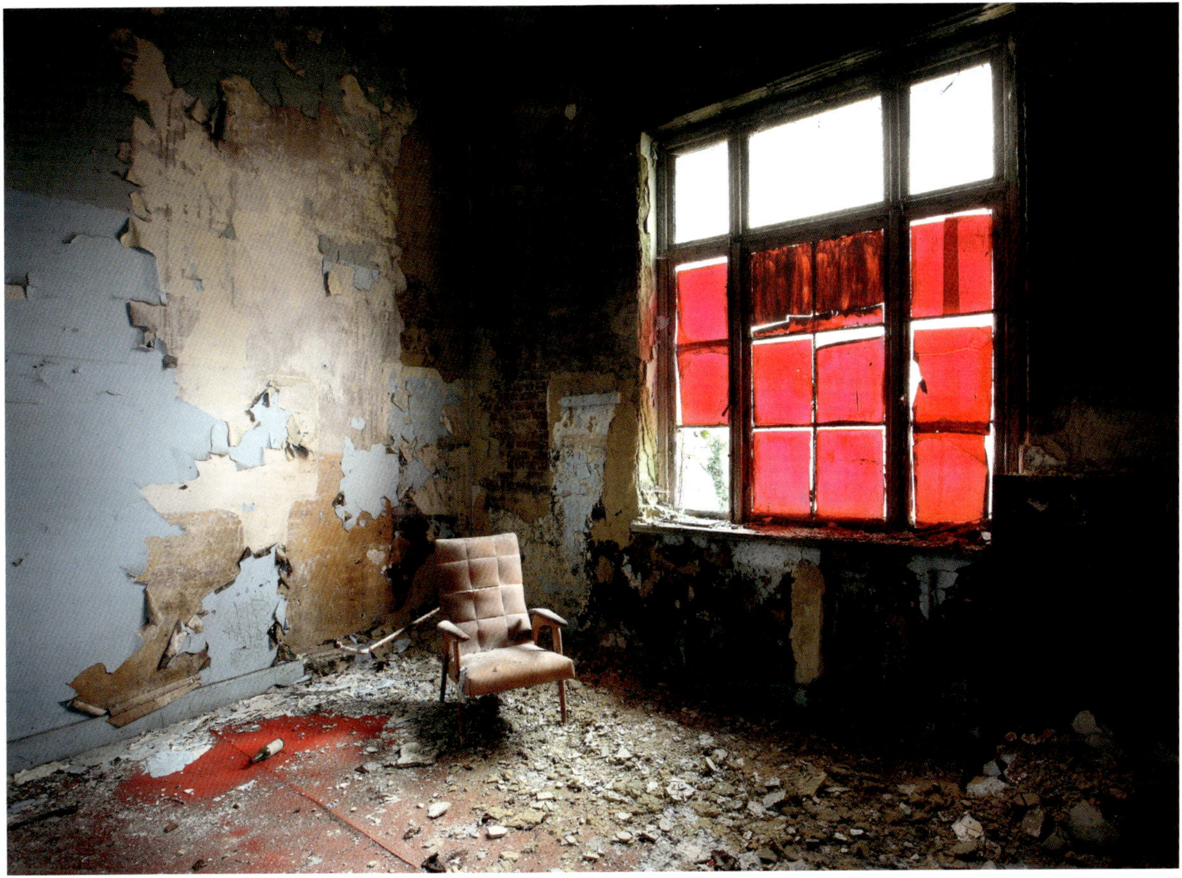

Train drivers' resting area, Belgium, 2006

MONTGOMERY MALL

ALABAMA, USA, 2012

This huge mall has been abandoned for some years. Even the larger parking lot was deserted when we arrived... except for one car with two occupants sitting half-hidden in a corner of the parking lot. Tough luck: security!

Almost immediately, they got into action and trailed us. We stopped. They stopped too. We turned left, they too. Right... right. We decided to leave the parking lot, drive around the block and return via the other entrance. But who was standing right there waiting for us? You've got it.

Plan B: talk to them, explain, and hope they might look away while we try and enter the building. We parked our car, got out, walked towards them and watched the hesitant maneuvering of their car. Inside it were two women. We looked at each other: we invitingly, they uncomprehendingly. They reversed, parked again. The older woman explained something to the younger one. They had already forgotten about us. Such is life when a mother is teaching her daughter to drive. ◆

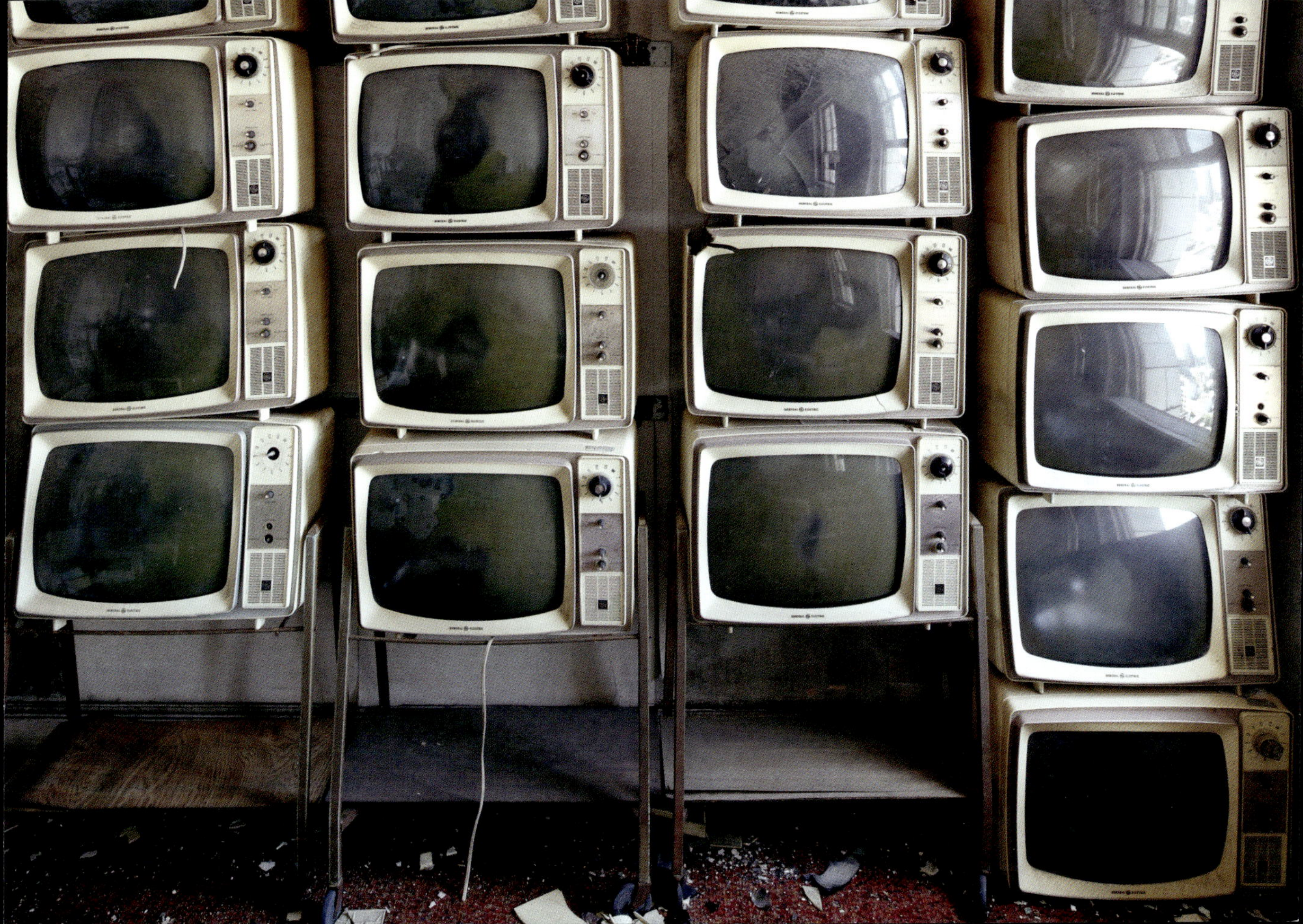

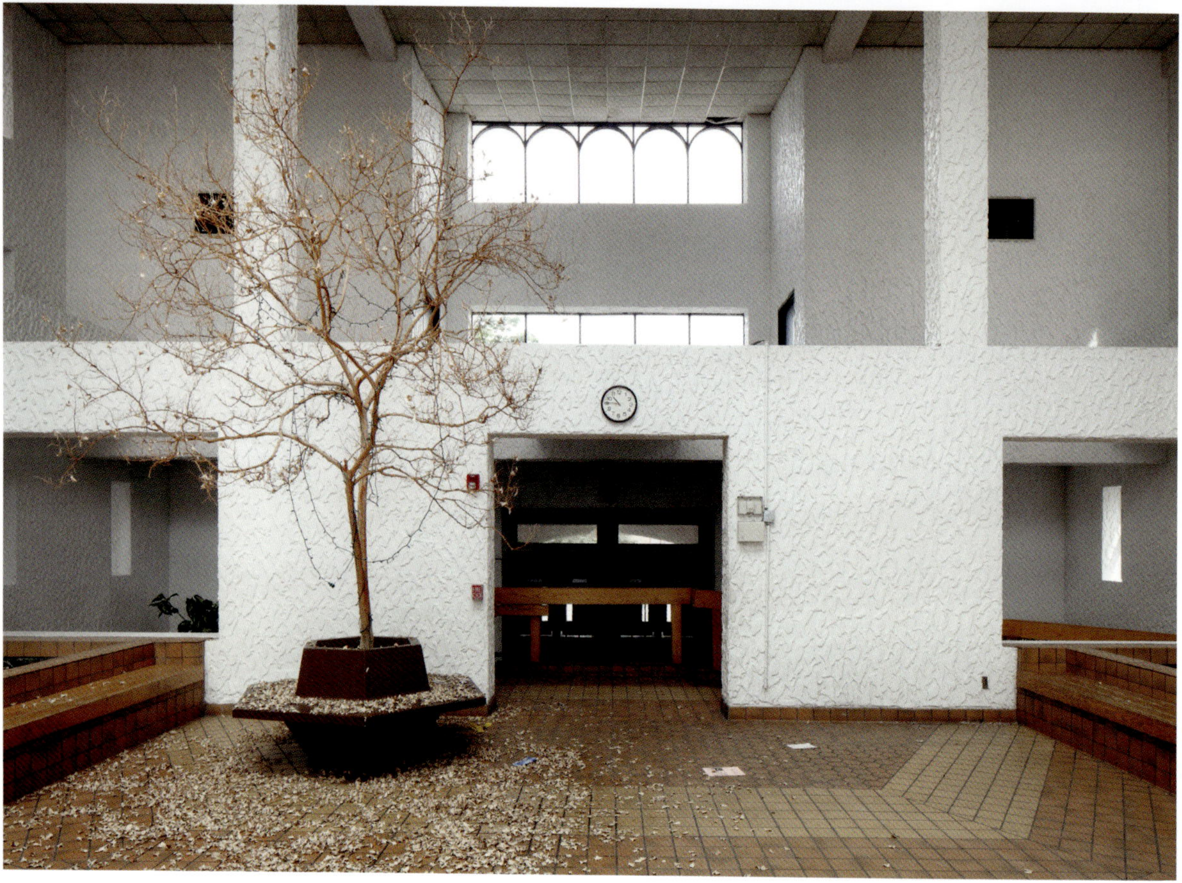

Highland Park, Detroit, USA, 2012

Montgomery Mall, Alabama, USA, 2012

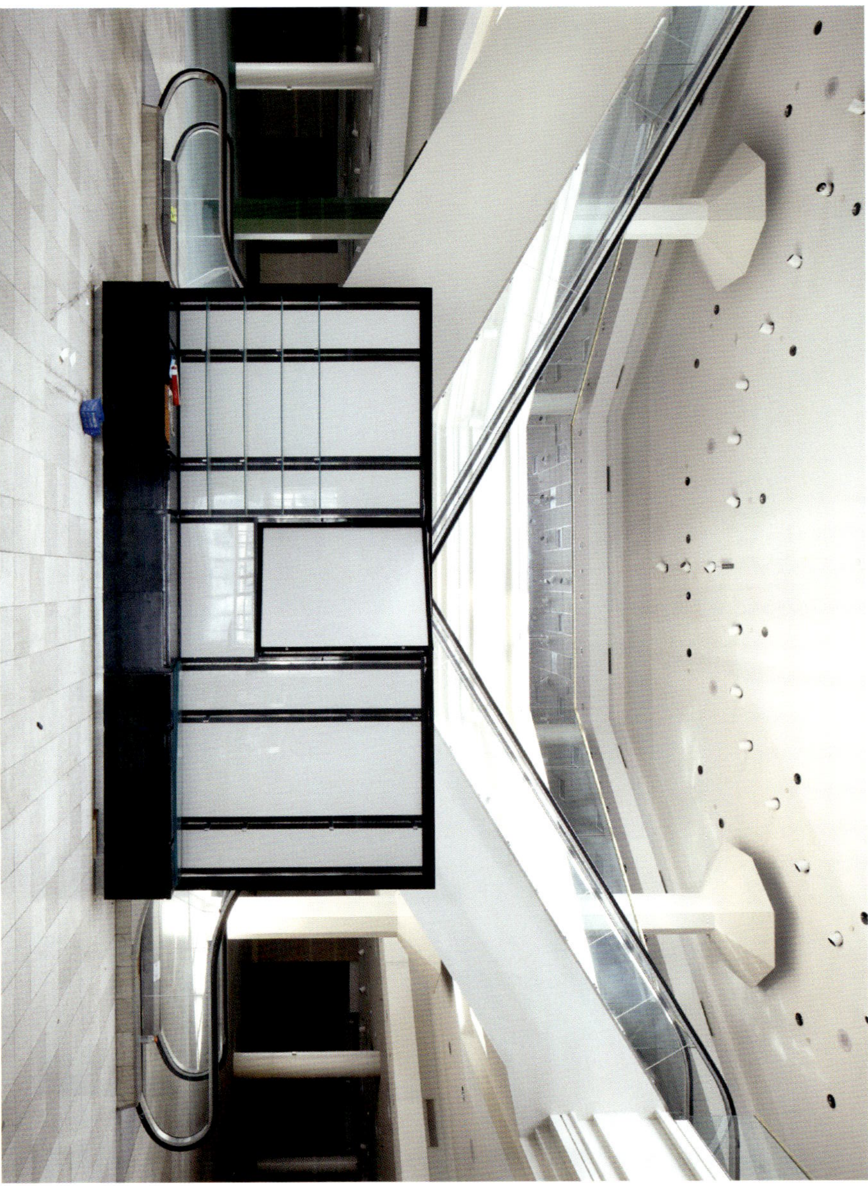

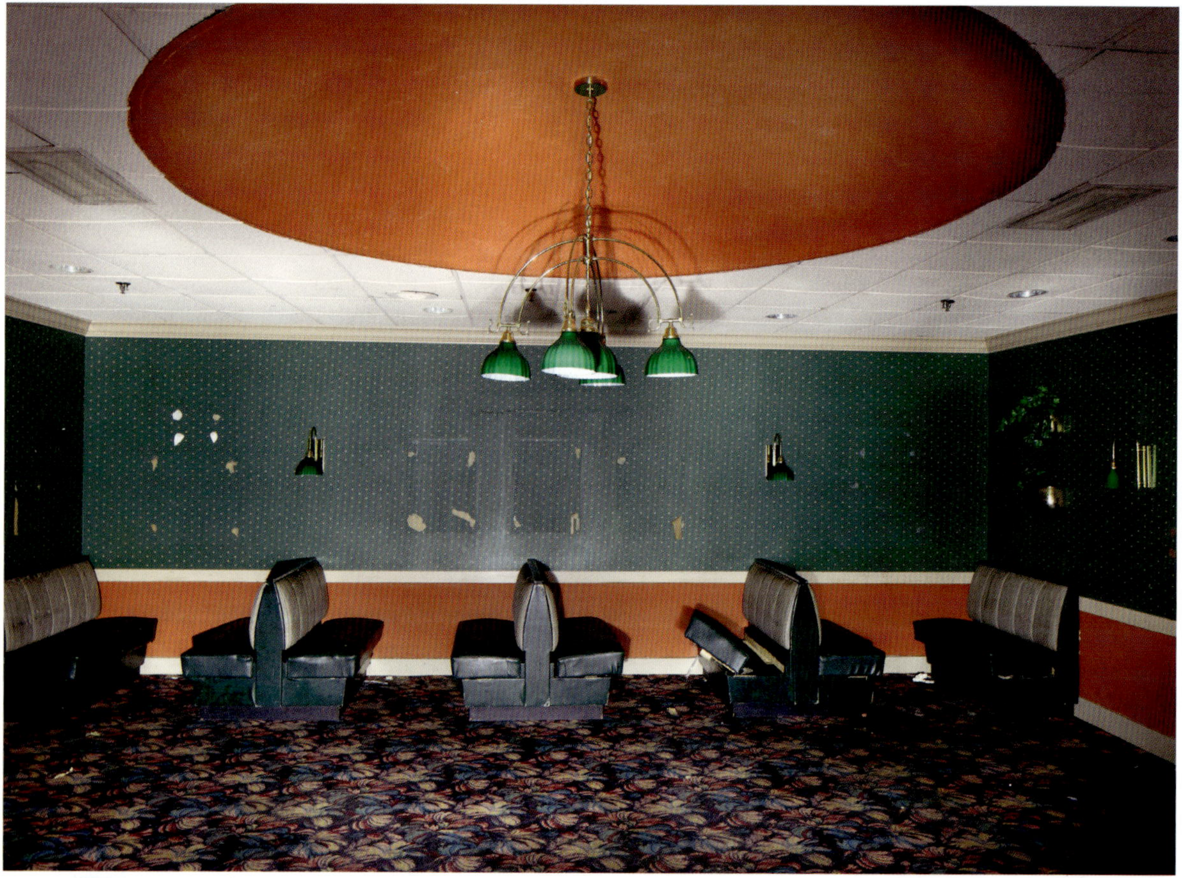

Montgomery Mall, Alabama, USA, 2012

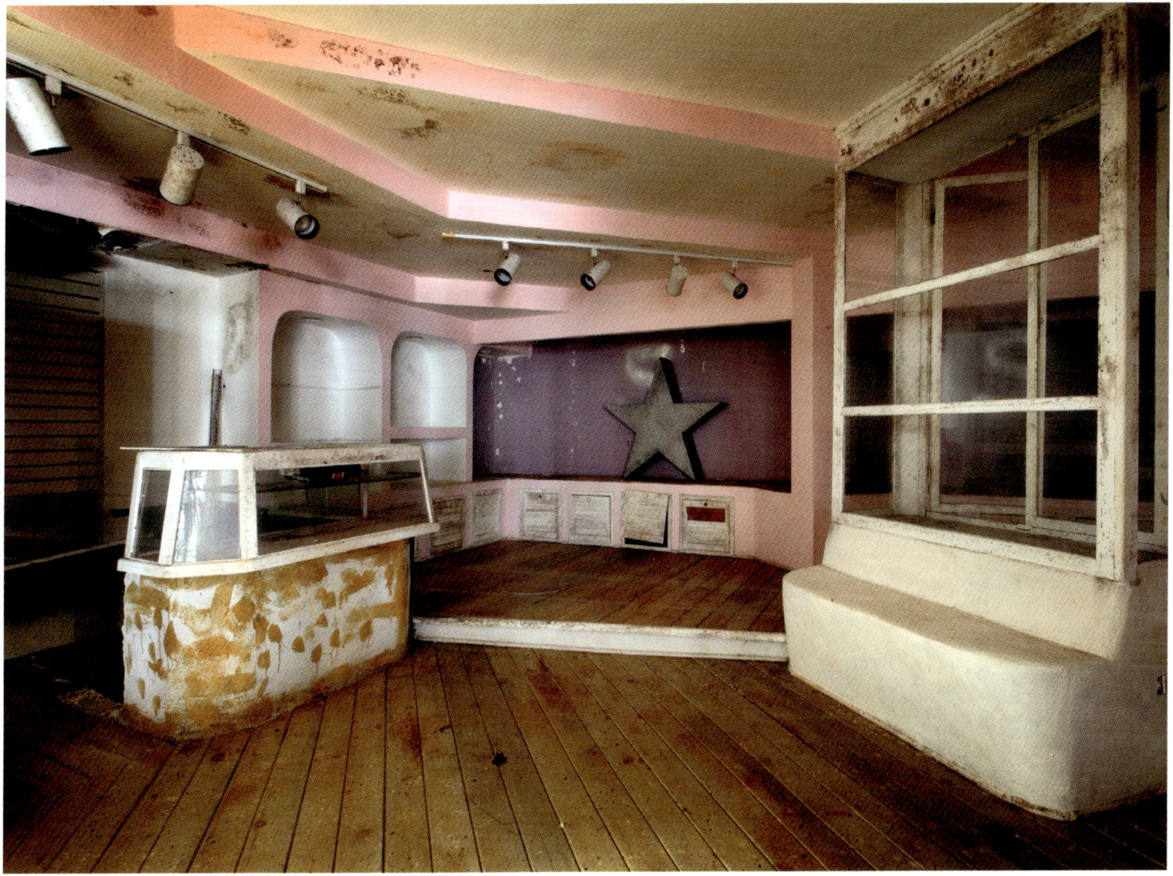

Disco bar, Cancun, Mexico, 2009

KURIOSHI INN ▹

JAPAN, 2012

If you manage to fend off the stray dogs that regard this establishment as their territory, the first part of this stunning hotel that you come into contact with is the lobby. The view over the ocean is endless and the seventies atmosphere immediately envelops you.

For me, this photo is the Abandoned Places version of a Swiss cuckoo clock.

How long had this hotel stood empty? Twenty years or so? The lamps have a loop in their cables and hang neatly at the same height. Over the course of those twenty years, seven of the loops have come loose. Roughly once every three years, one of the lamps drops down a meter with an audible clunk, followed by the metallic sound of the hook. For a minute or two, the lamp will swing to and fro, enjoying its short-lived freedom. It will then return to its motionless state, until the next cuckoo call.

I sat for a while, actually quite a while, hoping, in vain, for the tick of the clock. ◆

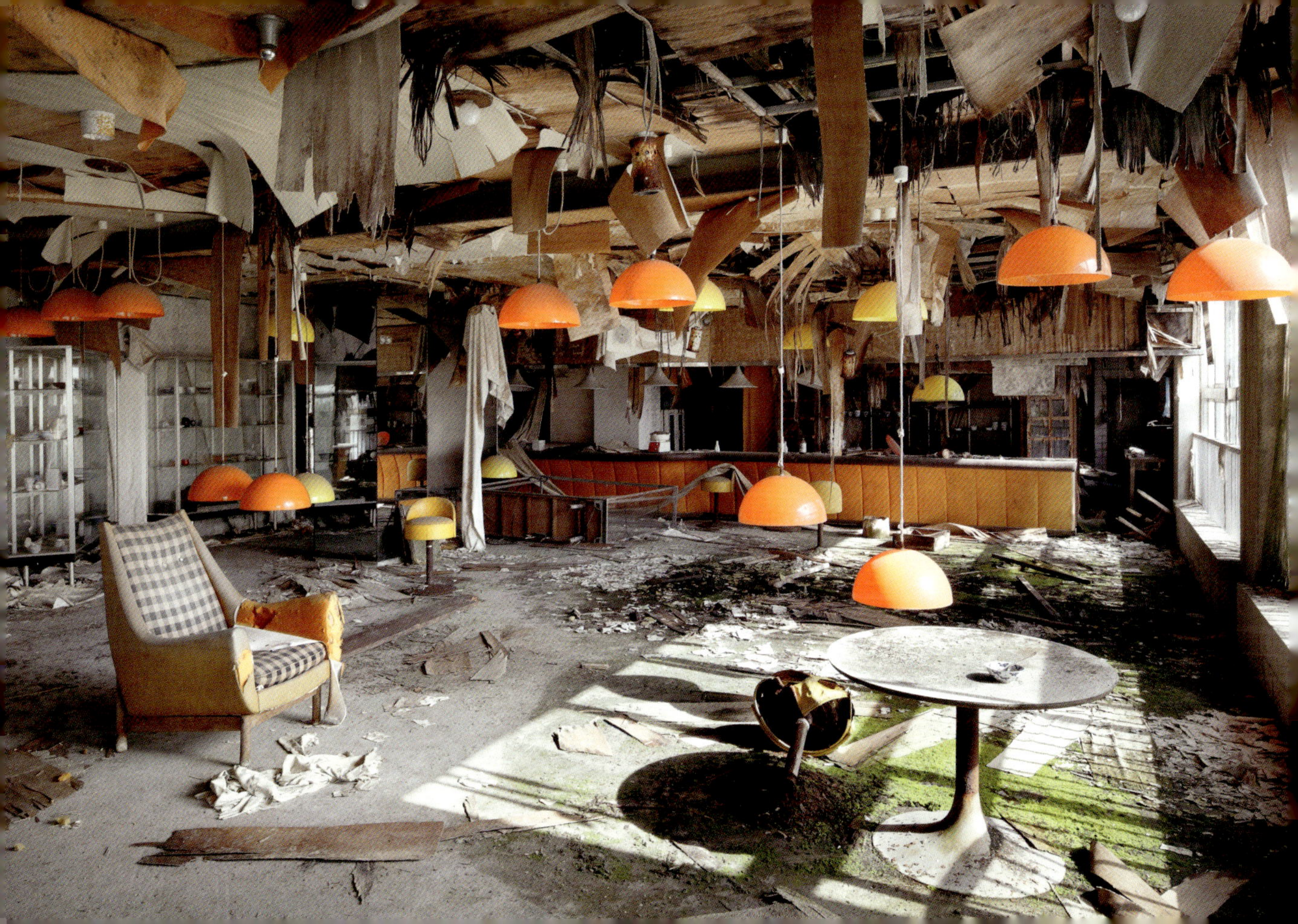

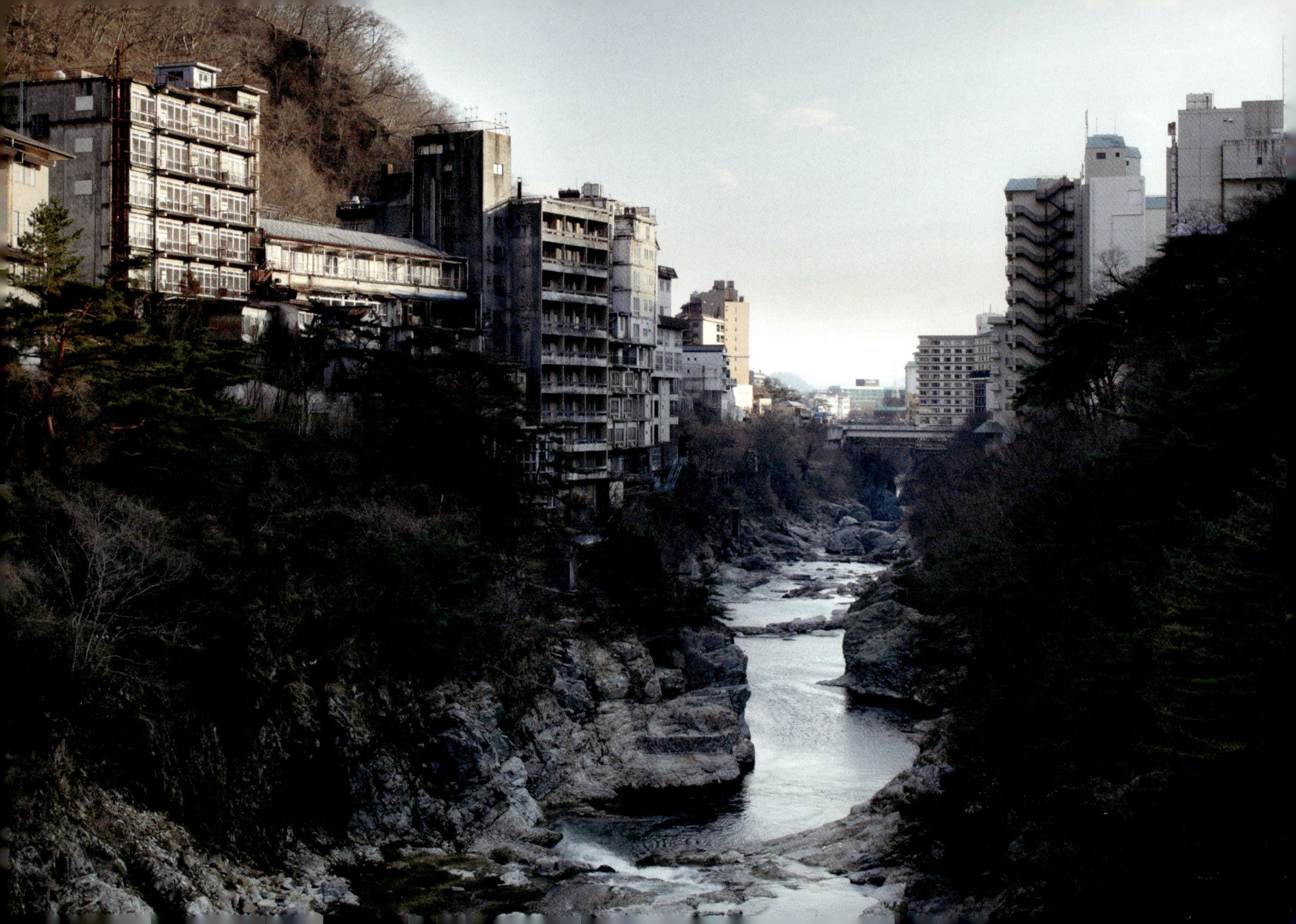

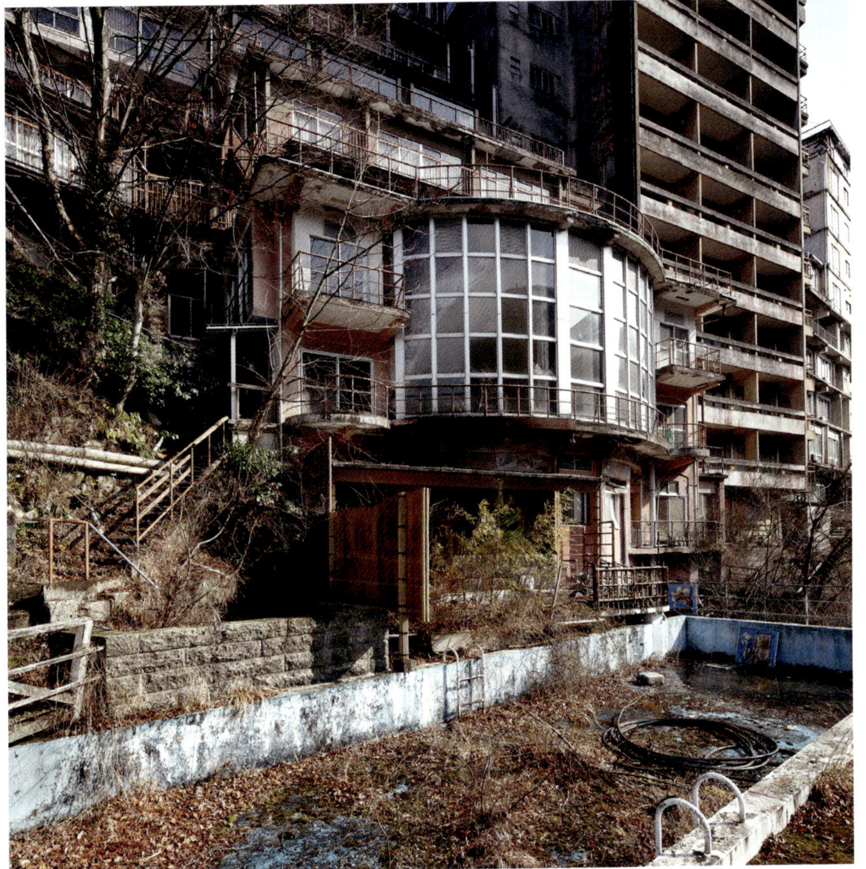

△▽ Kappa Onsen, Japan, 2012

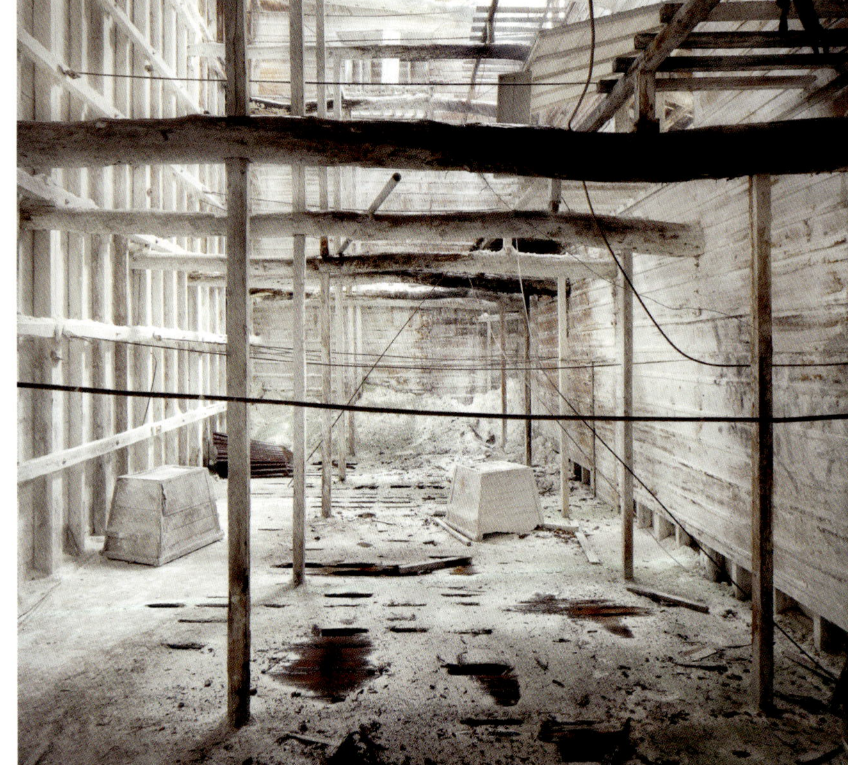

△ Shiraishi, Japan, 2012

▽ Kappa Onsen, Japan, 2012

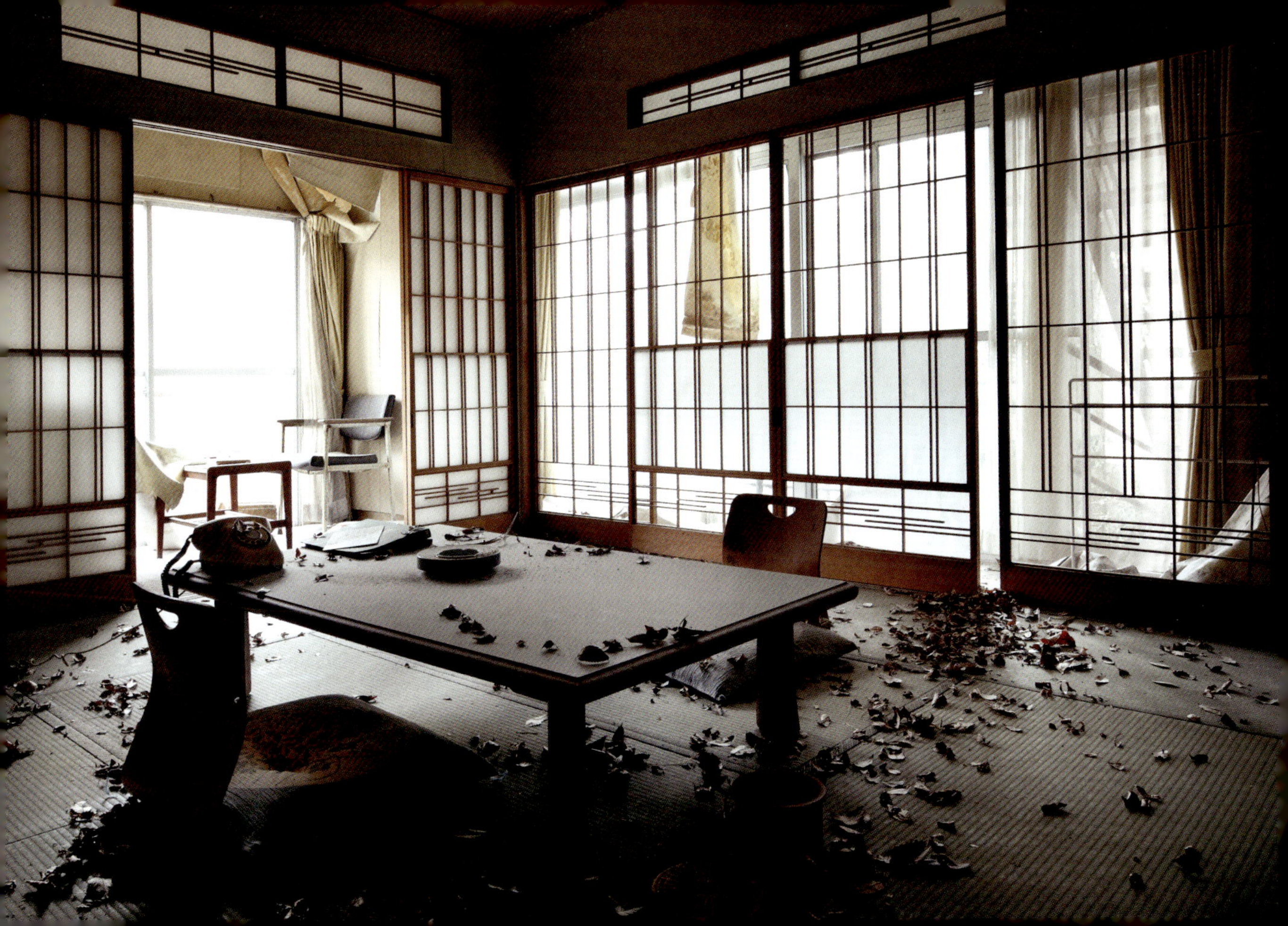

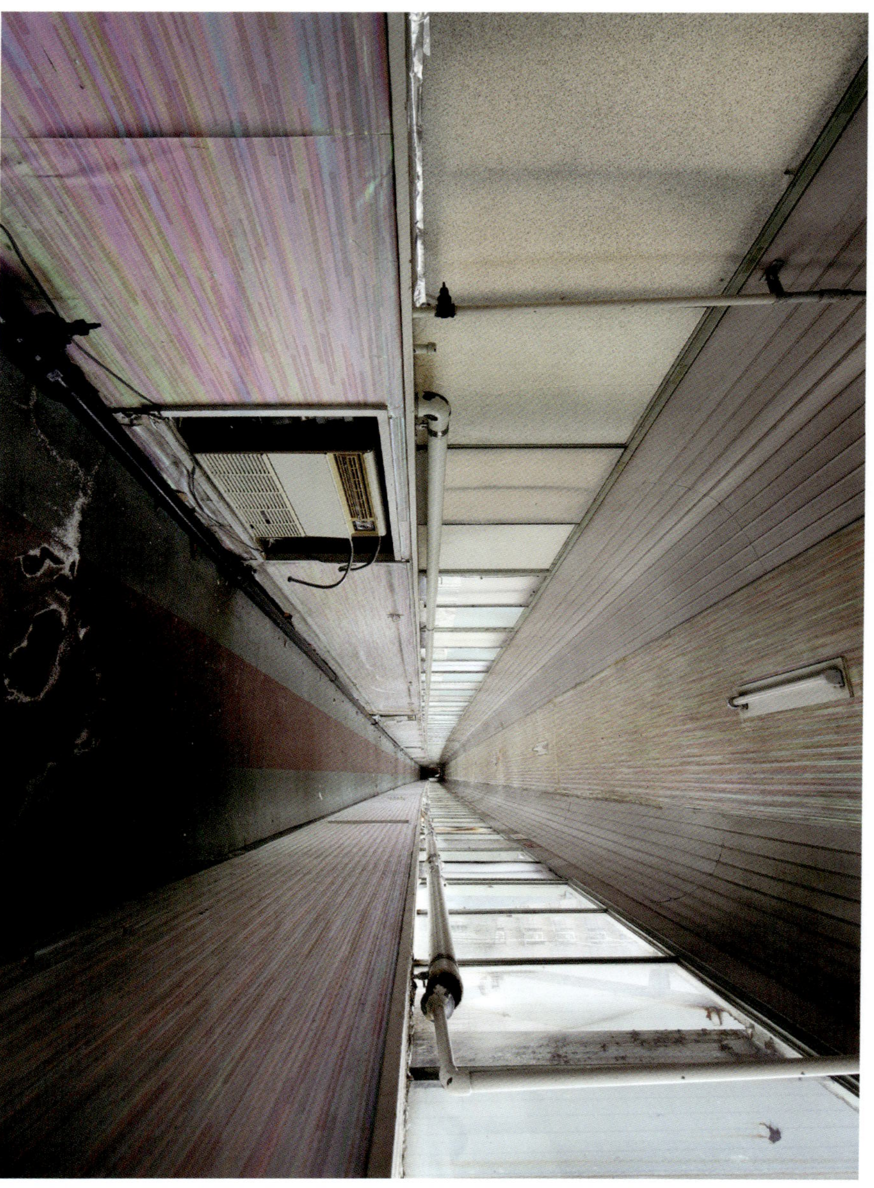

 Air Bridge Hotel, Japan, 2014

Kappa Onsen, Japan, 2012

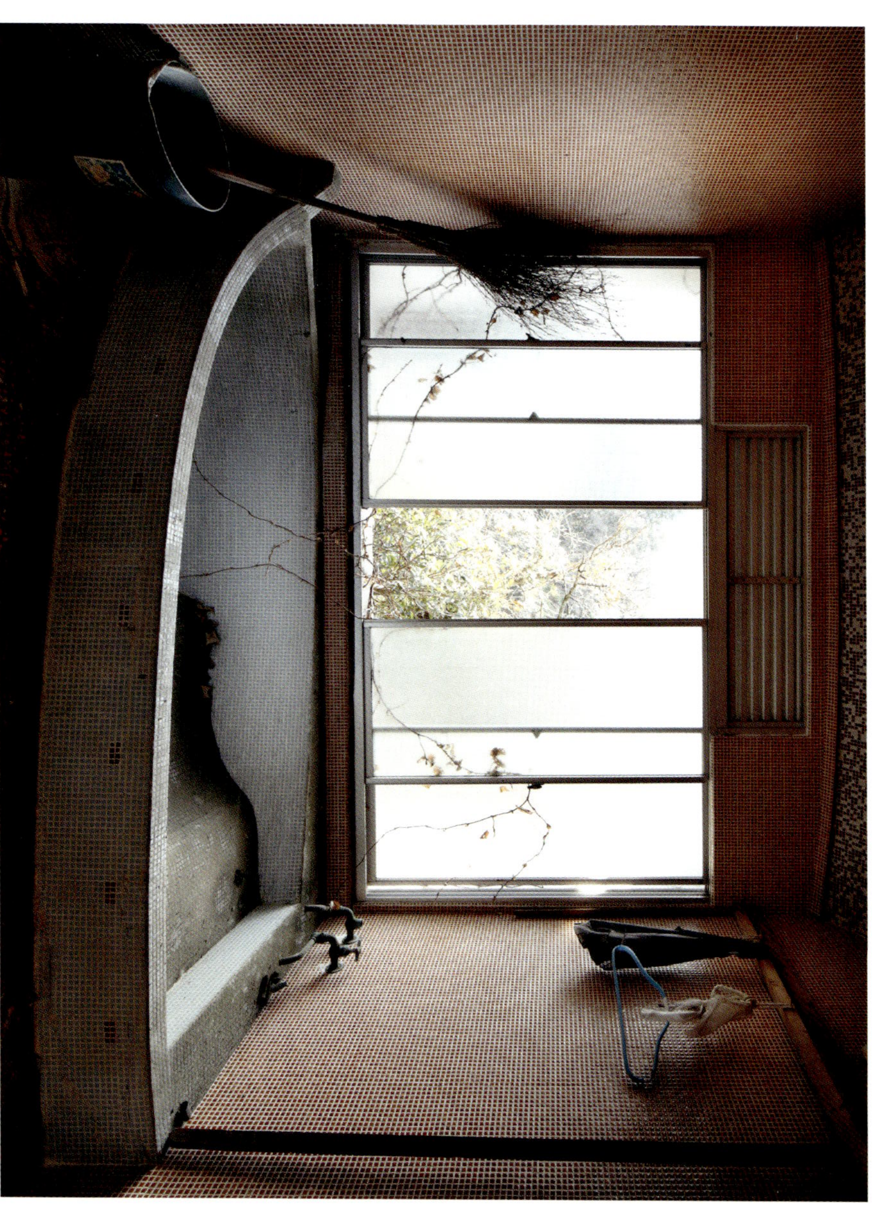

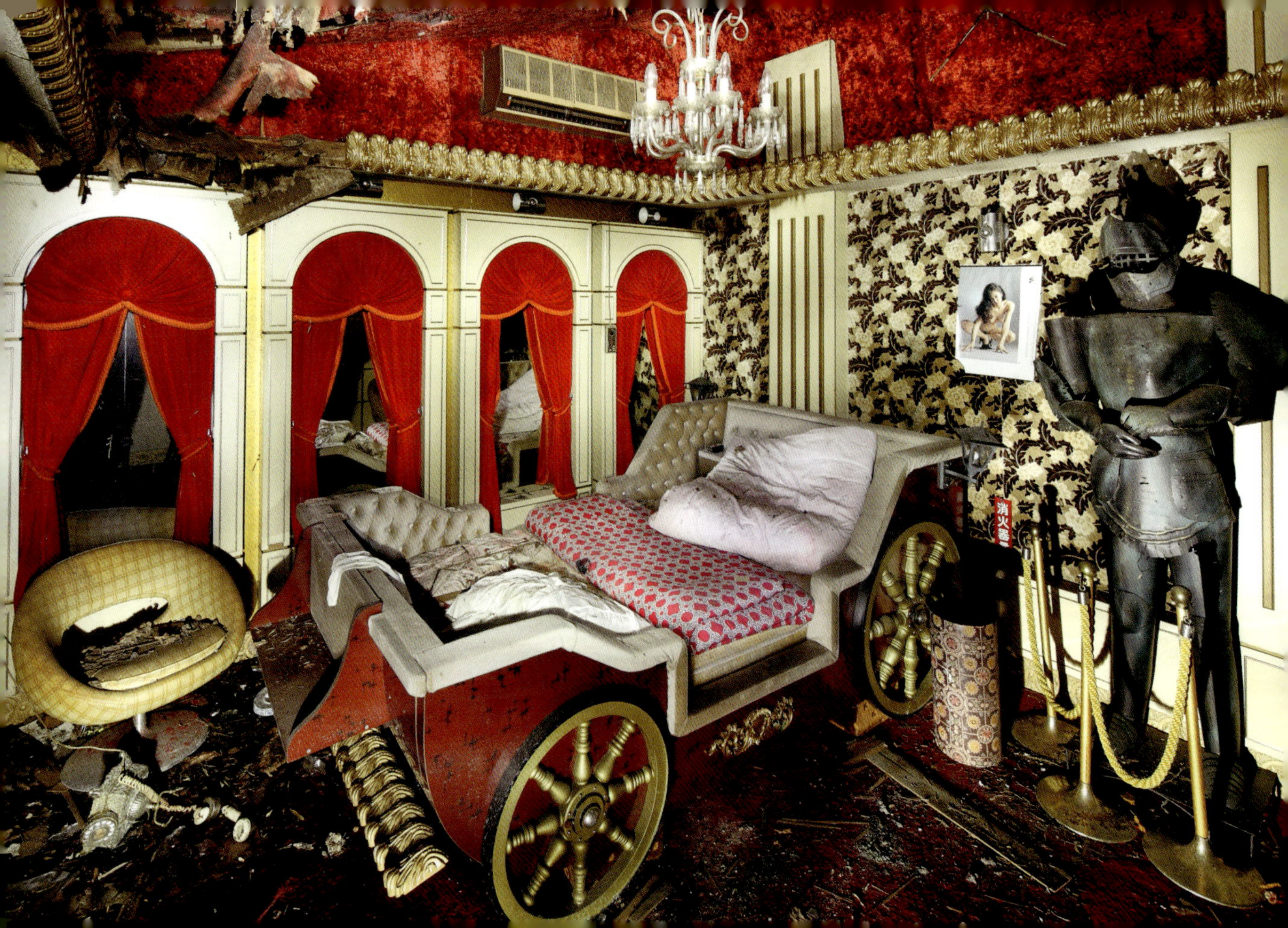

◃ FUU MOTEL
JAPAN, 2012

Some of the most amazing forgotten places lie in everyday residential neighborhoods. Boarded-up windows and doors surrounded by impenetrable bamboo, barbed wire covered with prickly plants.

From the street it looks like a piece of nature in the city, but crawl through the jungle and tumble inside – the worse for wear – through a hole in the roof, and you have found the way into the forgotten Fuu Motel.

This 'love hotel' was one of many love nests, a safe little place of respite in the overcrowded city. Its visitors were couples, married or not, looking for discretion, as well as customers wanting to experience their paid sex in optimal conditions.

You paid by the hour, for a whole night, or a special day price for a luxury room with kitschy decoration, fantasy bed, Jacuzzi, TV and karaoke machine.

The hasty shedding of clothes, squeaking mattresses and suppressed panting have been replaced by the giving way of rotten floors and the rustling of mice behind the ceiling decoration. The place itself still hasn't lost any of its charm… or its discretion for that matter. ◆

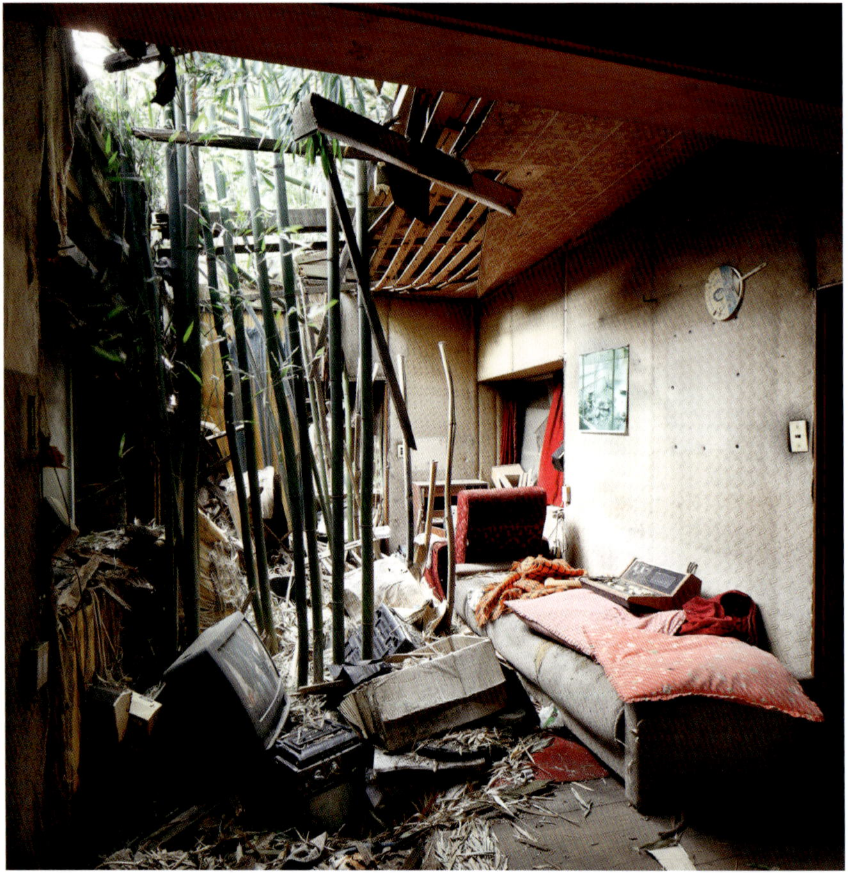

Fuu Motel, Japan, 2012

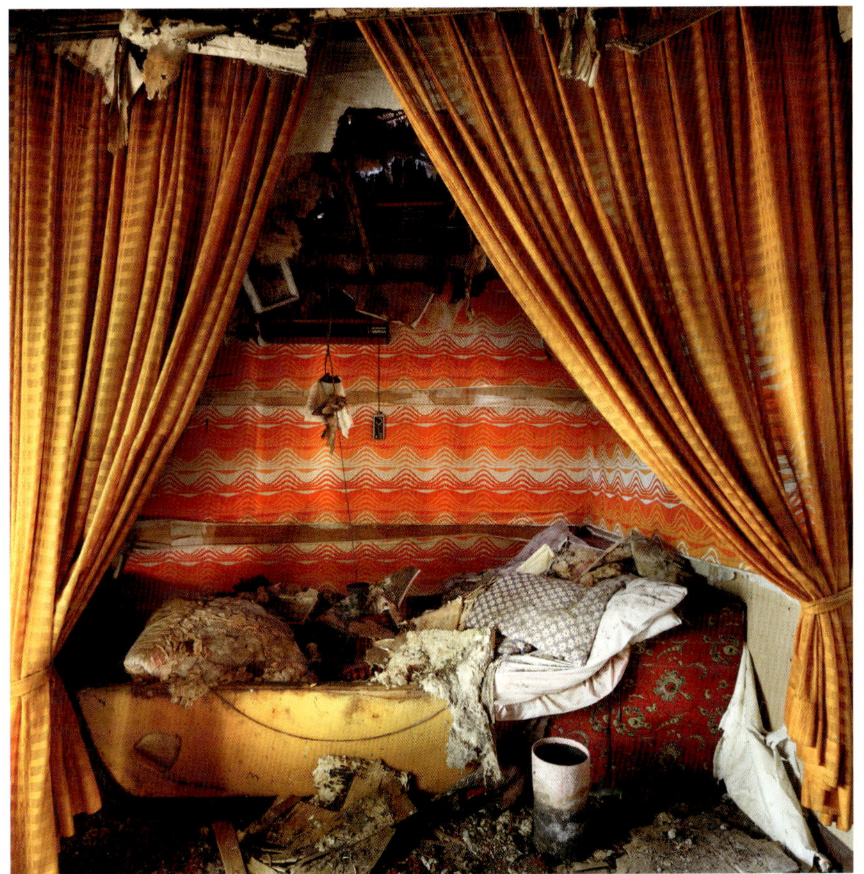

Fuu Motel, Japan, 2012

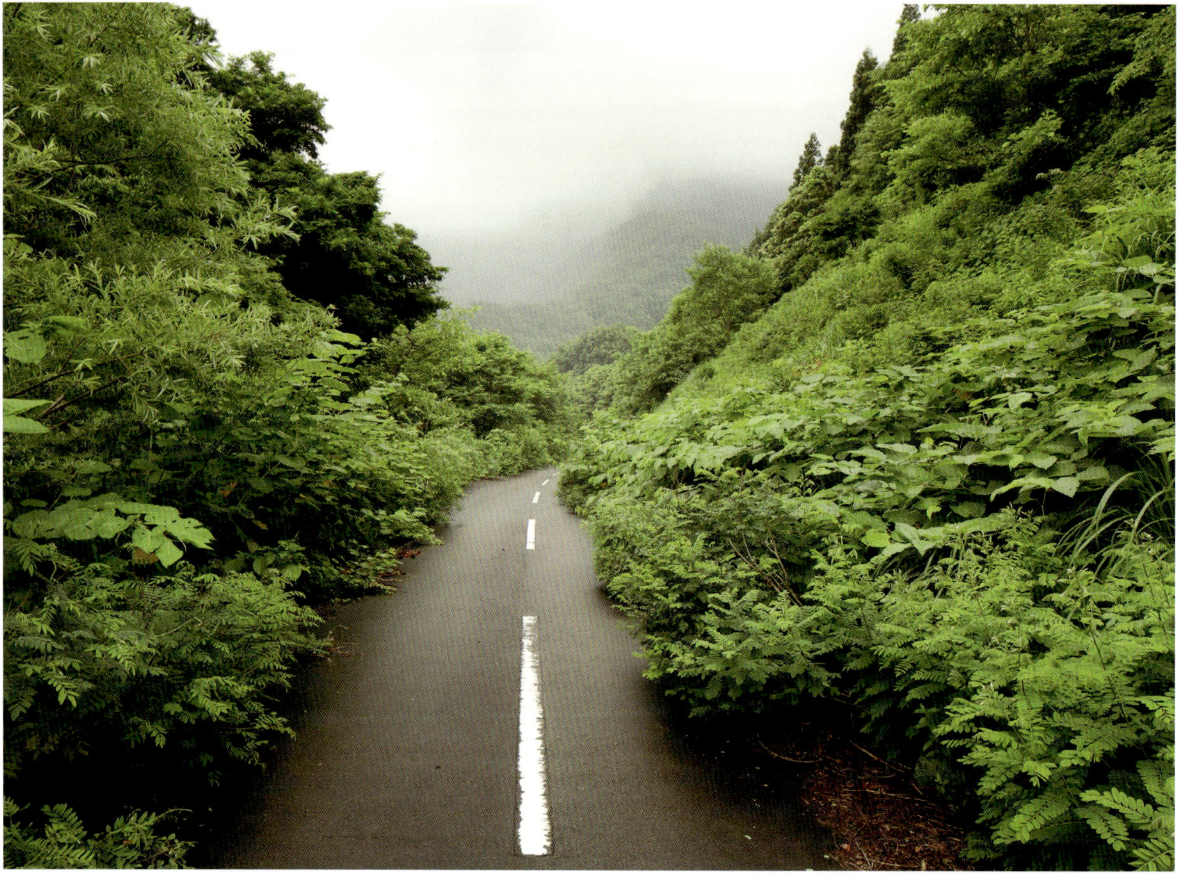

Wagakawa Highway, Japan, 2013

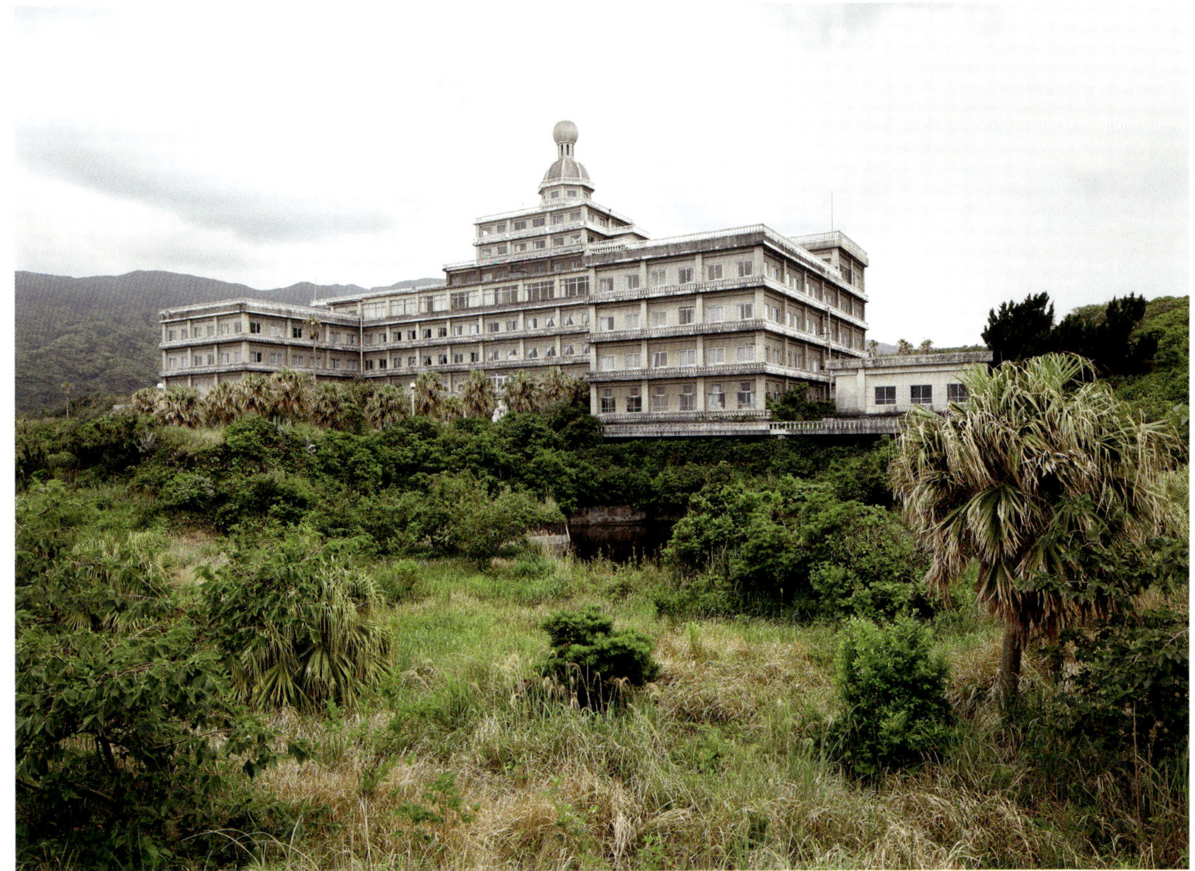

Black Sand Beach Hotel, Japan, 2014

△ Kappa Onsen, Japan, 2012

▽ Black Sand Beach Hotel, Japan, 2014

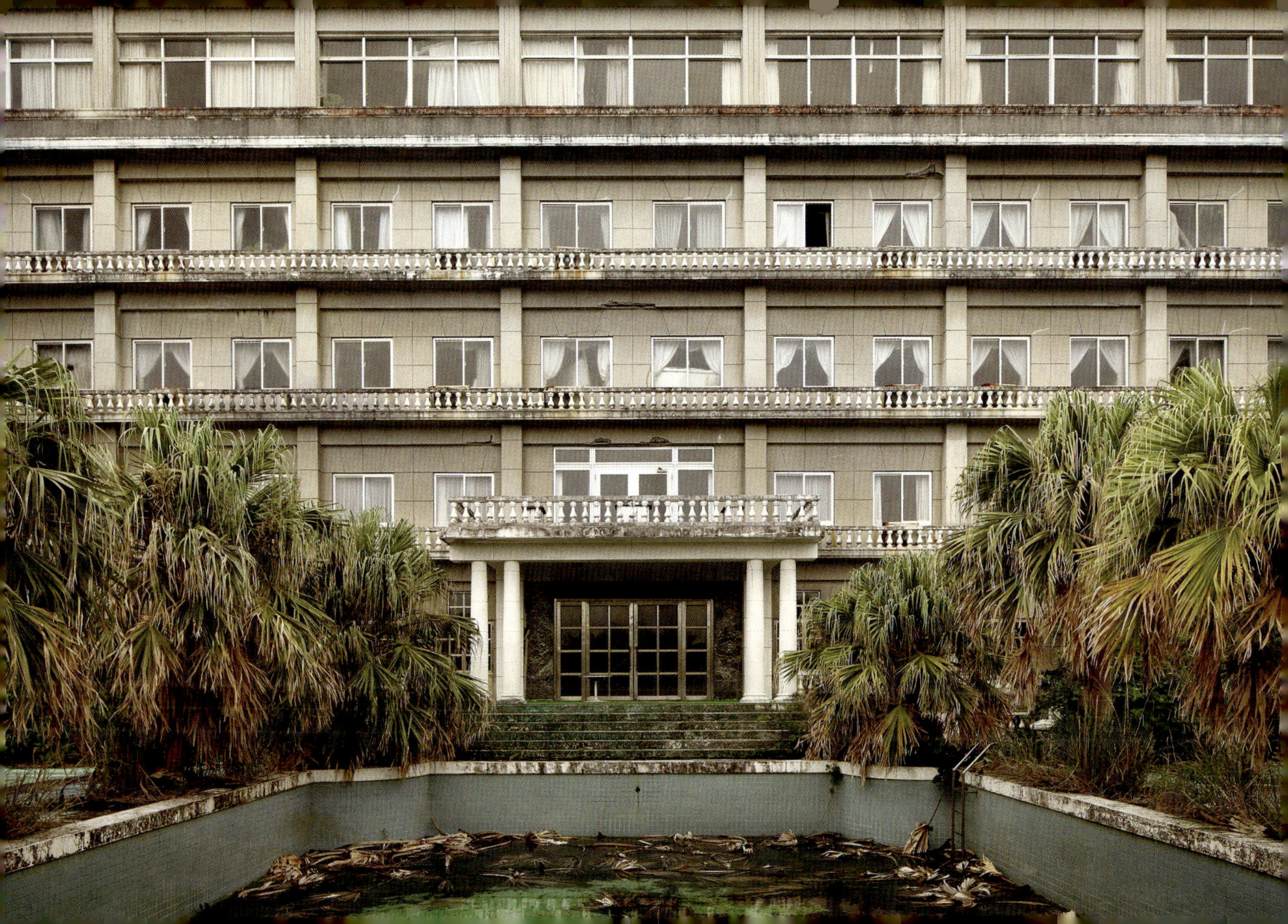

NARA DREAMLAND ▷

JAPAN, 2012

A nocturnal exploration is always special. Darkness sharpens the senses, the animal in man surfaces: seeing without light, walking without noise, climbing like a Ninja, blending invisibly into the environment (and yet you get scared stiff by a life-size dummy of a cowboy in the bushes).

At the highest point of the roller coaster, balancing between vertigo and ecstasy, I saw the guard's car. He stood in front of the gate with the four blinking lights, but had no chance of catching us, even though this could earn him 100,000 yen.

The park was pitch-dark. A quarter-moon was visible and the sky was slightly lit by the city lights in the background. I placed my camera on the tripod and set a minute's-long exposure. At first sight it gave an ordinary daylight picture, but with incredible light. We remained in the park for six hours in all; a surreal visit that ended with enjoying a can of beer, the view and the silence. Unreal. ◆

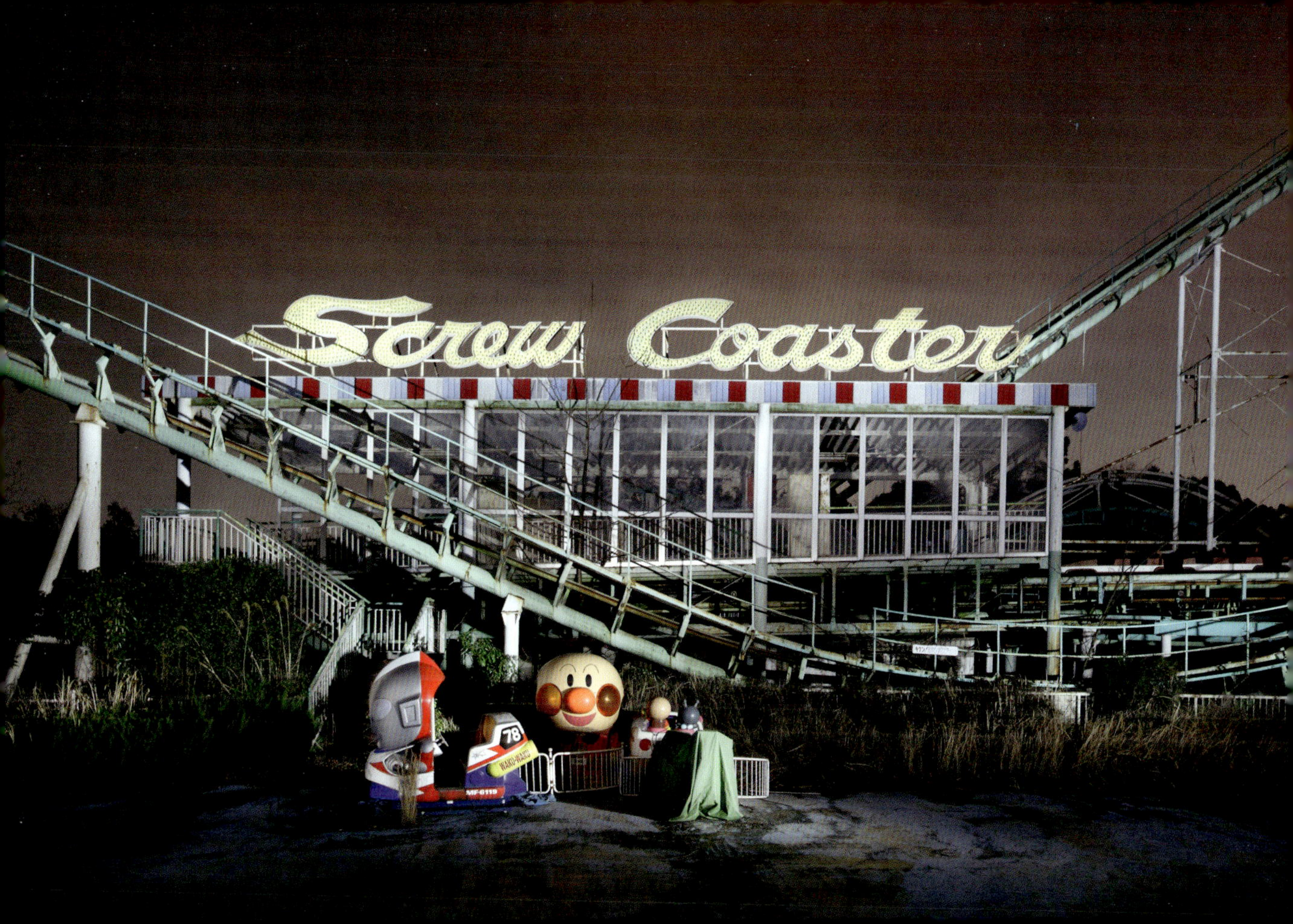
Screw Coaster
78

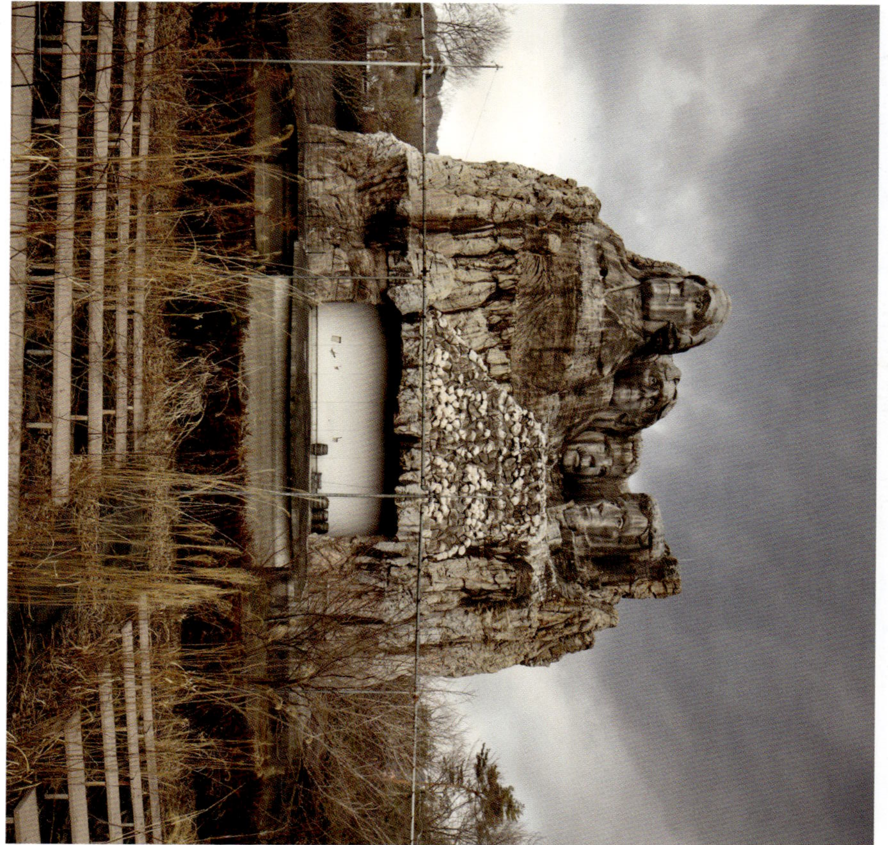

 △ Western Village, Japan, 2012 ▽ Nara Dreamland, Japan, 2012

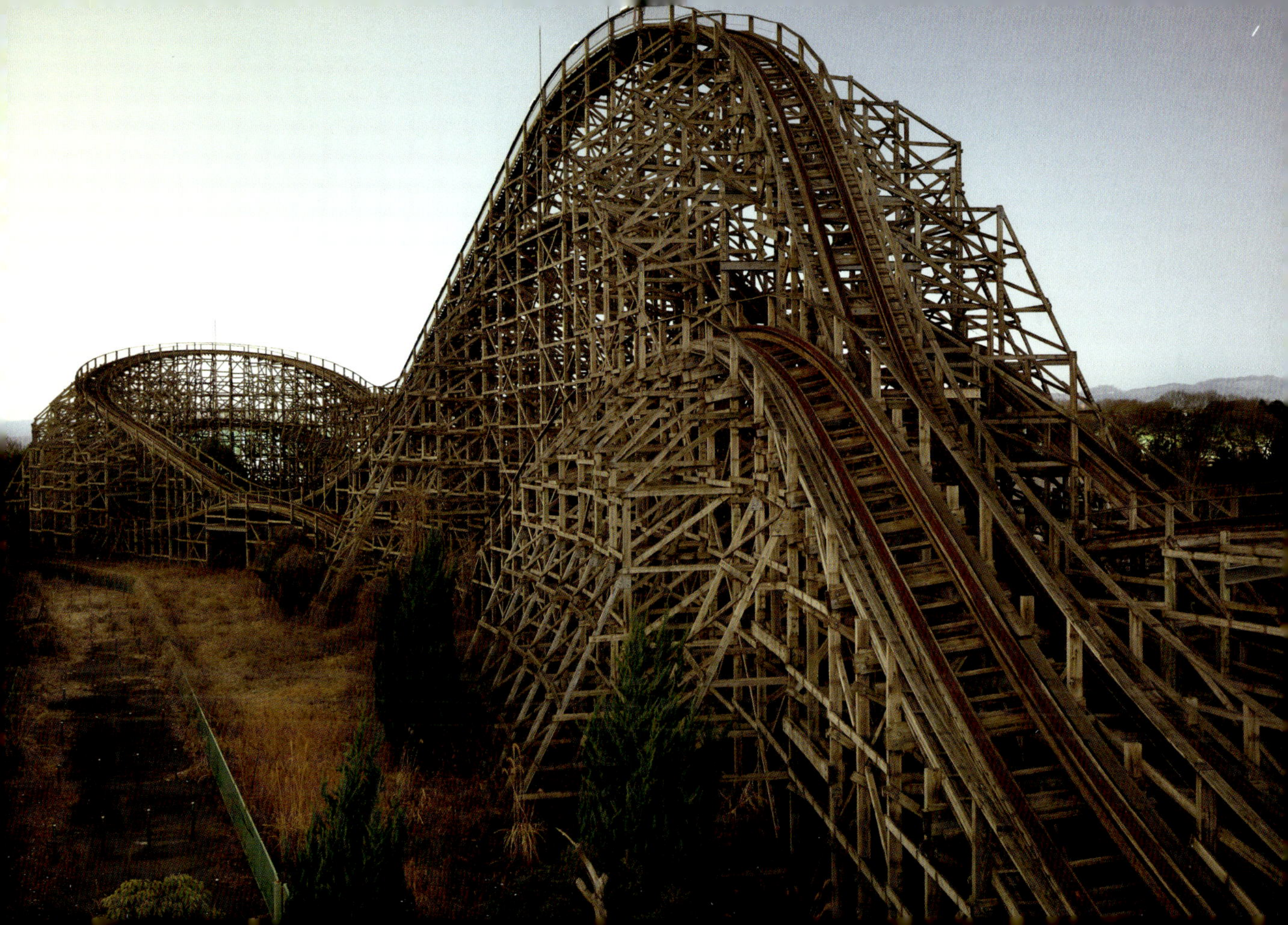

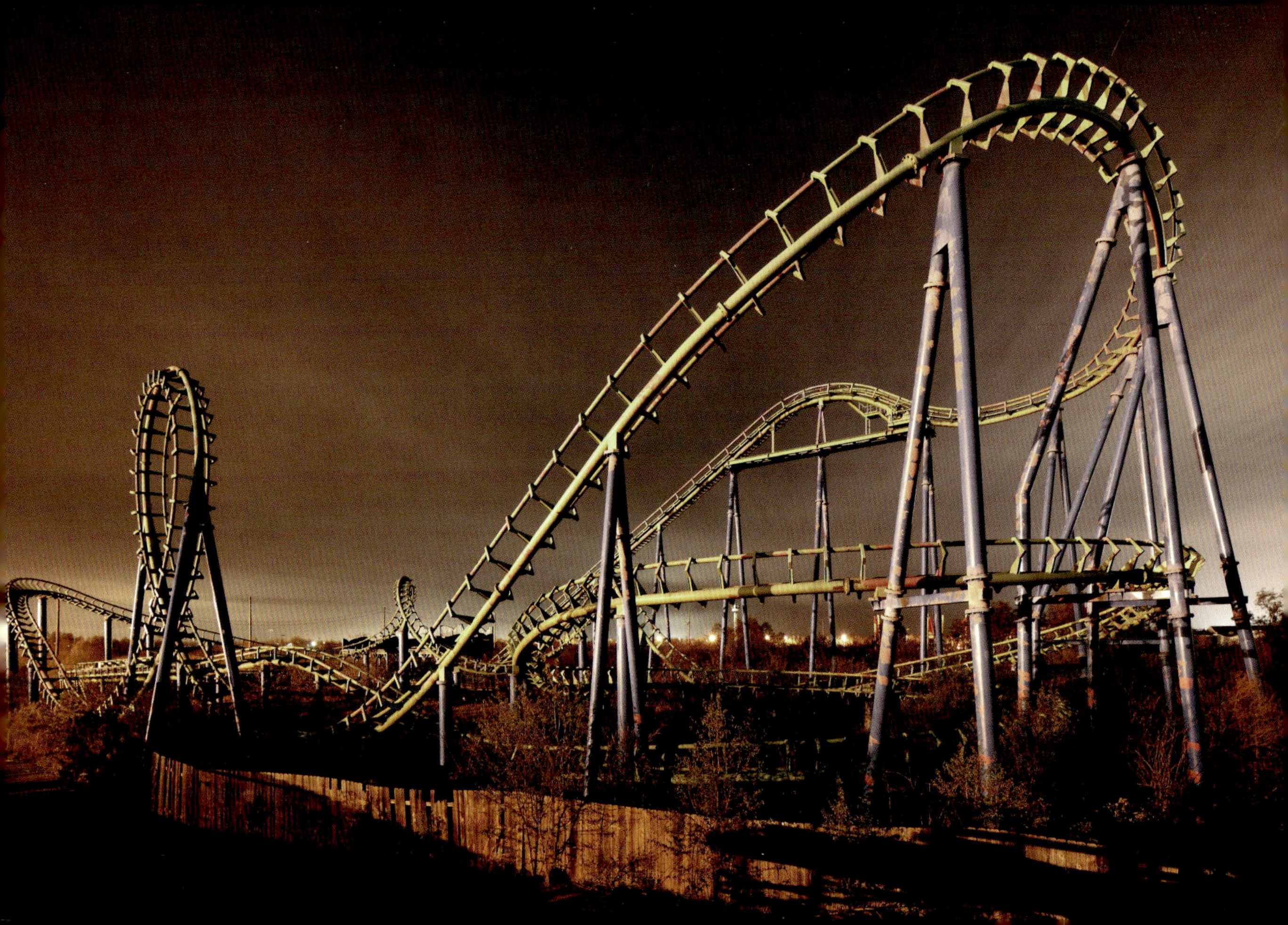

◃ SIX FLAGS NEW ORLEANS

USA, 2013

Six Flags New Orleans has been closed since hurricane Katrina struck in August 2005, flooding and destroying the theme park.

The park is guarded and the police regularly patrol it to keep out curious visitors. The plan was to explore the potential access points during the day and to return in the evening for the real visit.

Most of the park is encircled by swamps. Using rubble from an abandoned villa, we built a bridge up to the fence, where we found a hole. Further on we still had to cross a stretch of a swamp until we arrived at the large parking lot.

During the day, everything looked easy-going, but when we came back at night, the entire place was suddenly transformed. The street lamps created eerie shadows over the swamps as if alligators were lying about everywhere. The rubble that we used for crossing the swamp had sunk so deep in the mud that we barely made it to the other side, let alone returning over it in order to exit the park.

On the way, we were surprised by a pack of coyotes that had dug their burrow behind the bumper cars. Their whining, snoring and gnashing teeth gave us the chills. The image of these beasts running around cowardly with their tails between their legs, made each one of our imaginary primal hairs curl.

It was only once we stood safely near the roller coasters, that we could finally breathe freely again. The tension and the magic of the night blended with the endless buzzing of mosquitoes. And then time stood still. ◆

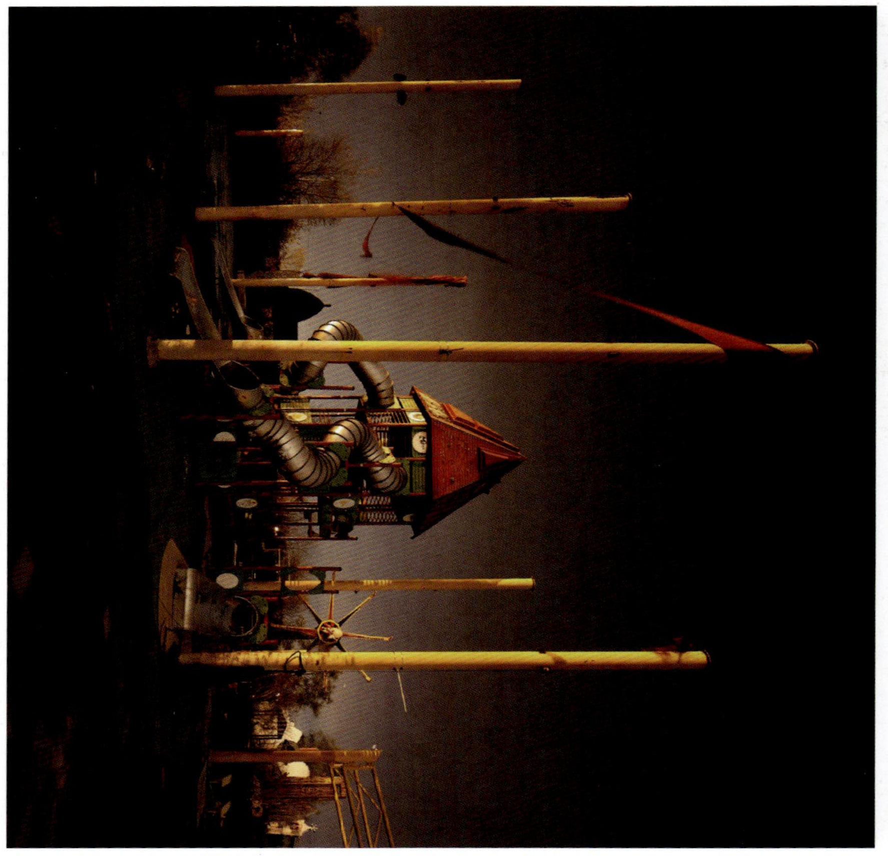

 △▽ Six Flags, New Orleans, USA, 2013

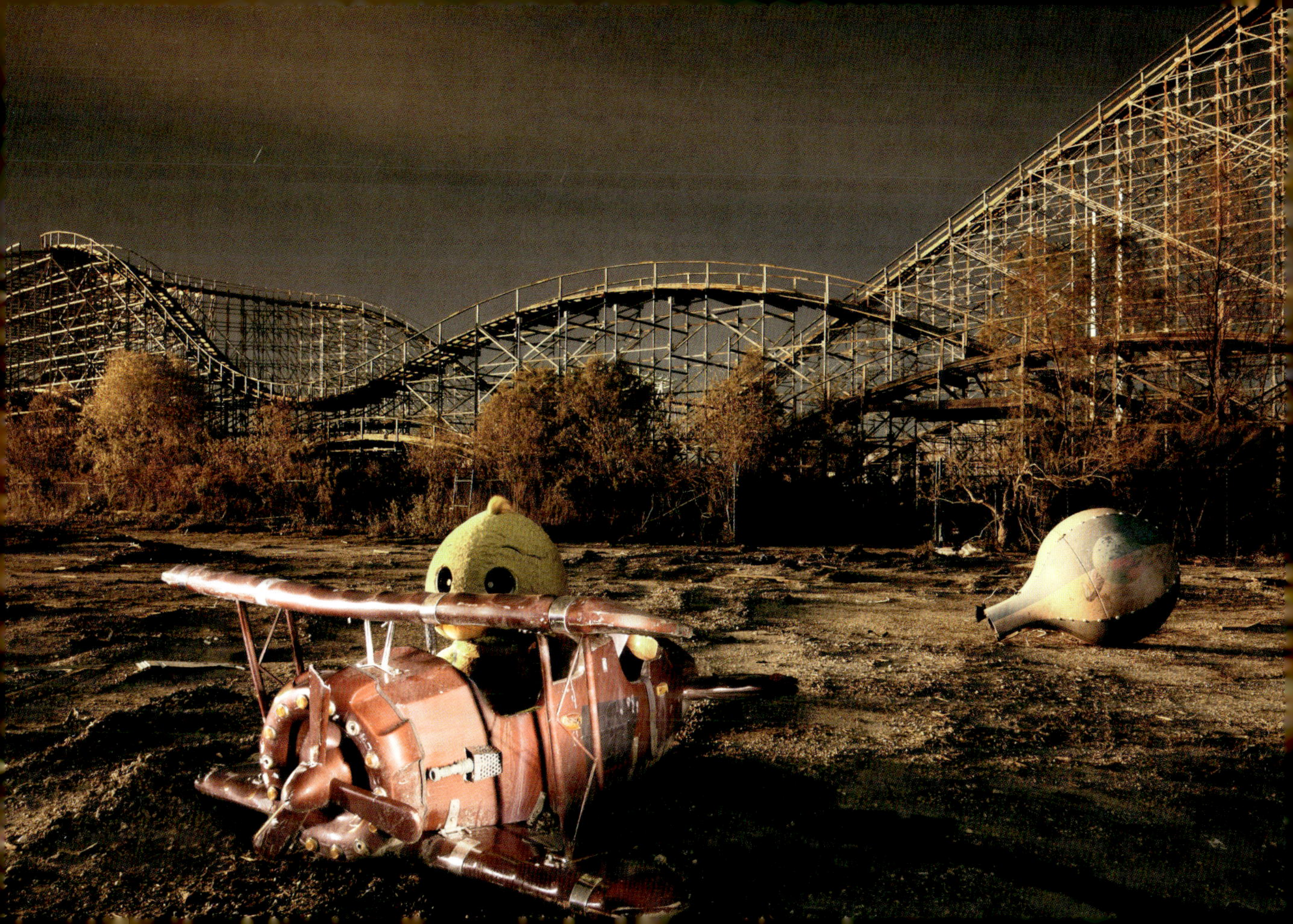

ADAM'S THEATER ▹

NEW JERSEY, USA, 2009

In this area with its homeless people and vagrants, everything is carefully sealed off. I had a chat with the parking lot security guard. I won his trust and he showed us the easiest place to climb over the barbed wire. He warned us that the fire escape was rusty and on the point of collapse.

It was impossible to do this discreetly, and we made a terrible racket as we climbed over the rusty, sharp wire. The rubbish belt behind the fence mirrored the dark side of this city, with its broken bottles of cheap liquor, its cans and needles.

The iron of the fire escape crumbled beneath our feet. I went in front as I weighed the least. The doors on the first and second floors were closed. On the third floor, two steps broke off and clattered to the ground. I clung to the railing and asked myself what *on earth* was I doing in that place. The last door at the top was jammed but not locked. When I put pressure on it, it opened a little way, but at the same time I felt the fire escape give way beneath my feet...

I slowly pushed open the door. Cool, damp air wafted out to greet me. As my eyes adjusted to the darkness, I could make out the contours of the gigantic theater. ◆

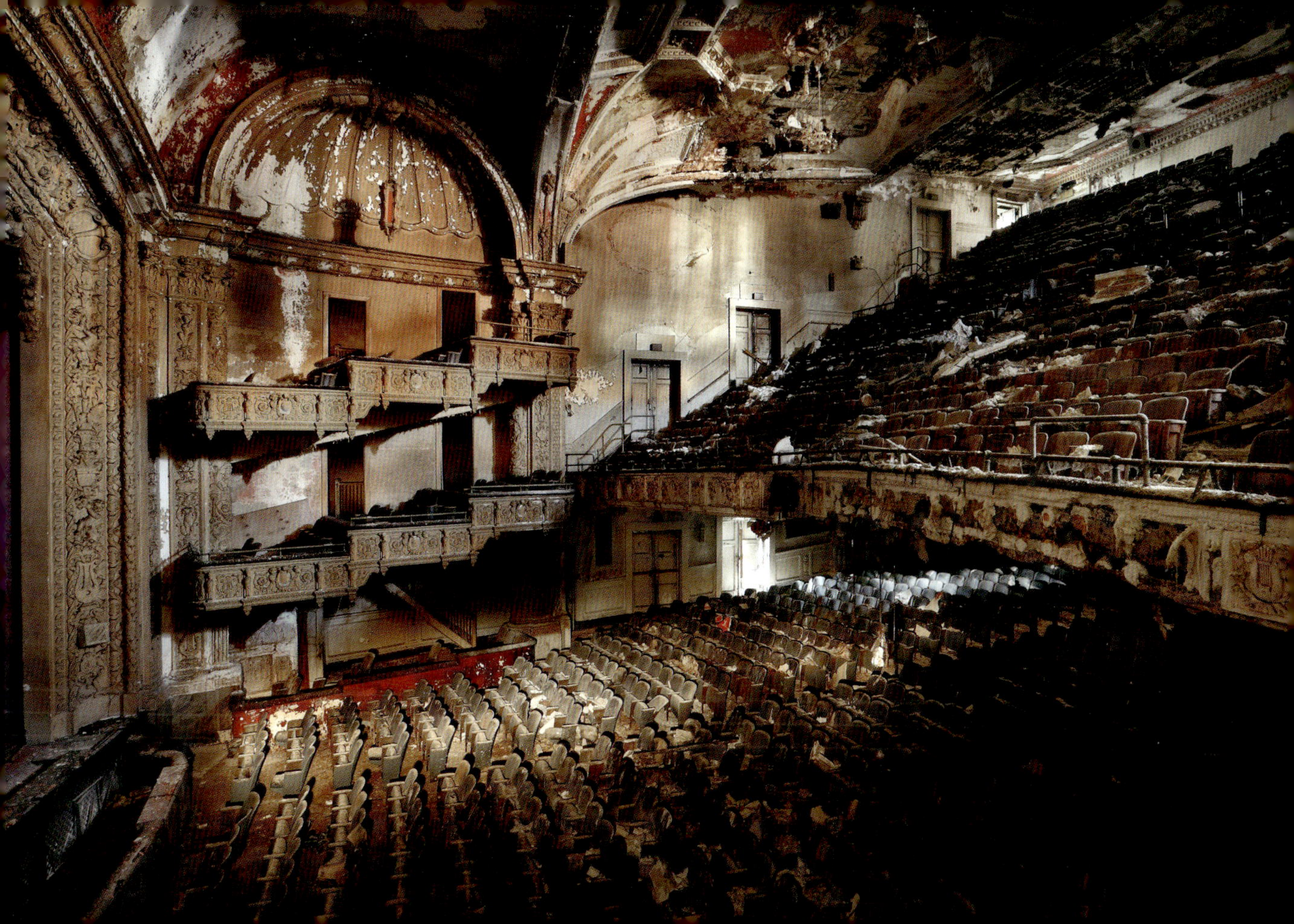

Maya 'Roof Tire' Hotel, Japan, 2012

 Lee Plaza Hotel lobby, Detroit, 2010

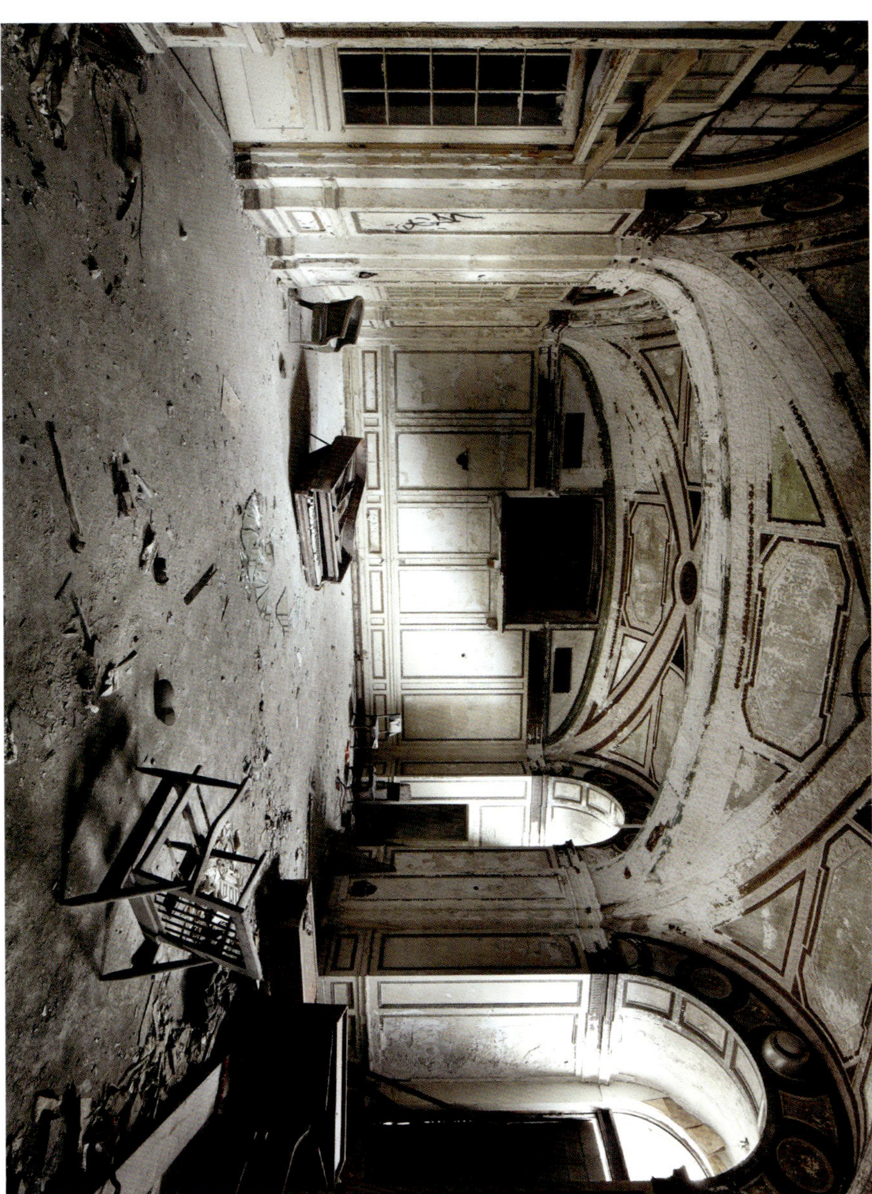

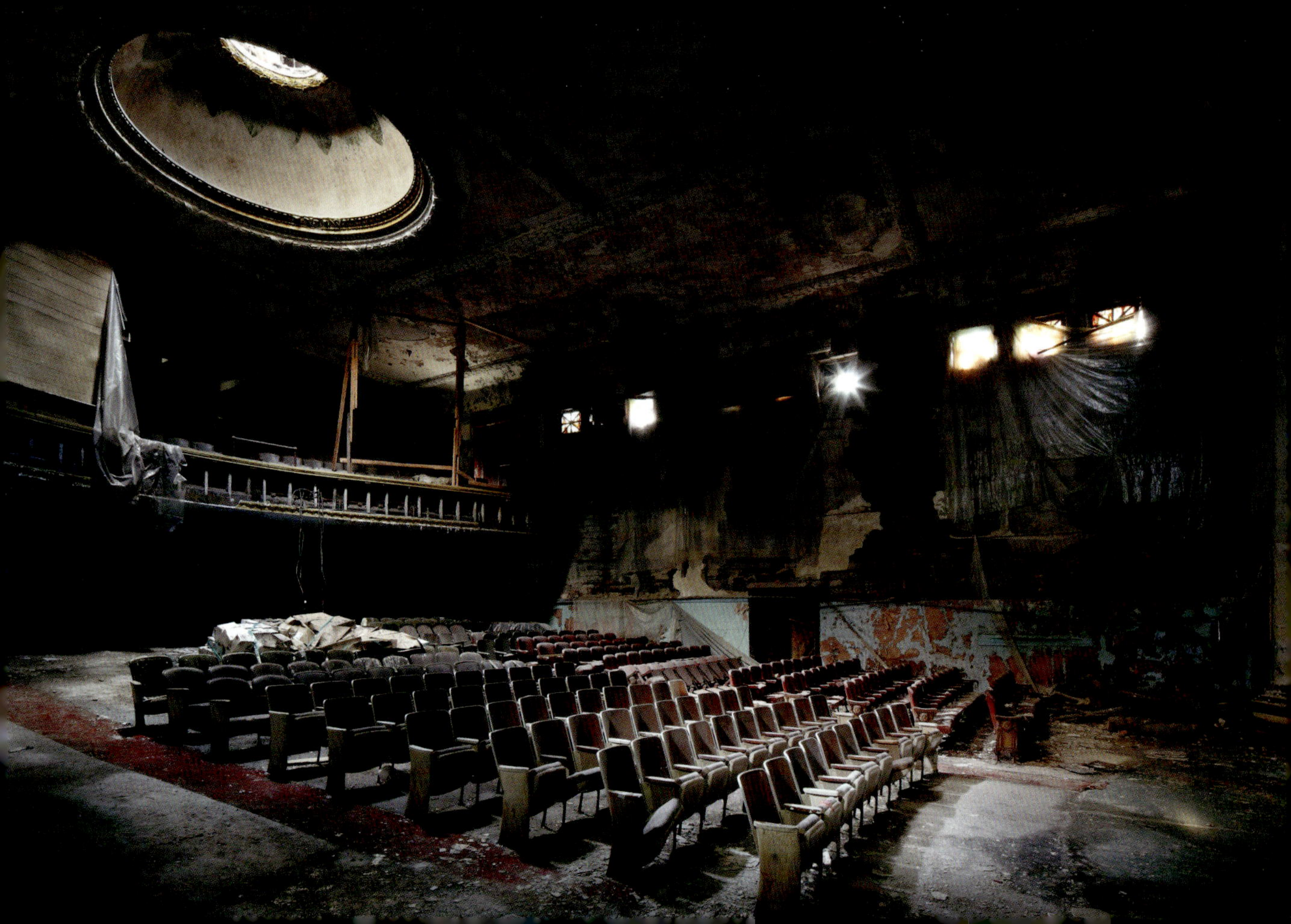

△ Sattler Theater, Buffalo, USA, 2011

▽ Val Benoit projector, Belgium, 2010

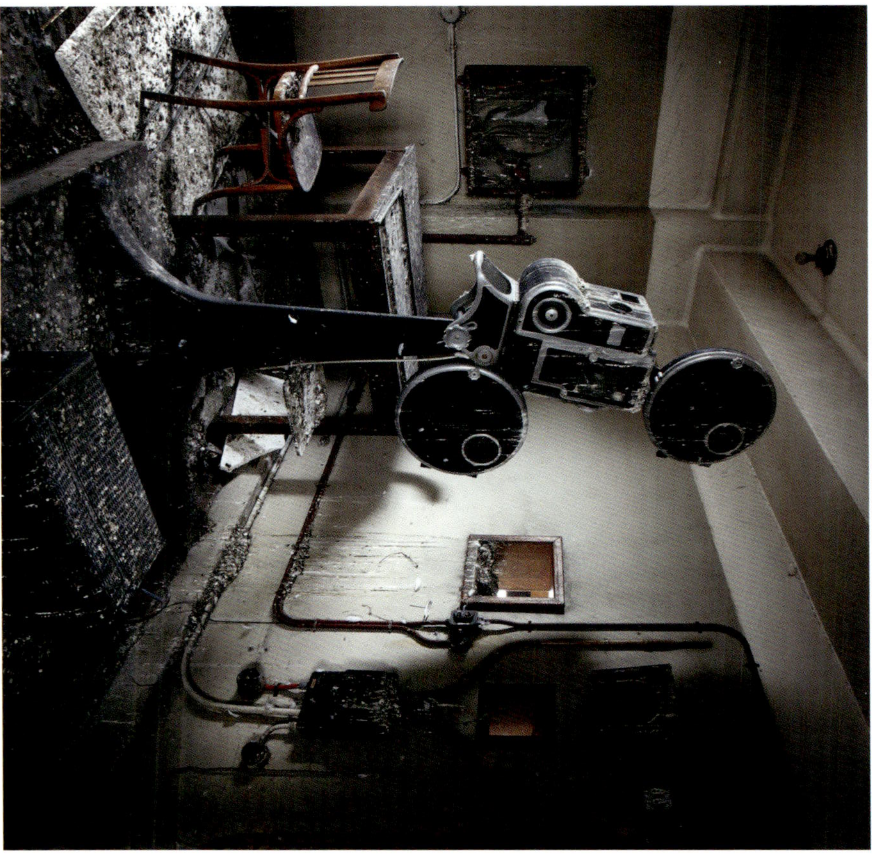

 △ The Hunting Party, Belgium, 2011 ▽ Aegidium, Belgium, 2012

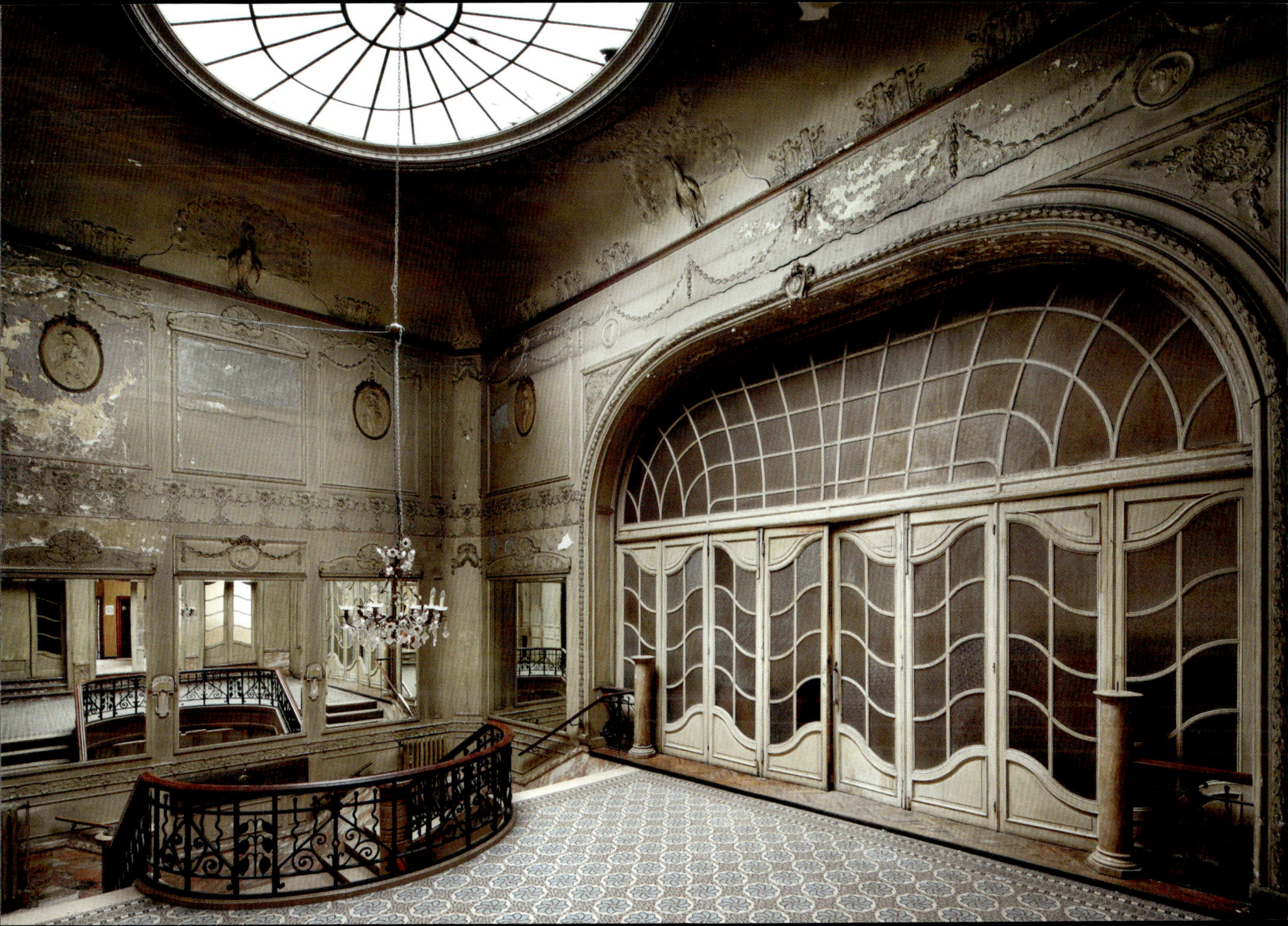

HUNTER'S CASTLE ▹

BELGIUM, 2008

This is a charming, dilapidated, 17th century country estate located amidst orchards and meadows.

In 1763 Mozart spent the night at the castle while touring, and aviation pioneer, Louis Blériot, found a bed here after an emergency landing in the park.

The last lord of this castle lived here until the end of his life, occupying only the scullery and a bedroom. The rest of the house was no longer heated, the roof leaked and the walls were covered with moss. There was no money for repairs and the lord's two nephews, the only remaining members of his family, couldn't afford to pay for the upkeep of the castle. An alarm system and a neighbor kept a watch on things. A farmer picked the fruits and used the stables for his equipment.

The silence inside doesn't really spoil the fun. In the living room, several animal heads mounted on the walls stare at each other while they muse over their glorious past. Every year, the layer of dust on their fur grows a little thicker. ◆

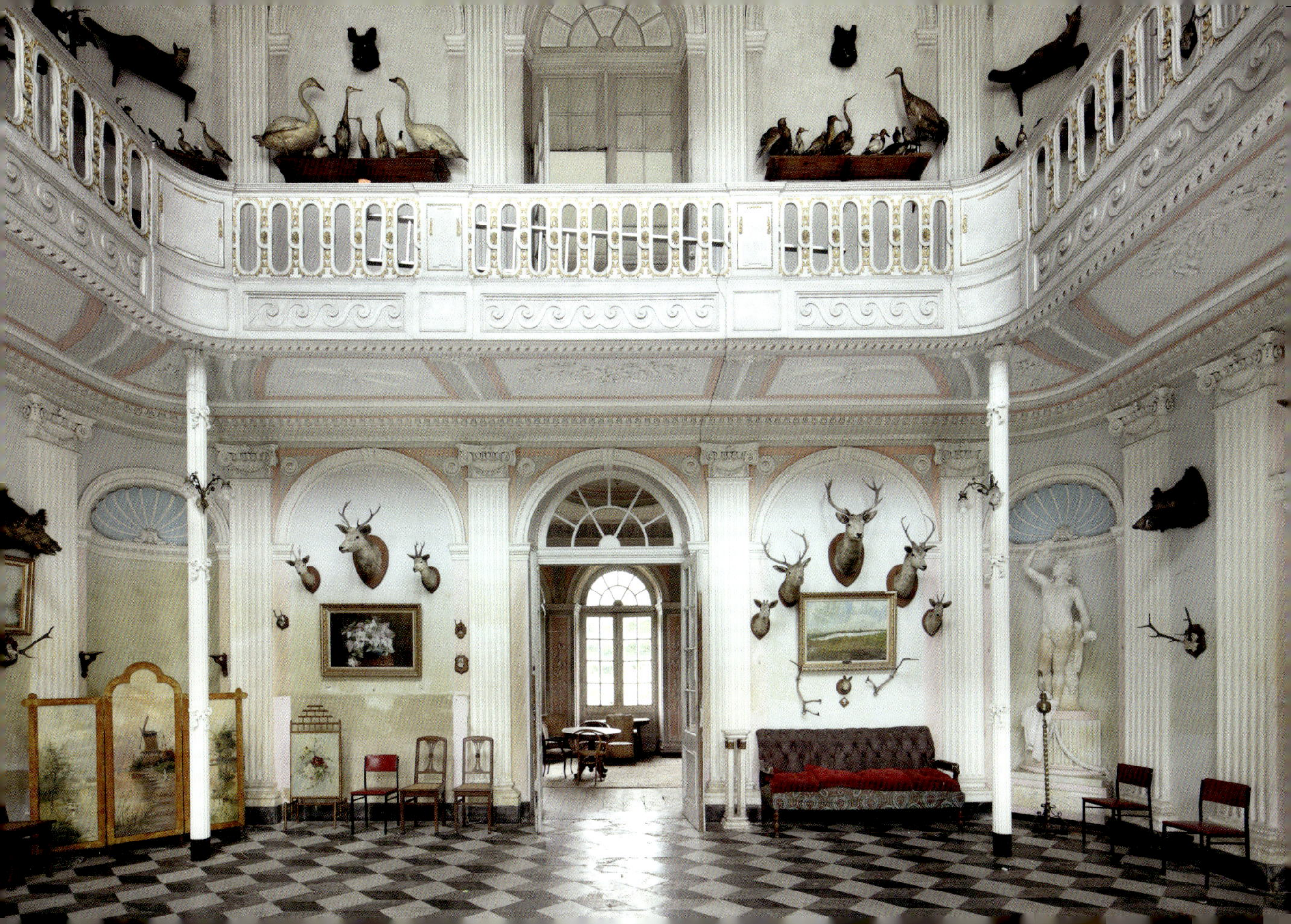

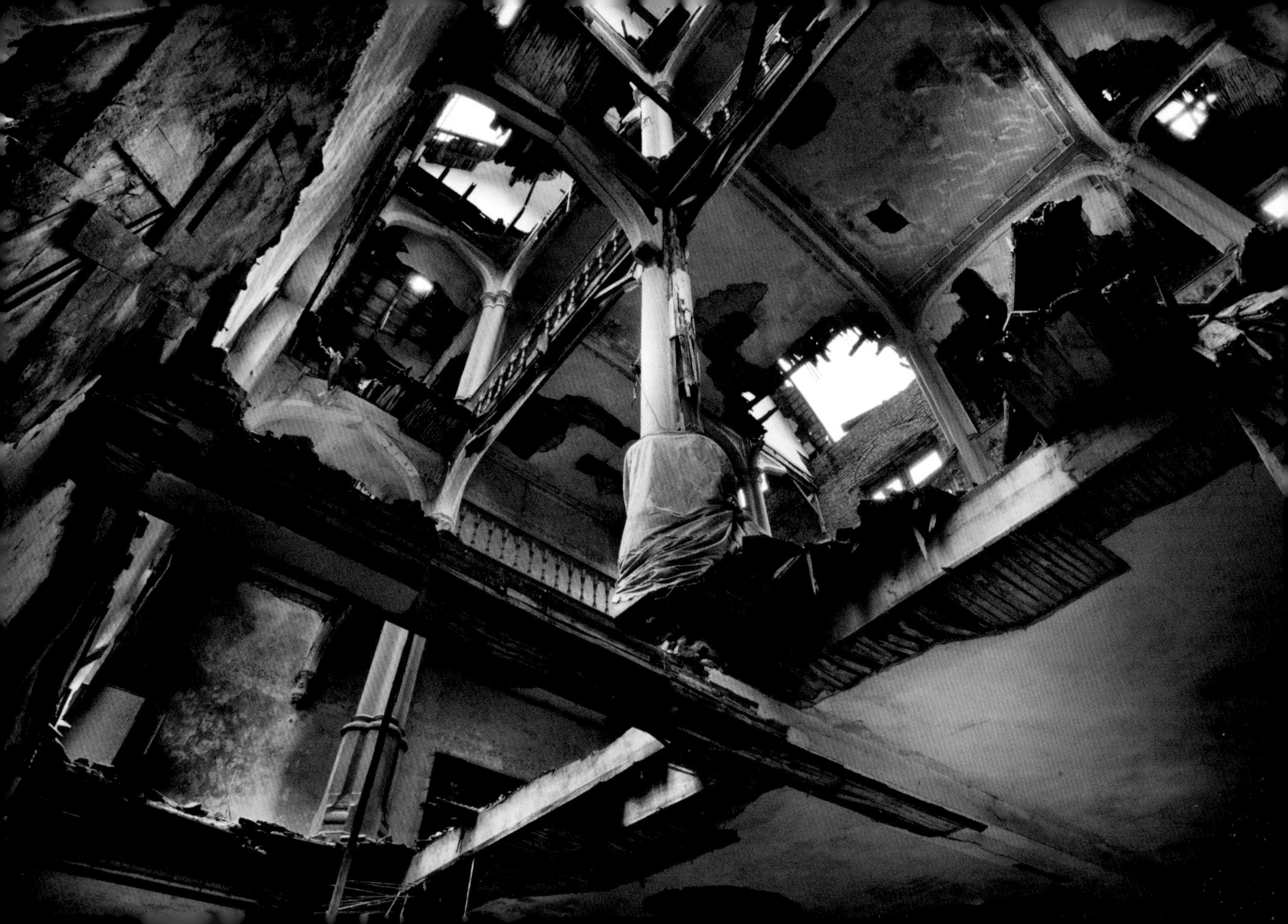

 △ Castle of Mesen, Belgium, 2006 ▽ Château Congo, Belgium, 2015

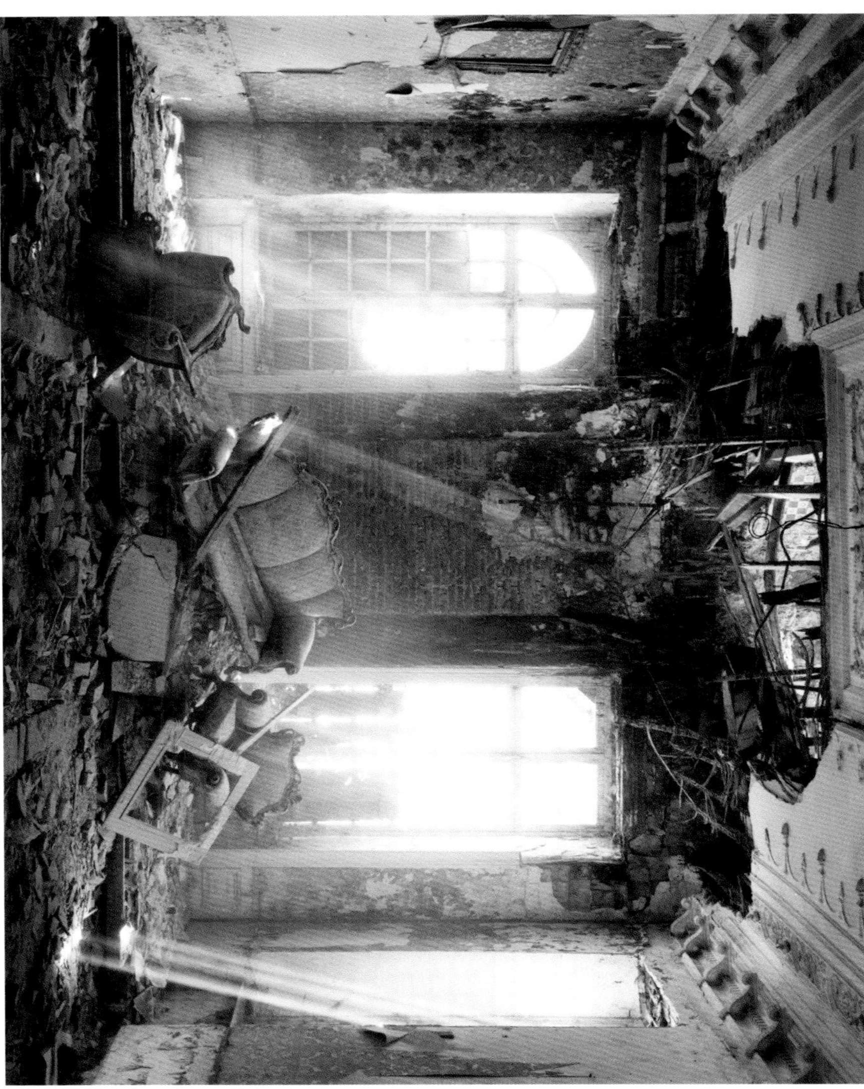

CHÂTEAU DE NOISY ▹

BELGIUM, 2007

Hidden deep in the woods, guarded by foresters and hunters, stands an old castle. Abandoned since the last of the railway children left in the 1980s.

The long climb to the castle on the hill was not without risk: showers of birdshot, aimed at unsuspecting pheasants, whistled past my ears. What was I to do? Put on a fluorescent jacket in an attempt not to become an innocent victim? Better to move stealthily, wait and chase away the pheasants around me!

Then suddenly I stood face to face with a fairy-tale castle, ravishing yet vulnerable. From a distance I wondered for a while whether the place was really abandoned, but the signs left no doubt: a broken window, a burnt roof, the front door boarded up, the driveway full of puddles and the park totally neglected. ◆

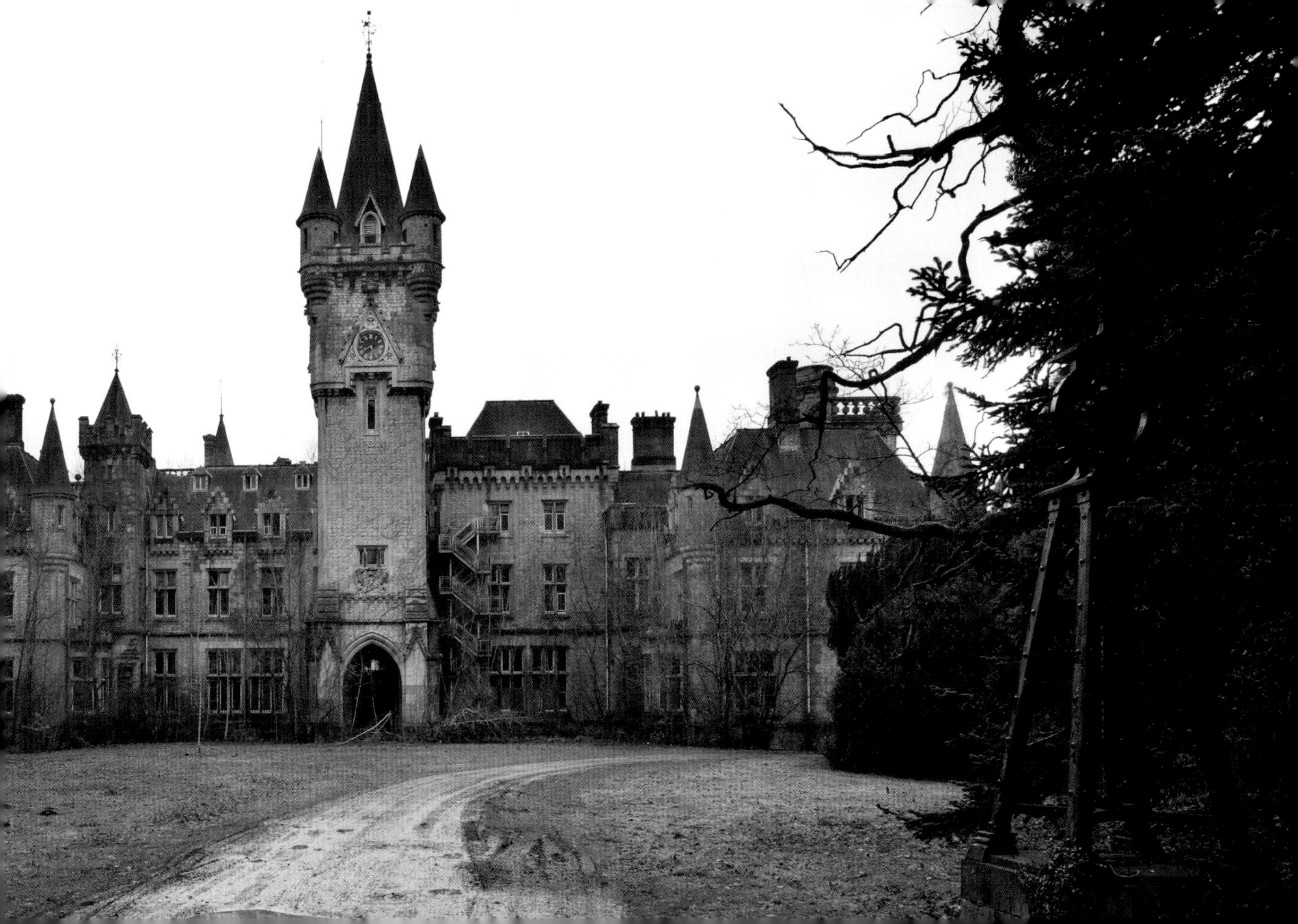

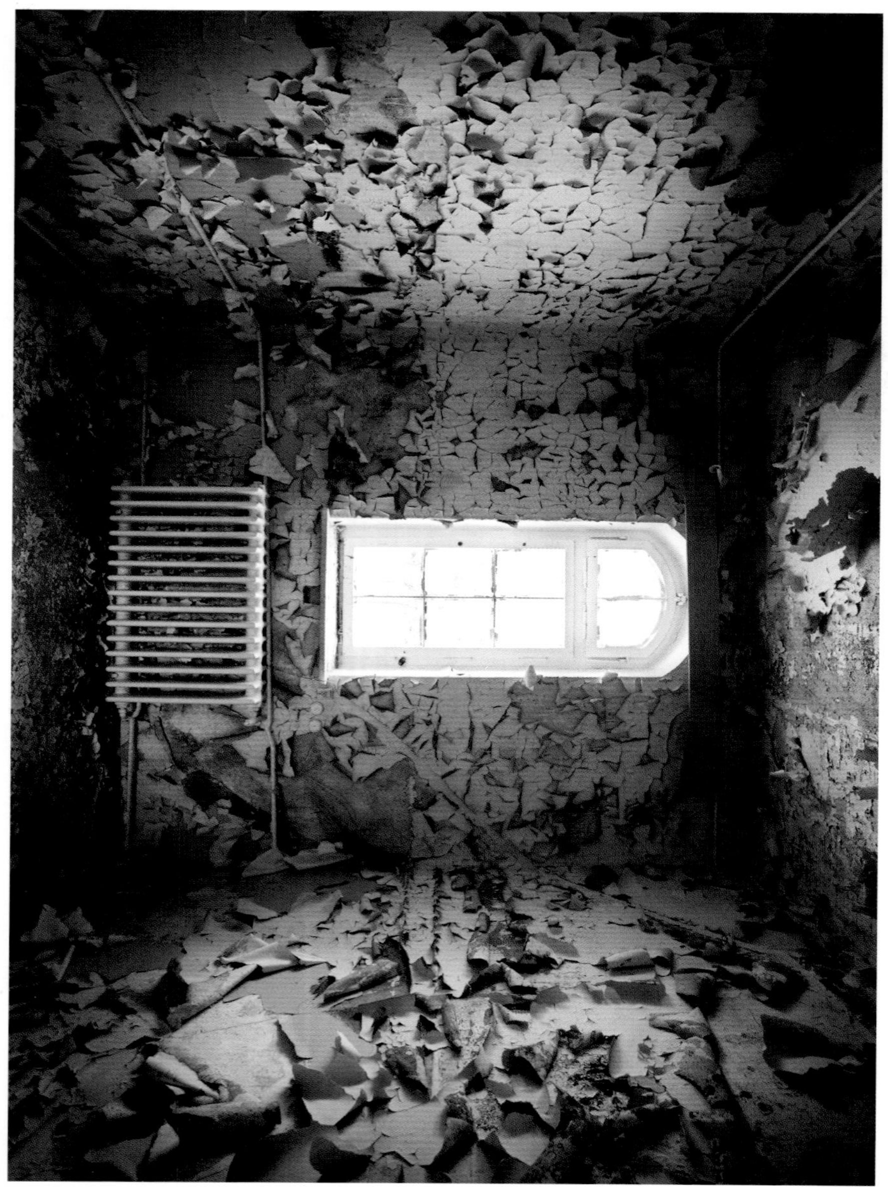

 Beelitz Heilstätten, Germany, 2007

Val Benoit, Belgium, 2010

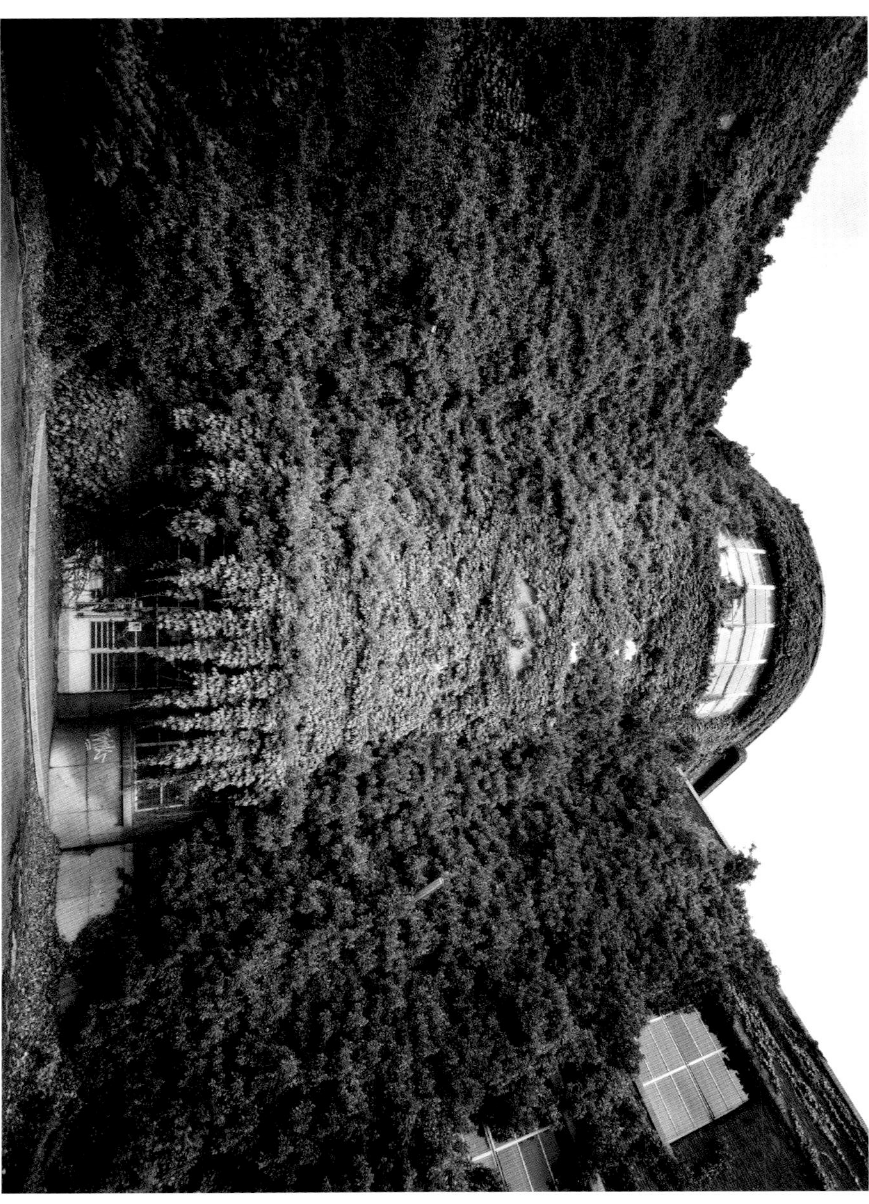

PLASTER STAIRWAY ▹

VILLA DECADIMENTO, ITALY, 2011

Down winding streets too tight even for the smallest Fiat, we were looking for Villa Decadimento. Trampled weeds, an iron gate, a hole in the high wall… and there stands the majestic villa in the middle of an arboretum with the best view ever of the Lago Maggiore. The garden is still maintained, the grass around the villa neatly clipped. Long ago thieves forced the door open, now climbing plants block the passage. Downstairs it is dark and damp. Over the years the decor has adapted itself perfectly to the 1970s Zanussi refrigerator, standing motionless like a chameleon in an upside-down world.

The large central staircase is a real beauty. The stairs are covered with a white layer of powdered plaster. Light penetrates through a landing window and a hole in the wall. It is dark and light simultaneously, as in a fairy tale.

Later that day, traveling by car, we found another villa that looked deserted. Just to make sure I knocked on the door, waited a minute, knocked again, but got no answer. I walked cautiously around the house. Coming back to the front door from the other side, a woman now stood there shouting out angrily at me. Behind her was a man with a shotgun! All I could do was look innocent like a silly tourist and ask if I could take photos of the villa, to which she responded: 'Get the hell off my property.' ◆

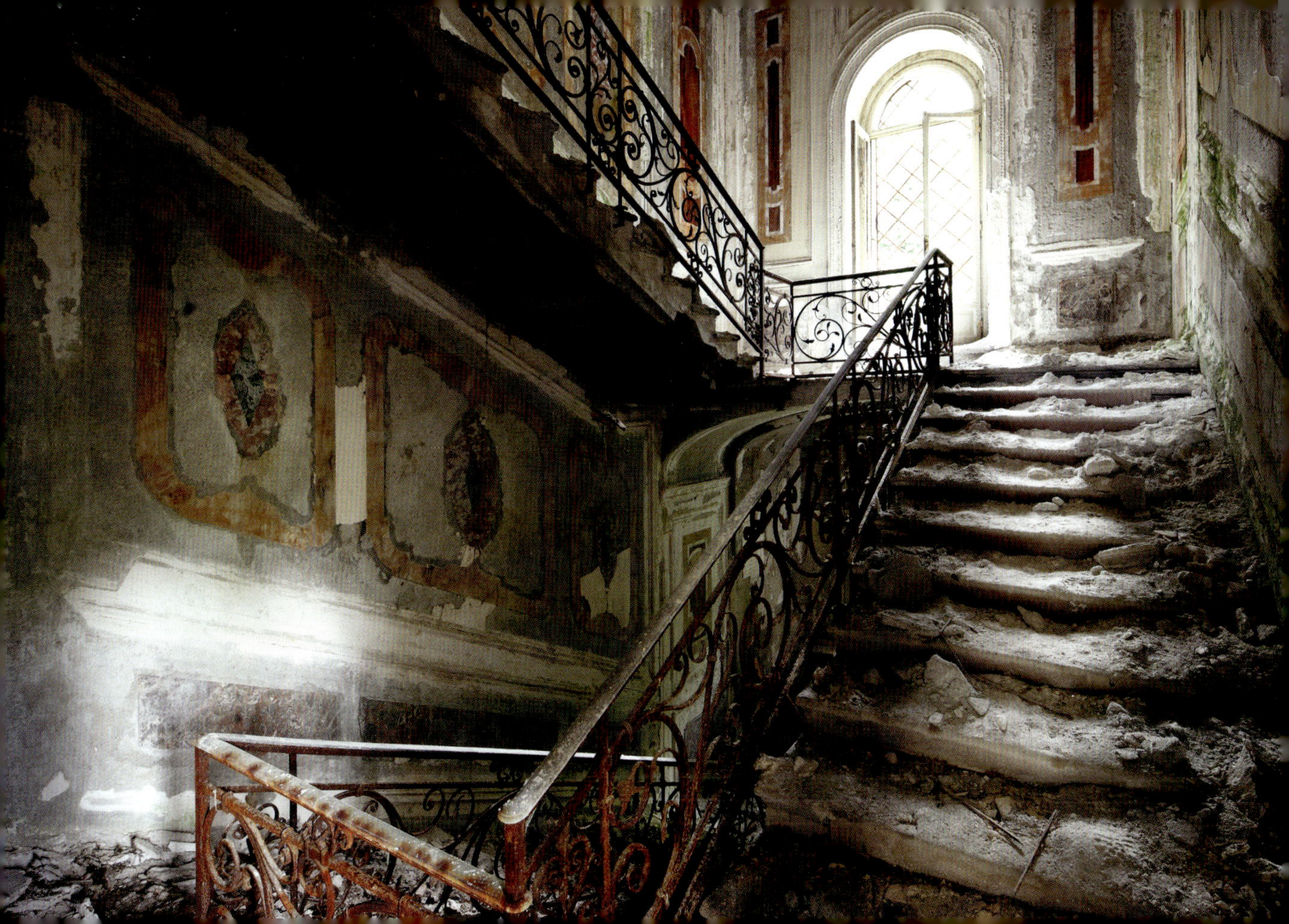

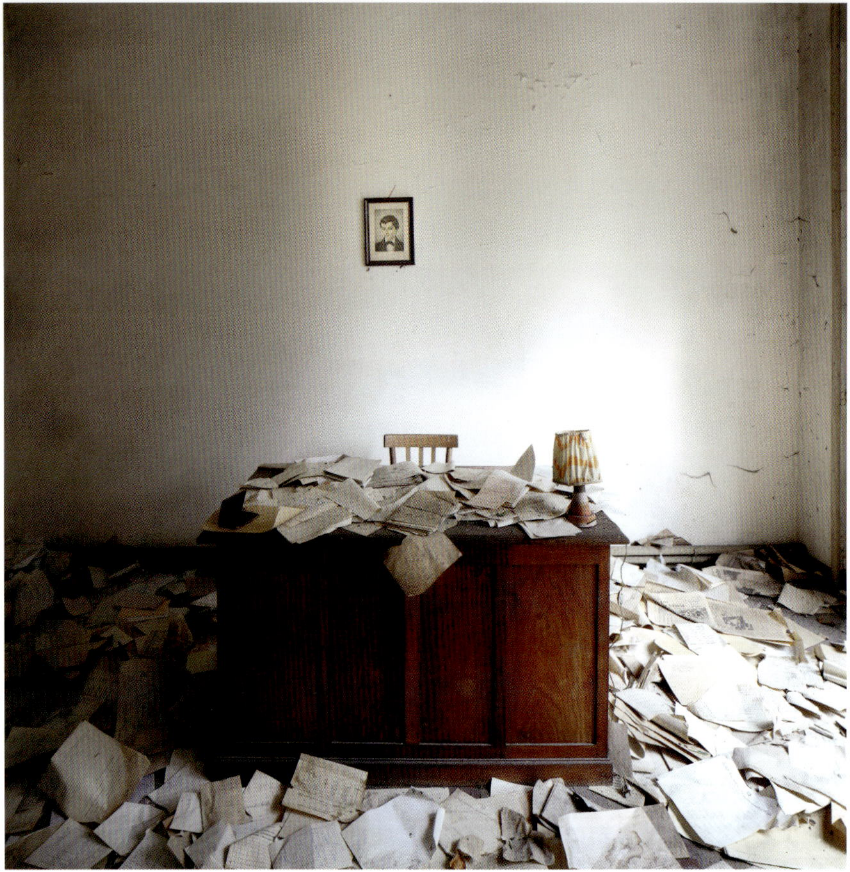

Colonia Montana, Italy, 2013

Château A, Belgium, 2014

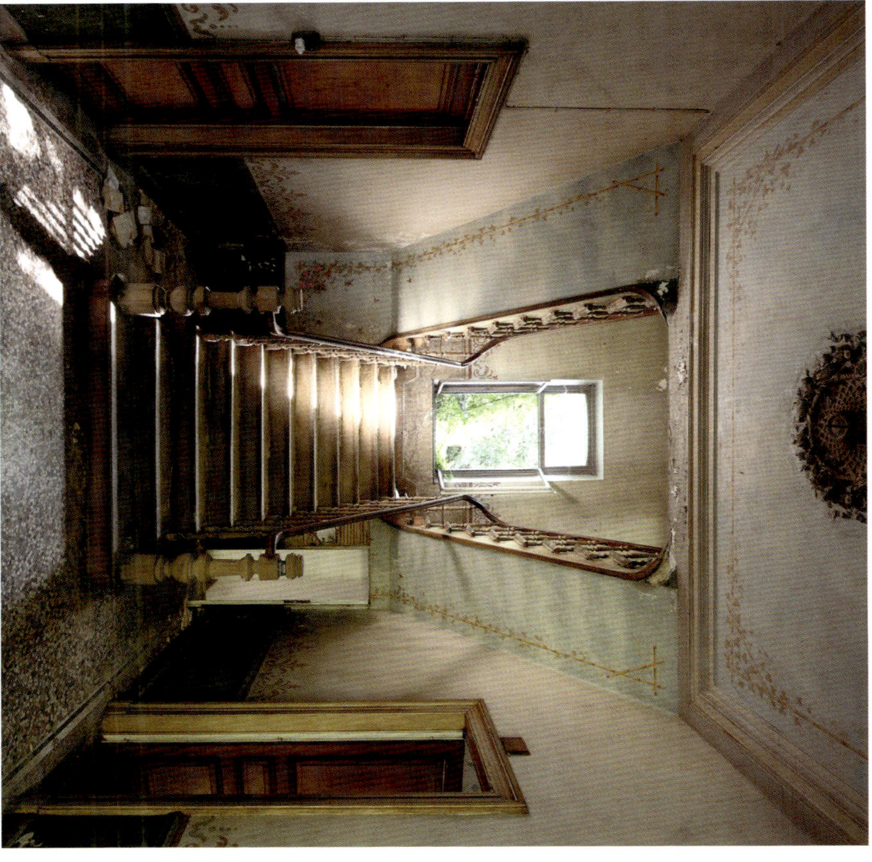

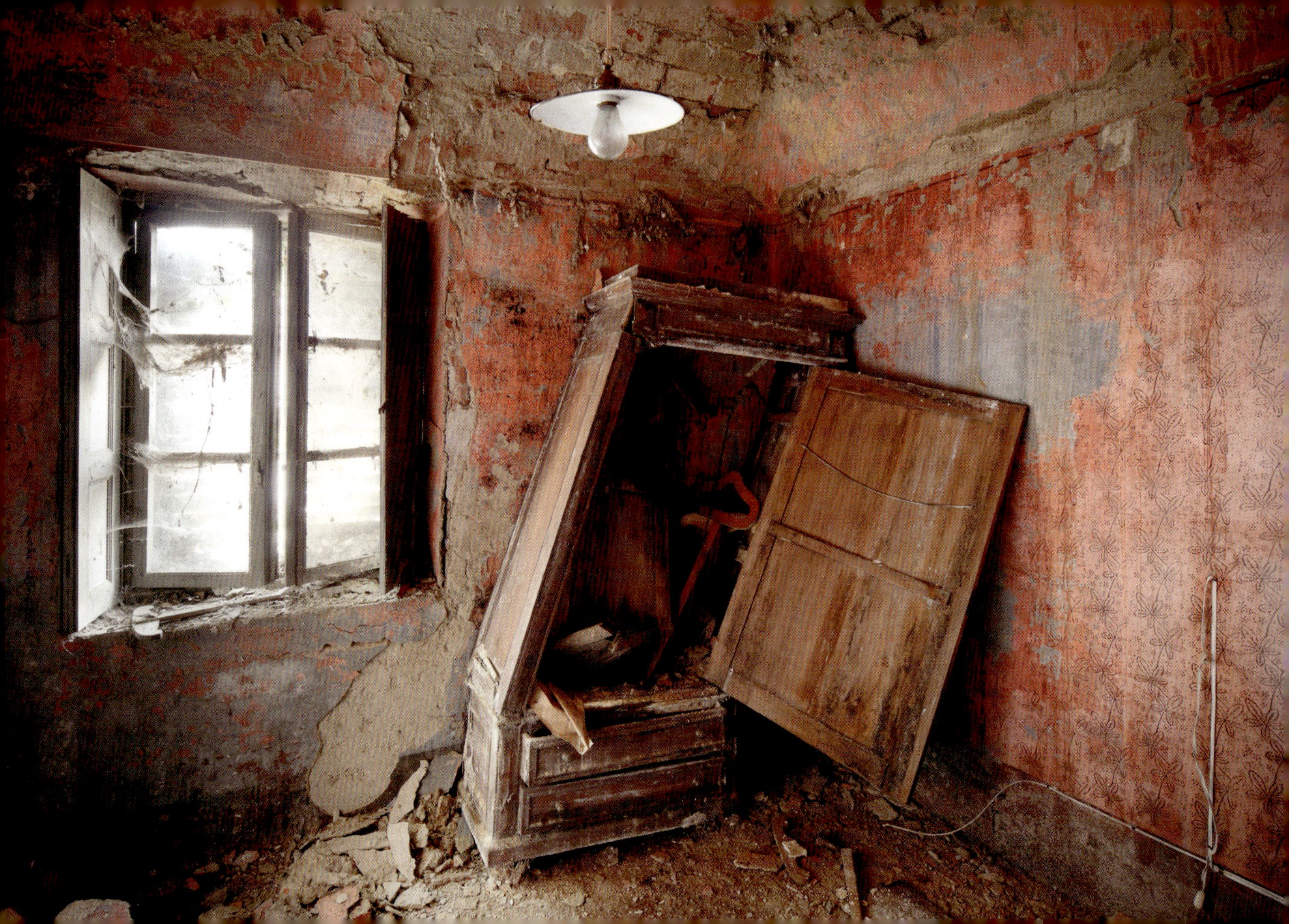

△ Castello Albano, Italy, 2011

▽ Castello Albano - Paris Match, Italy, 2011

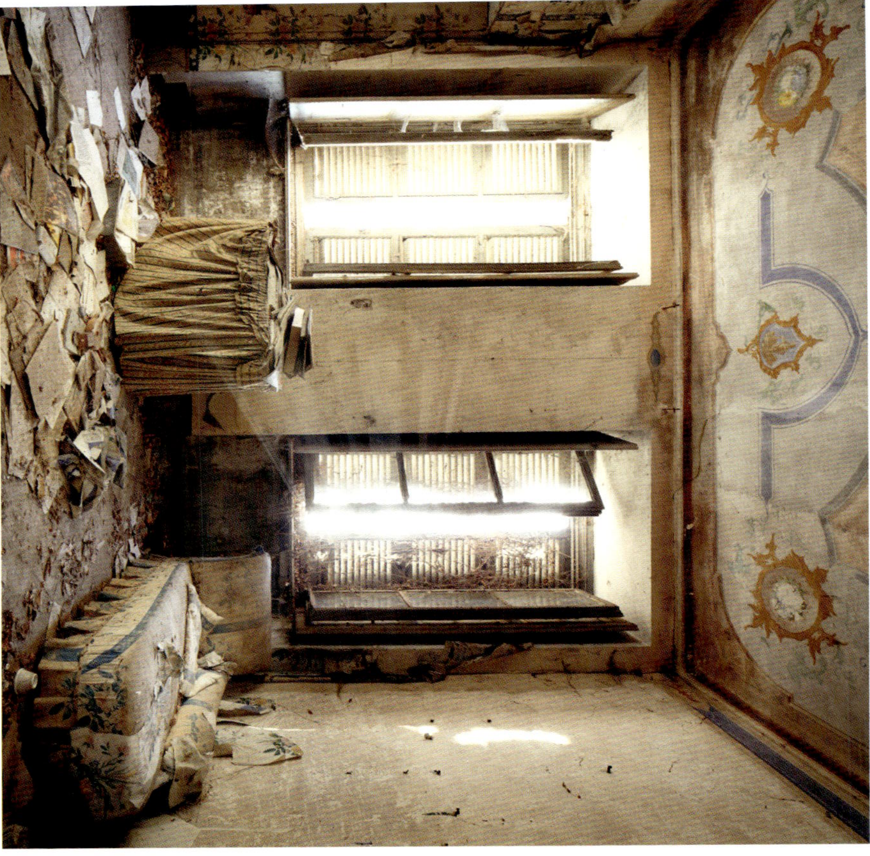

THE BURNT LIBRARY ▹
ITALY, 2011

CORRIDOR OF ZEN ▹
ITALY, 2013

In a small town in the Po Valley this hospital stands like an impregnable fortress.

Some of the newer buildings on the estate are easily accessible, but not very interesting. The shepherd, whose sheep graze the grass short on the lawns, was keeping an eye on things. While avoiding him, I stumbled upon a confused old man collecting dead twigs in the park. We shook hands and babbled mutually unintelligible Italian. I asked him if he knew a way inside. But he didn't seem to grasp why I wanted to enter a building which for years he probably wanted to escape… The solution ultimately appeared in the form of a rotten ladder hidden in the tall grass.

The reward tasted sweet.

The covered passageway radiated such improbable peace and harmony that a daily walk must have had more effect than the medicine of the day. I call it 'The Corridor of Zen'.

The old building is incredibly big. The fire was on the first floor. The story that goes around is that the archive contained mainly material about the mafia. An identical cupboard in an office next door was spared. Its doors stand haphazardly open as if a mischievous wind is blowing through the room. ◆

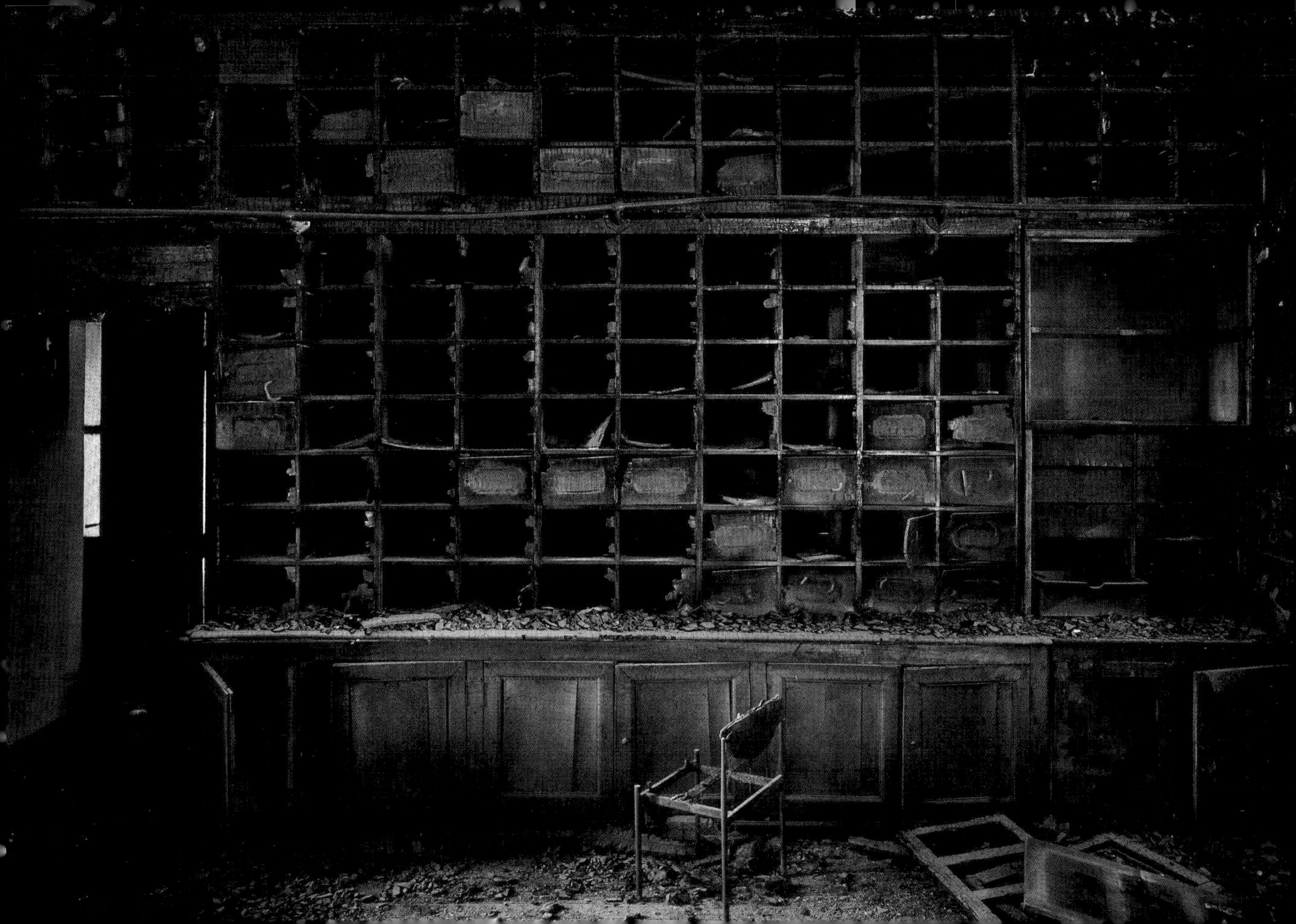

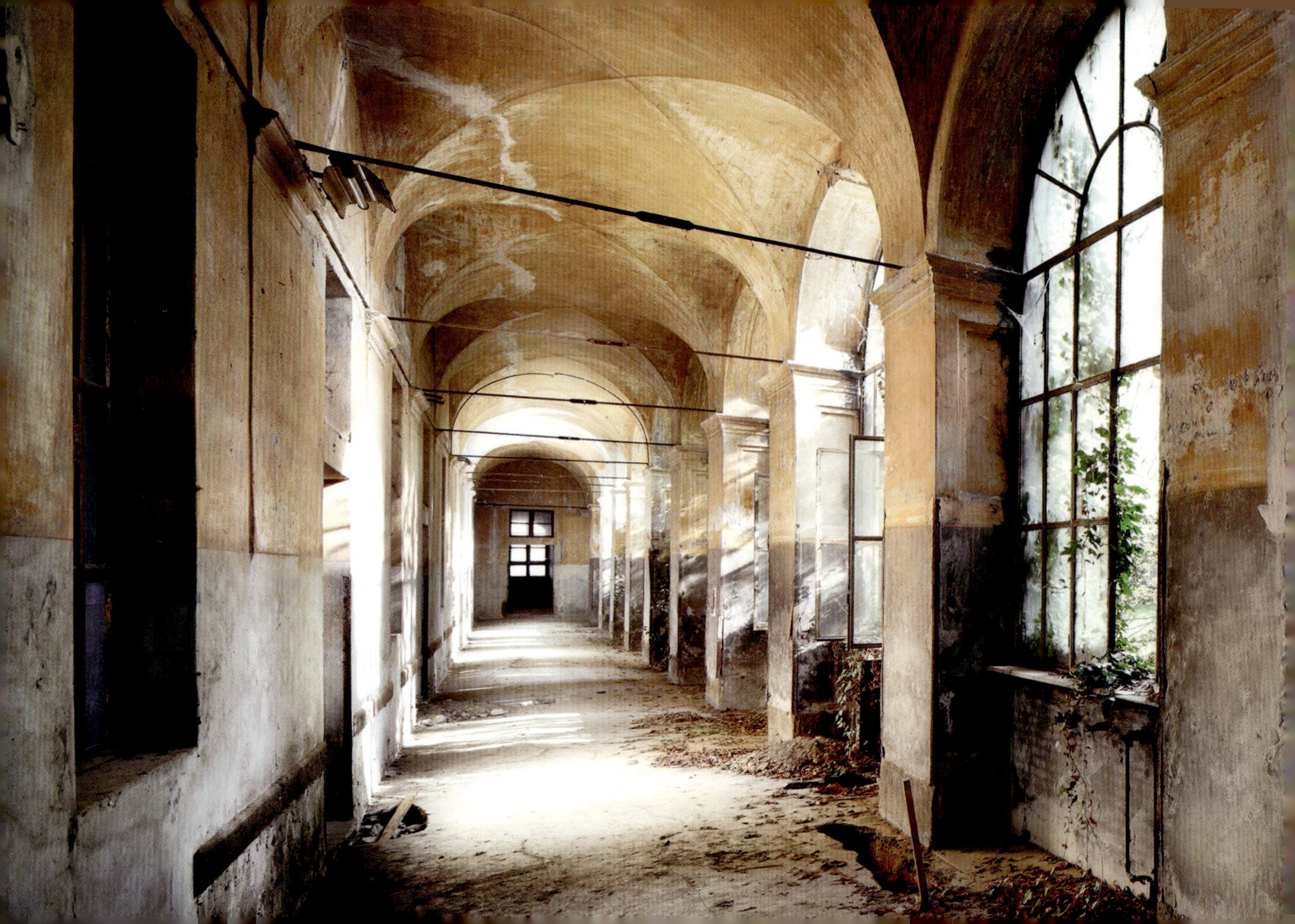

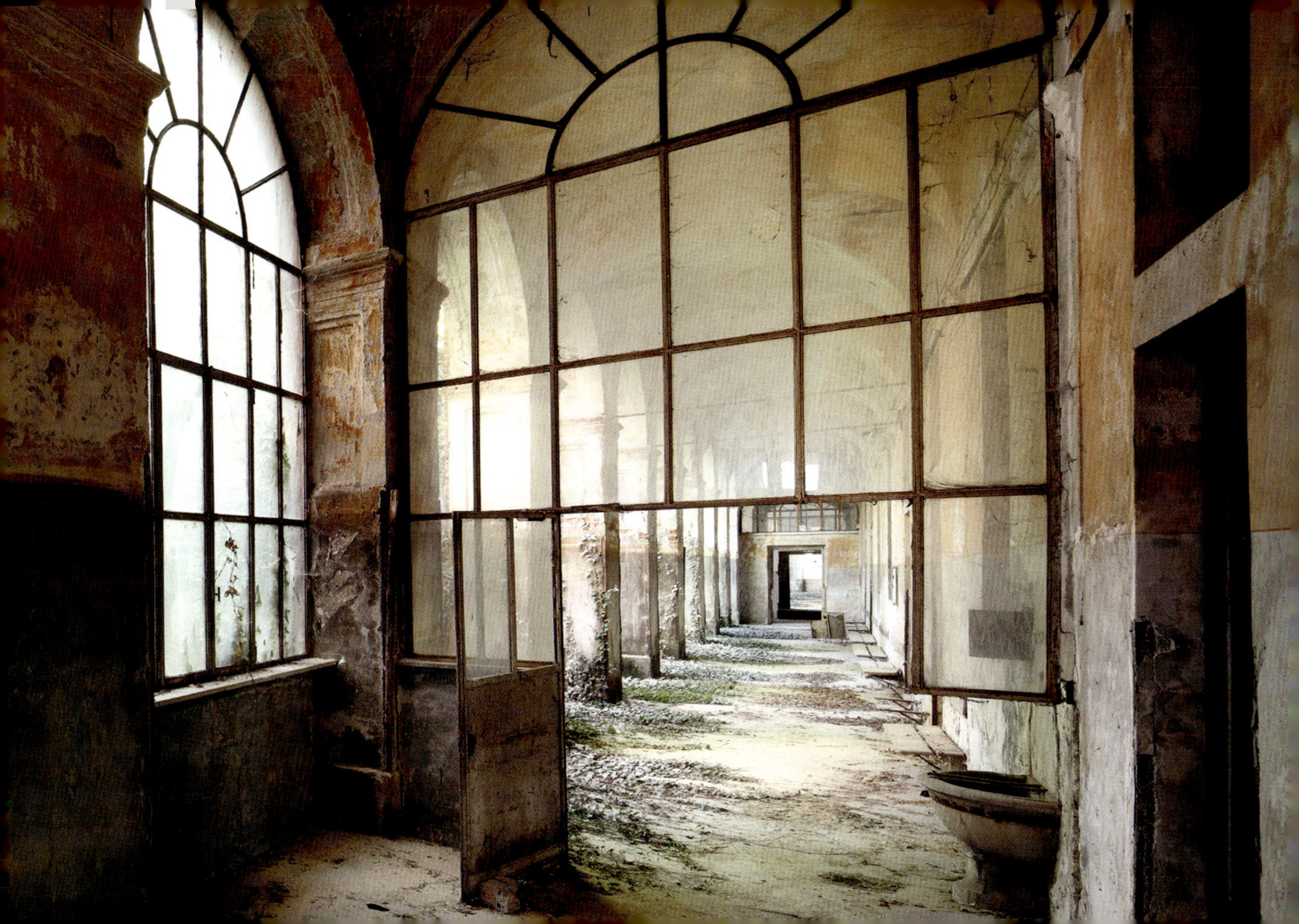

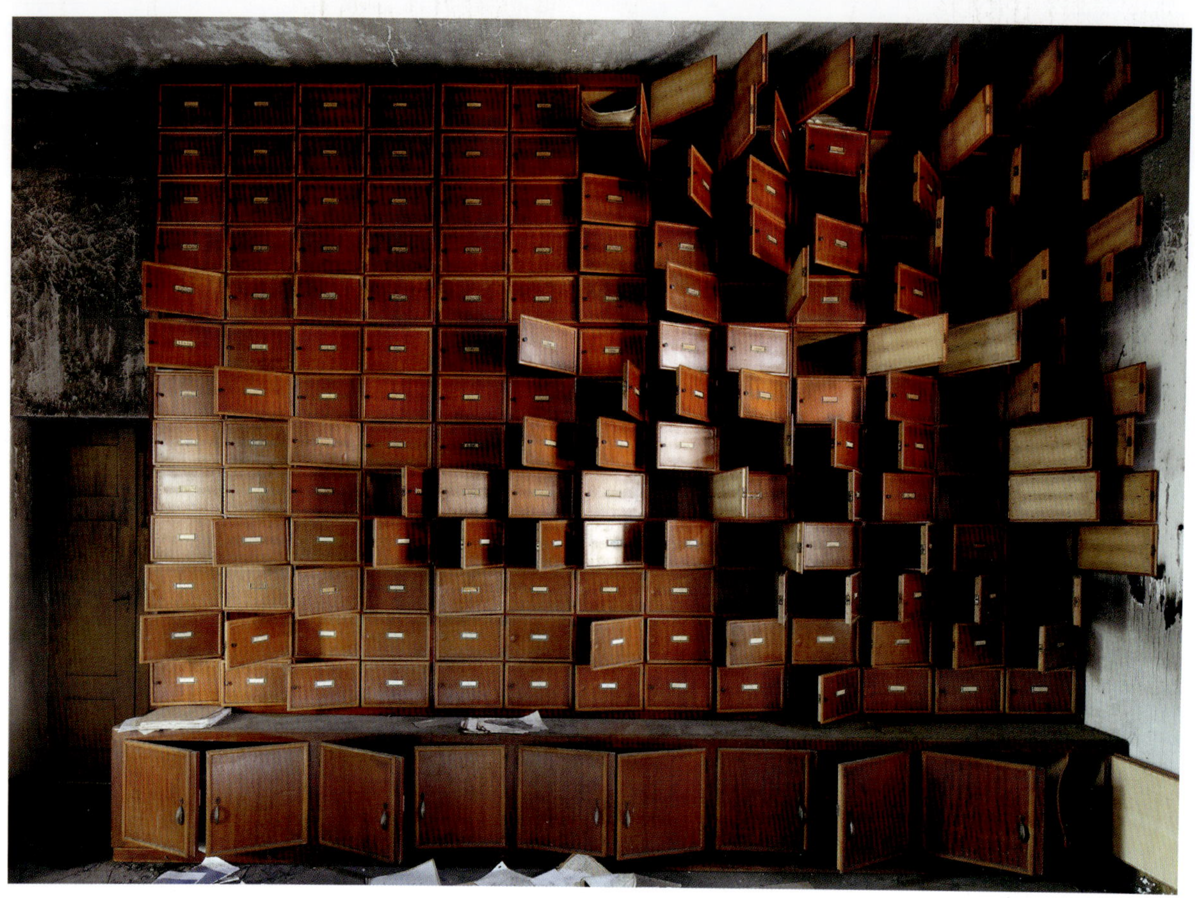

The Unburnt Library, Italy, 2013

Castello Duchessa di Genova, Italy, 2013

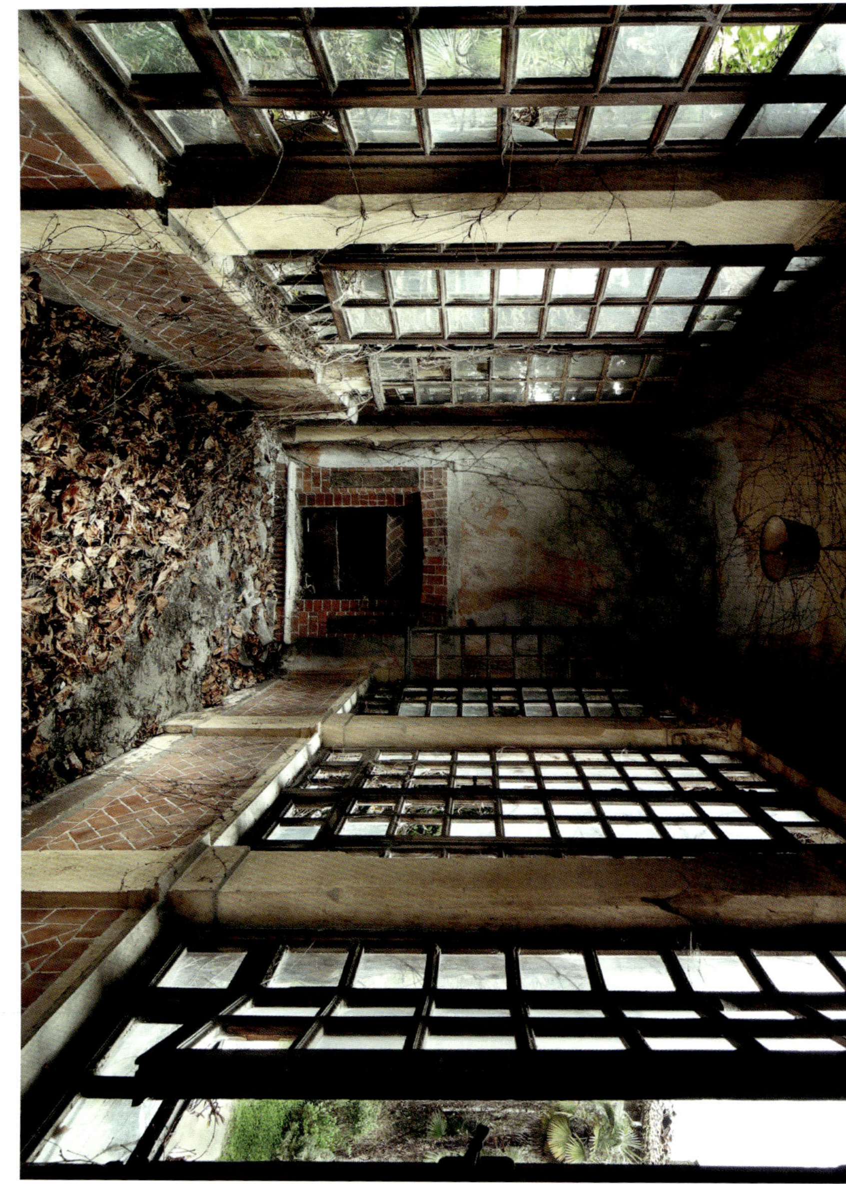

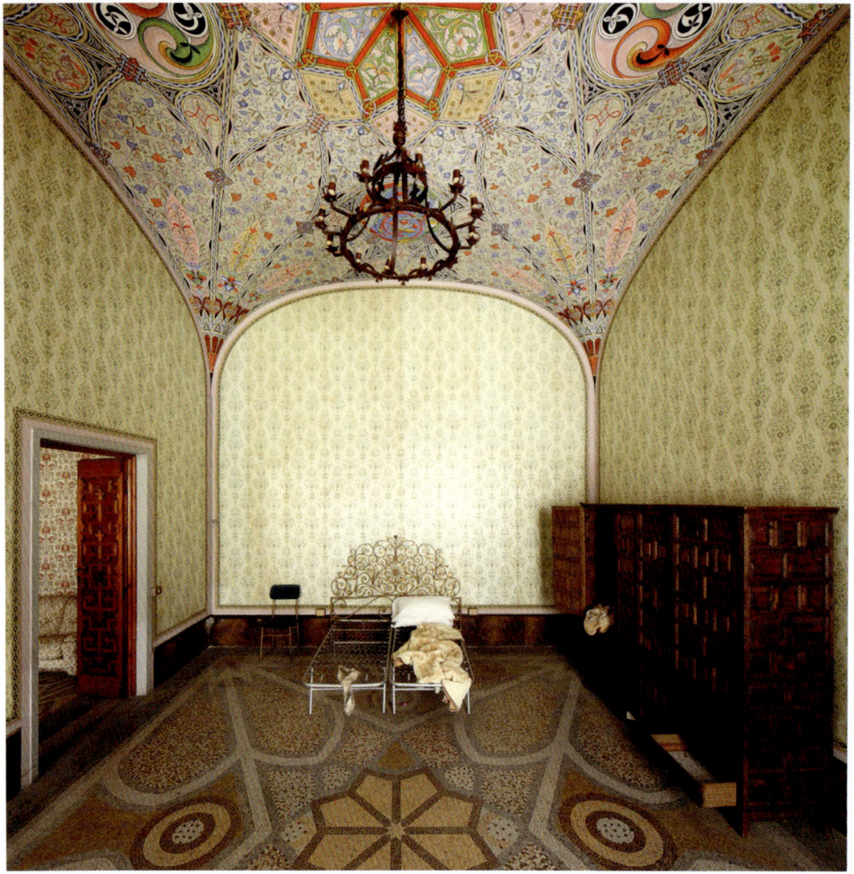

Castello di Sammezzano, Italy, 2013

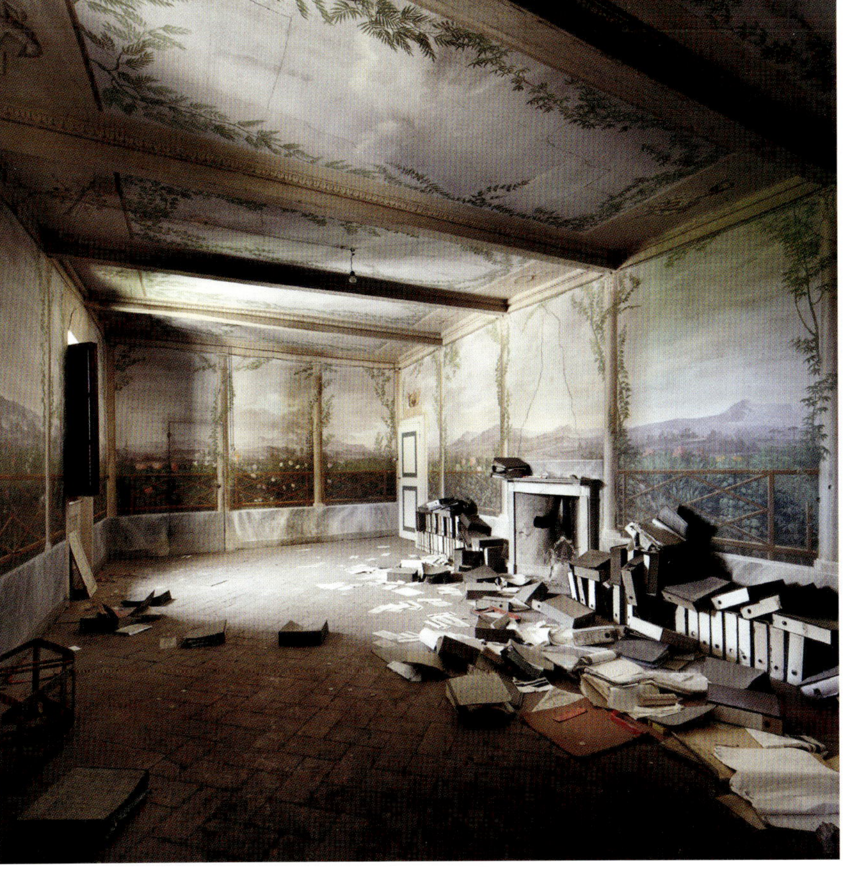

Villa Bastia, Italy, 2011

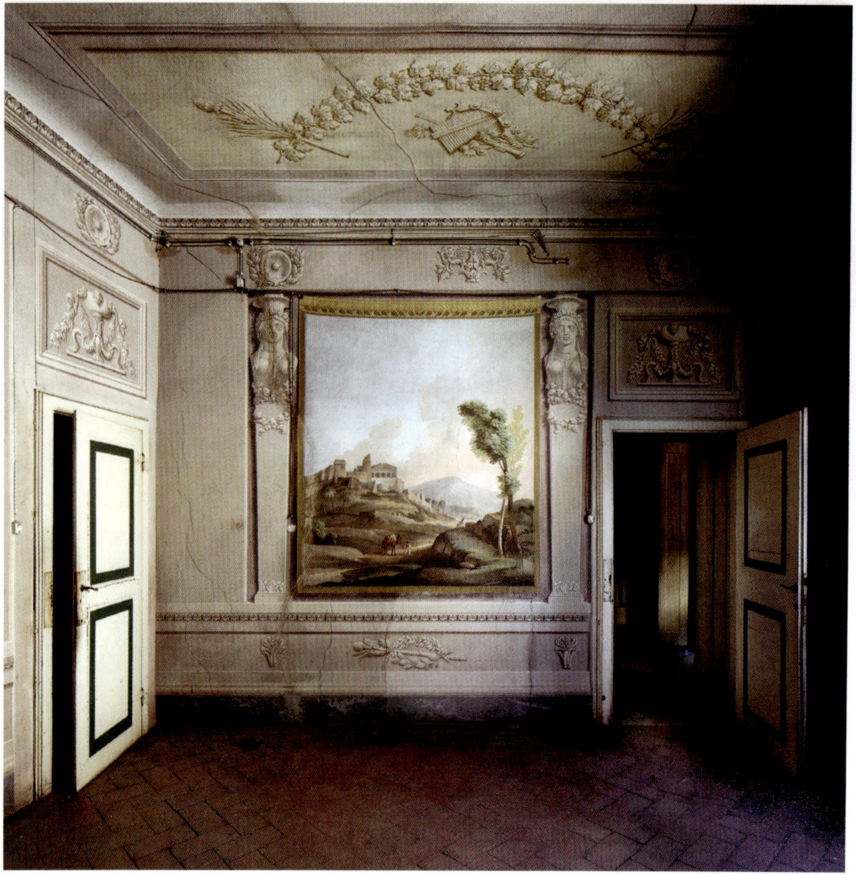

▵ Villa Bastia, Italy, 2011 ▿ Villa Quiete, Italy, 2013

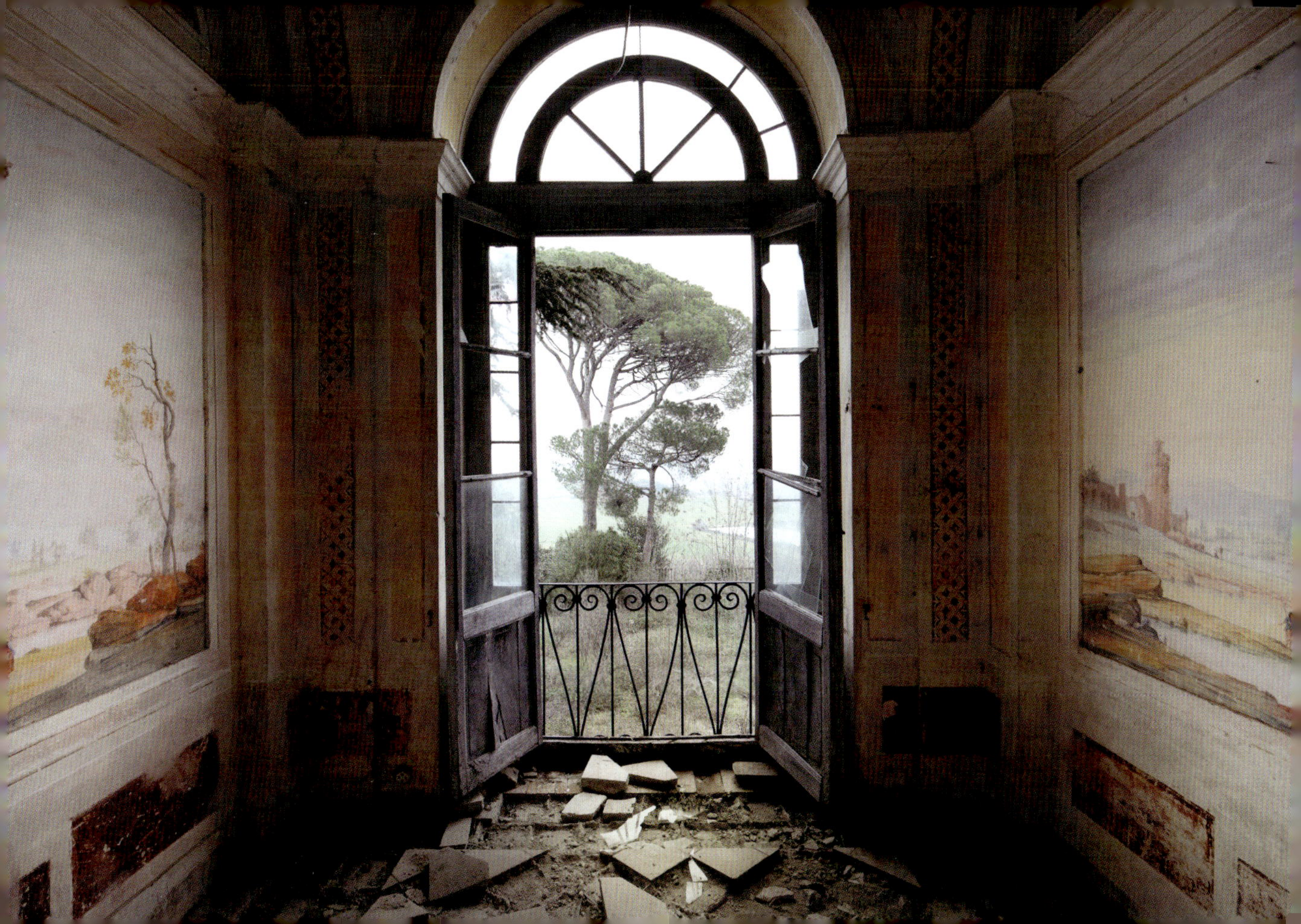

RAYS OF SUN ▹

ZELISZOW, POLAND, 2012

Just outside the village: a football field, a bus stop, a few houses, fields and a church. More reminiscent of a theater than a church, all in wood, with warm colors and graceful arches. The sun's beams are a sign that an empty church is never forsaken by God. Here once sounded the words of Martin Luther's German bible and the enchanting music of Bach's St. Matthew Passion. ◆

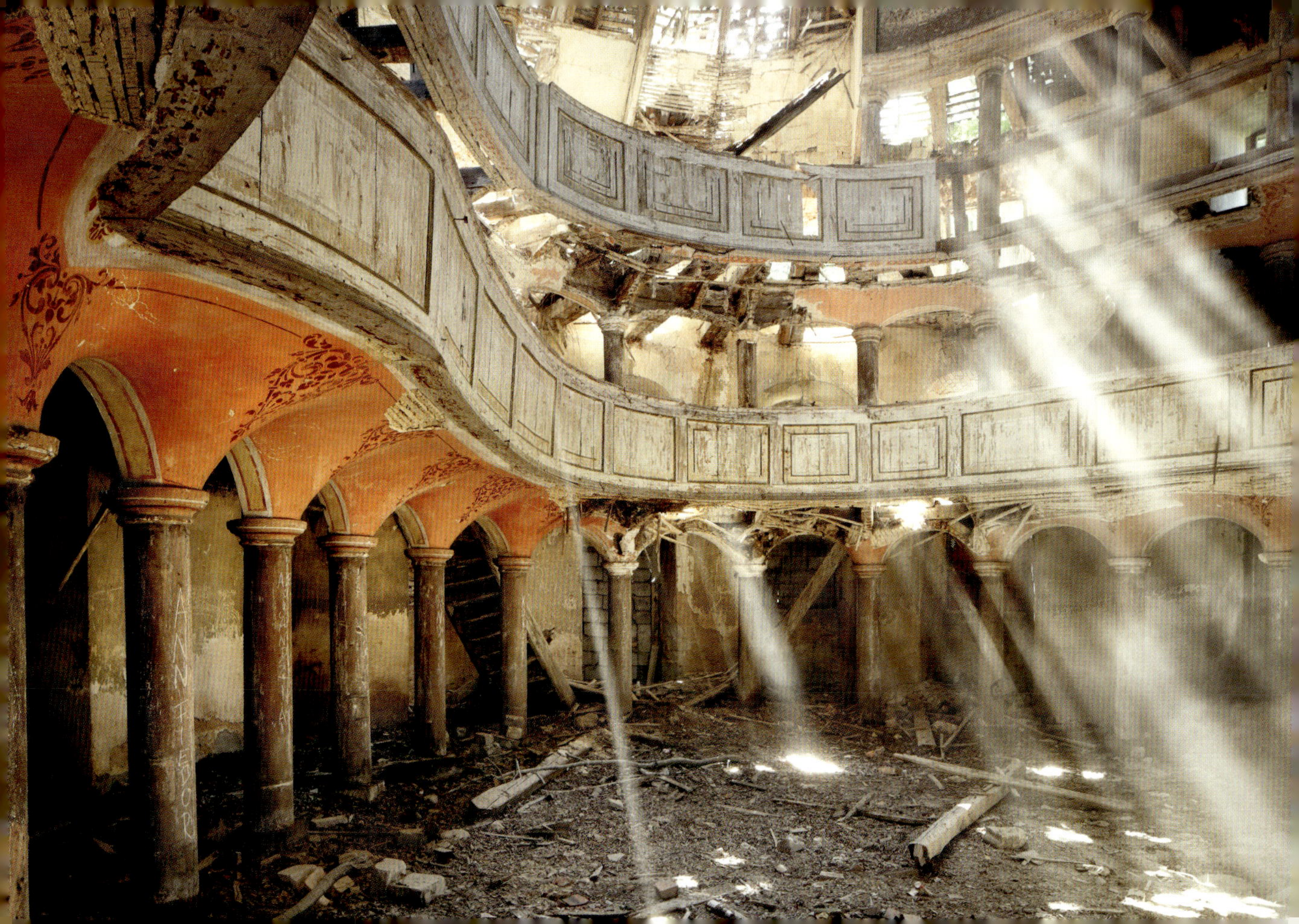

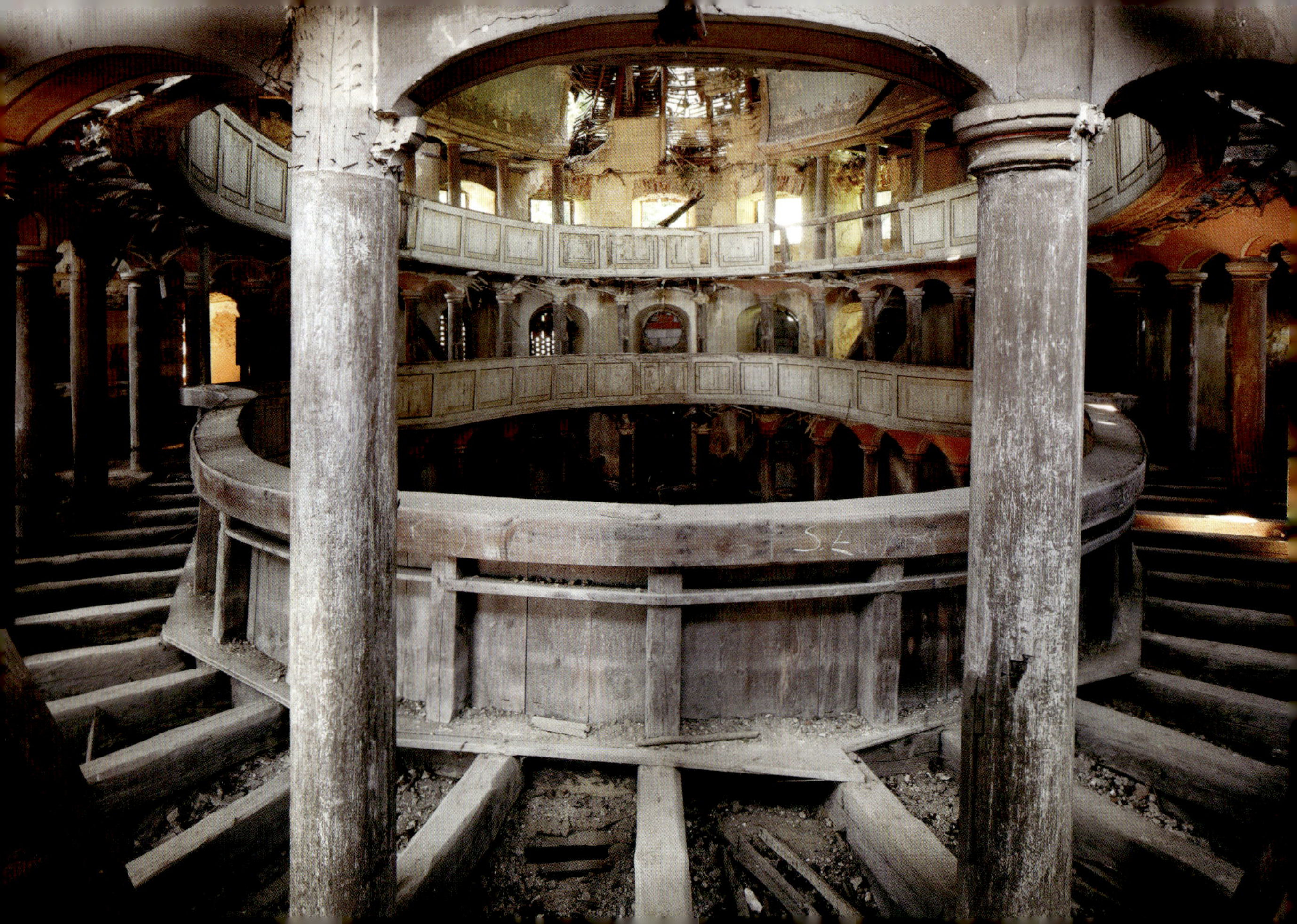

△ Rays of Sun, Zeliszow, Poland, 2011

▽ Oratorium, Italy, 2011

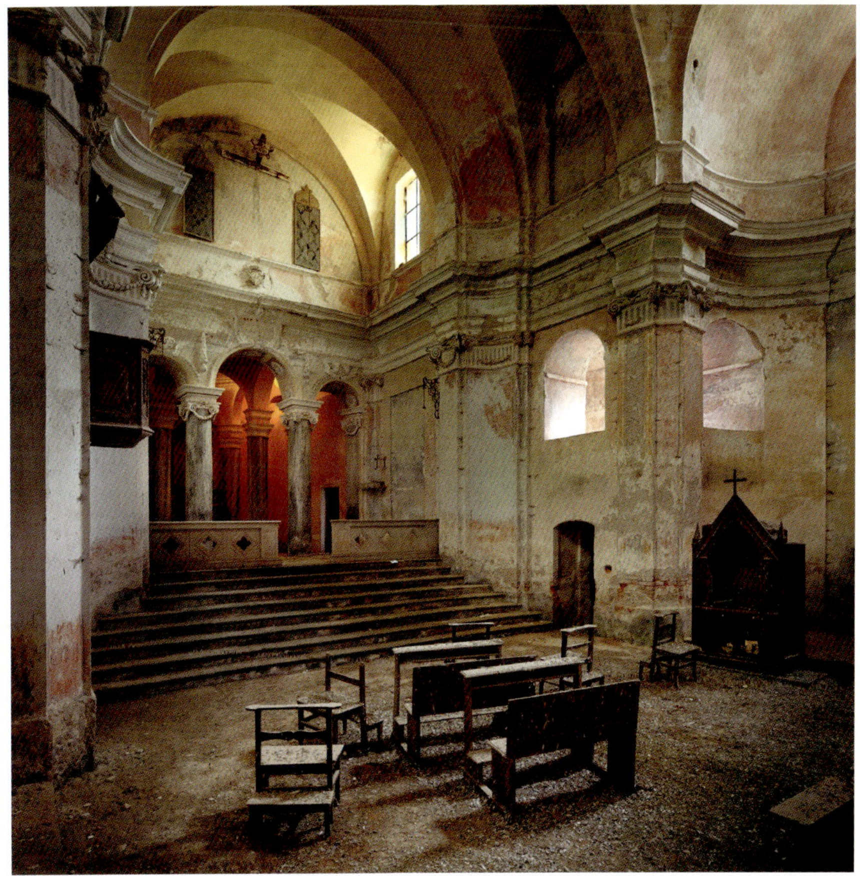

St.-Curvy, Detroit, USA, 2012

111 St.-Curvy, Detroit, USA, 2012

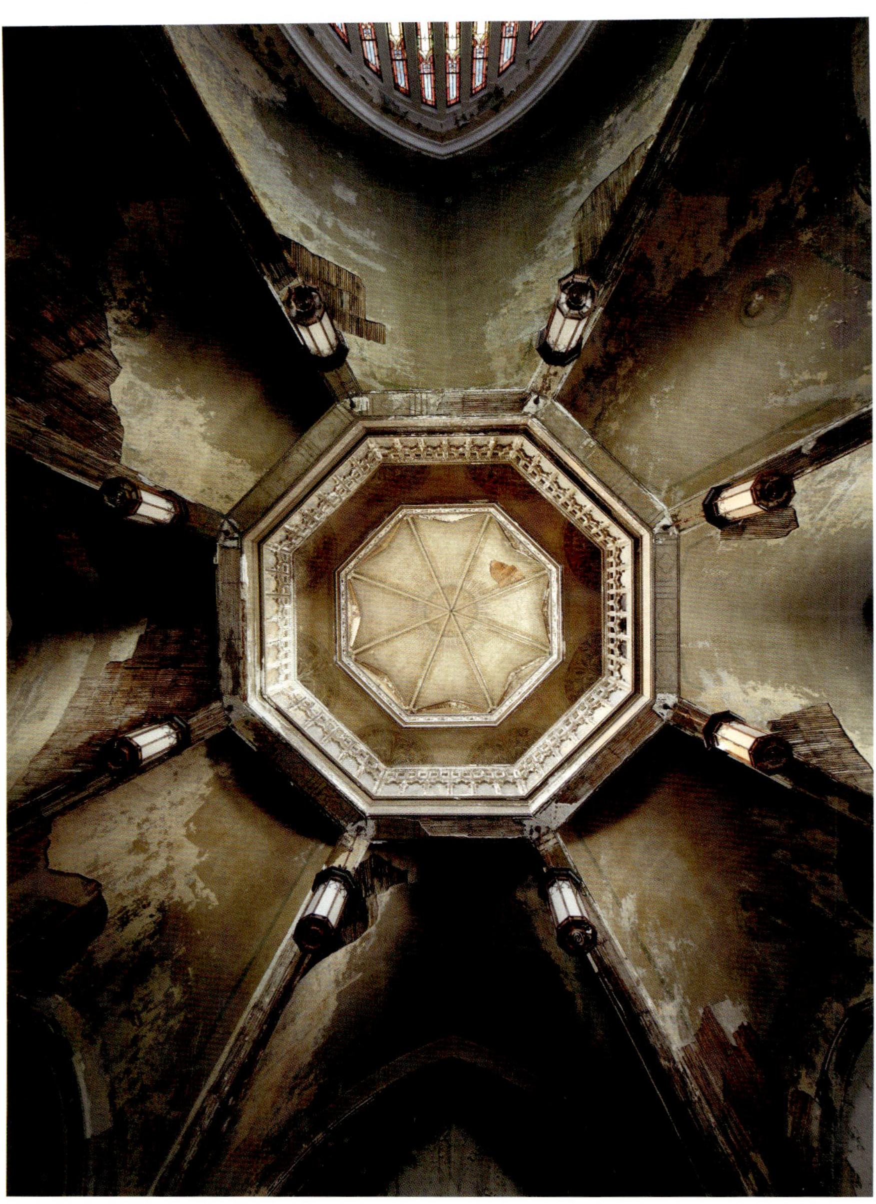

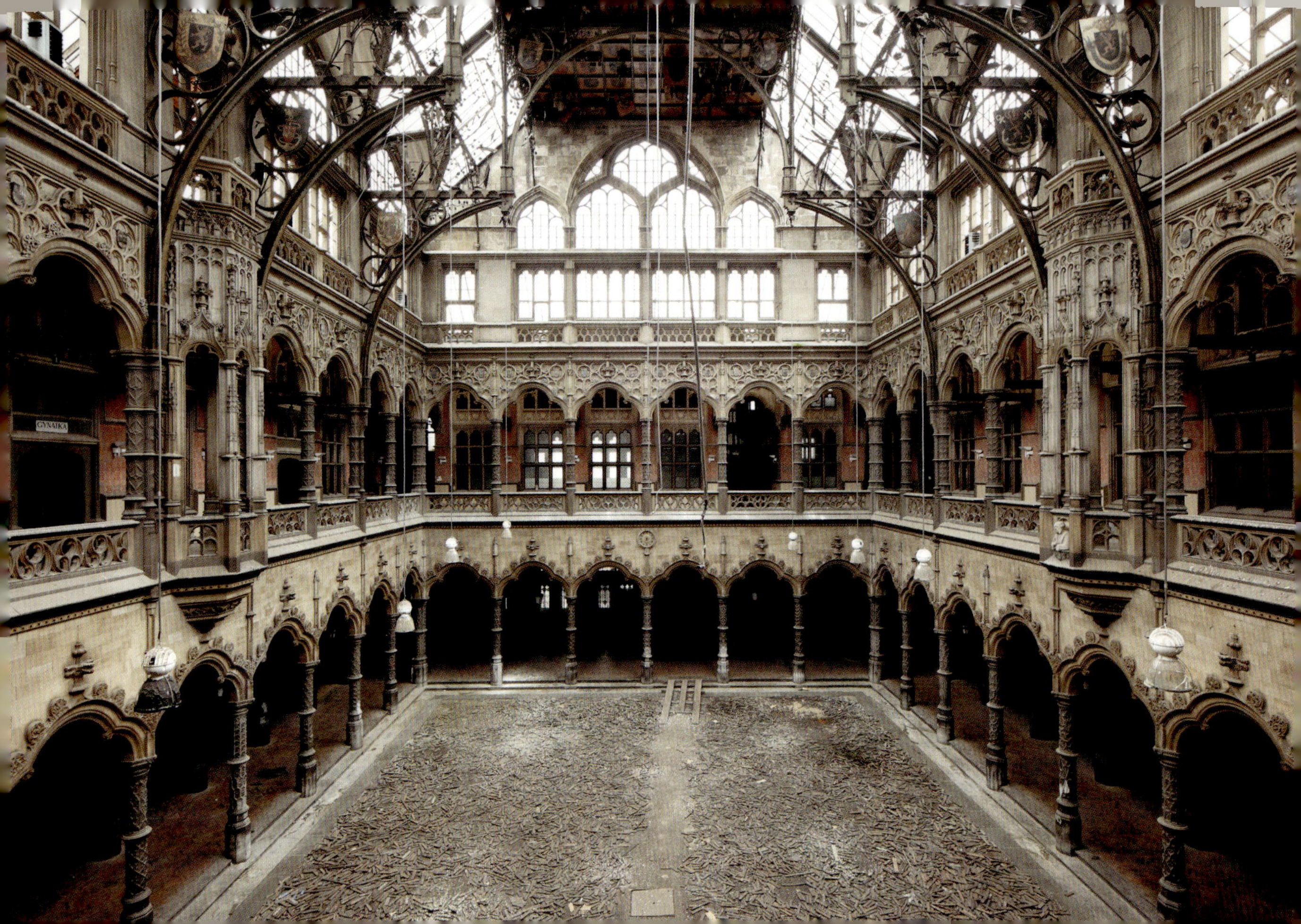
GYNAIKA

◁ ANTWERP STOCK EXCHANGE

BELGIUM, 2011

In five hundred years of history, the stock exchange enjoyed periods of glory, suffered devastating fires and underwent major reconstruction.

The structure was built in 1531, when Antwerp was the commercial and cultural center of Western Europe. Not until thirty years later did London build its own stock exchange, followed shortly after that by Rotterdam and Amsterdam. The Antwerp building burned down twice. What we see today is a reconstruction from 1872.

From the balcony I imagine myself looking down on a motley mass of merchants, shippers, brokers and bankers. Germans, Italians, Spaniards and Portuguese hurry around, negotiating with each other in small groups. But I also make out exotic figures from distant corners of the world. The talk is of shipments, weights, volumes, exchange rates, delivery times and advances. Names of boats are called out with departure dates, destinations and available space. Hands go up, deals are closed.

In a side street off the square stand the traders' horses. The servants crowd together, laughing. It starts to rain. The traders take shelter under the arcades, the servants pull up their collars.

Nowadays, the offices and assembly rooms are empty. High up in the building, in the ridge of the roof, I found a name: 'Sandow Piet 1899 1901 1900'. Who was he? A craftsman, a trader, a vagabond or a fellow urban explorer before the term was even invented? ◆

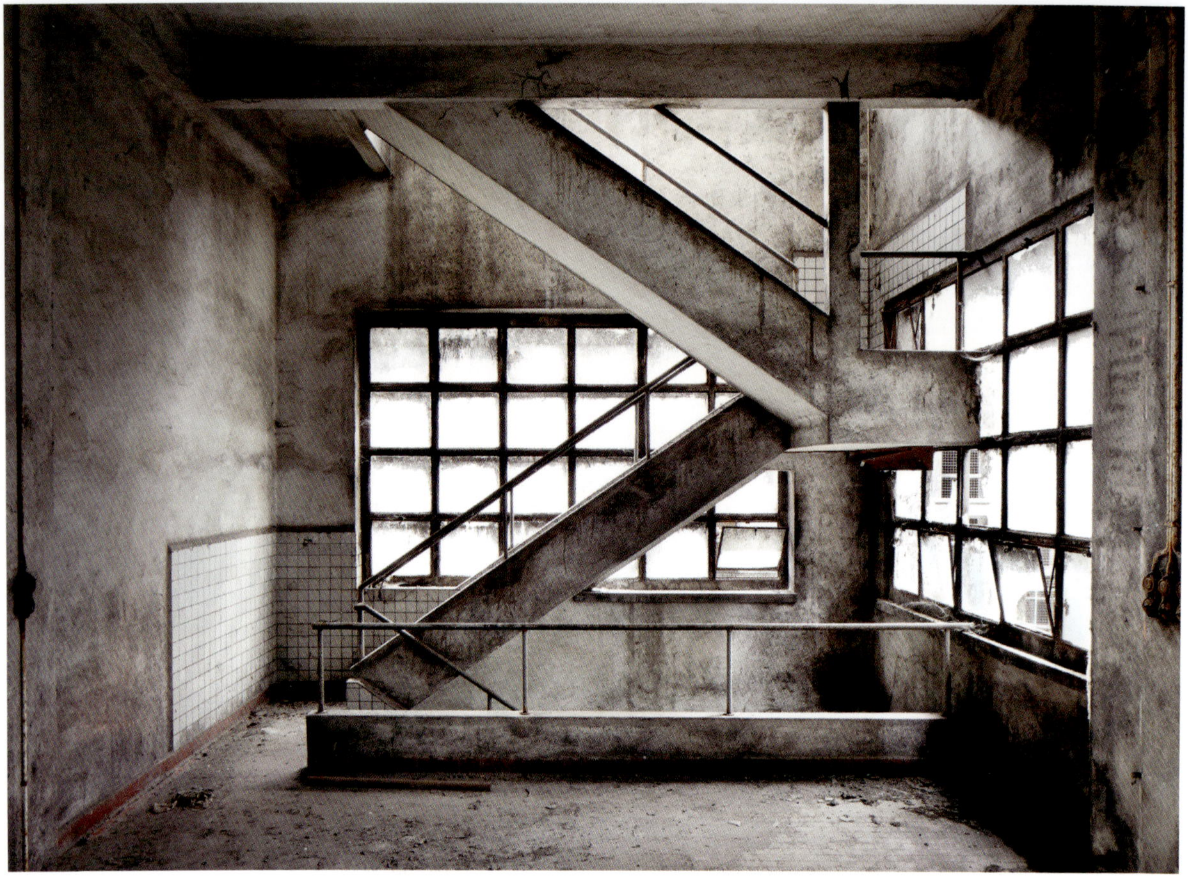

Factory with Great Round Tower, Italy, 2011

 Farwell Building, Detroit, USA, 2012

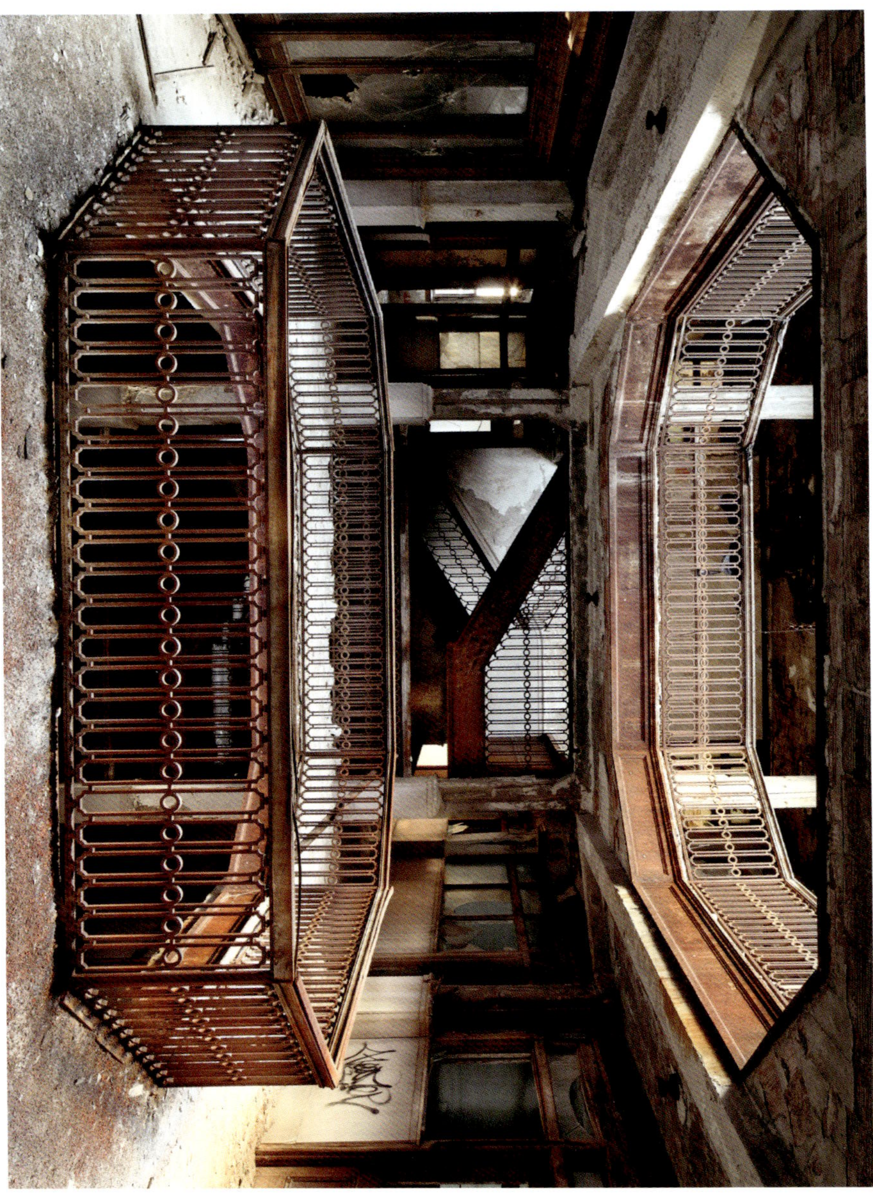

COLONIA MONTANA ▹

ITALY, 2013

The sky was clear, there was still a bit of snow on the ground, the mountain air was at its purest.

Not too much traffic at the border crossing. It's really not more than a village street. The guardsmen were hanging around the electric heater in their shed. The windows were fogged over so I doubt that they could see me creeping into the gigantic building that stands literally on the border. This is where children from the working class were sent on vacation to get away from the smog in the Po Valley.

Inside it was as still as a mouse. Just like it probably was the day before the vacation. ◆

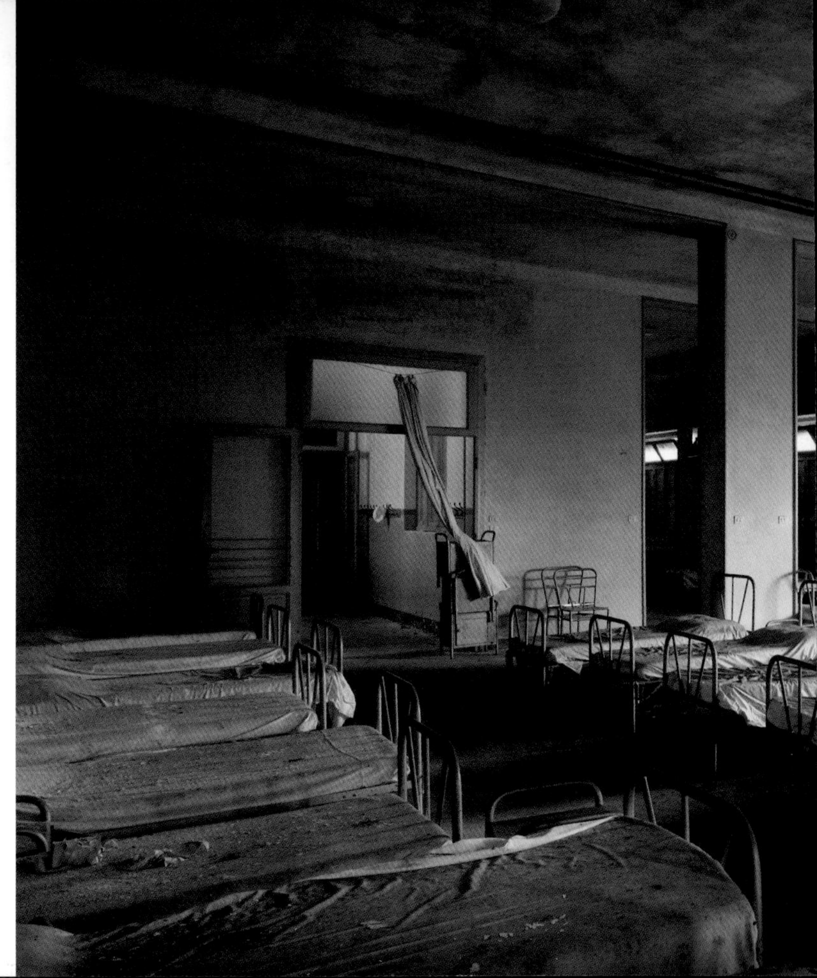

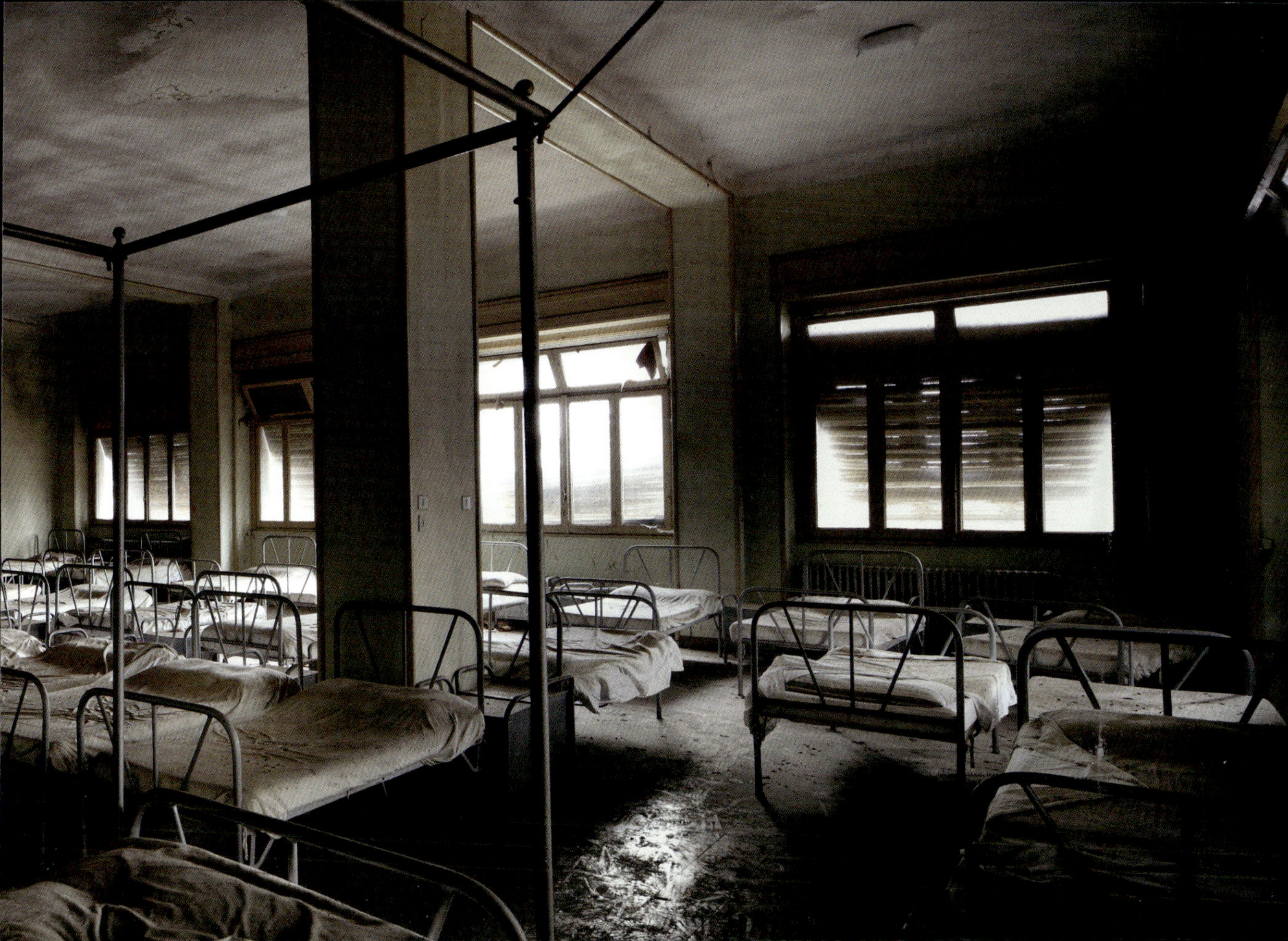

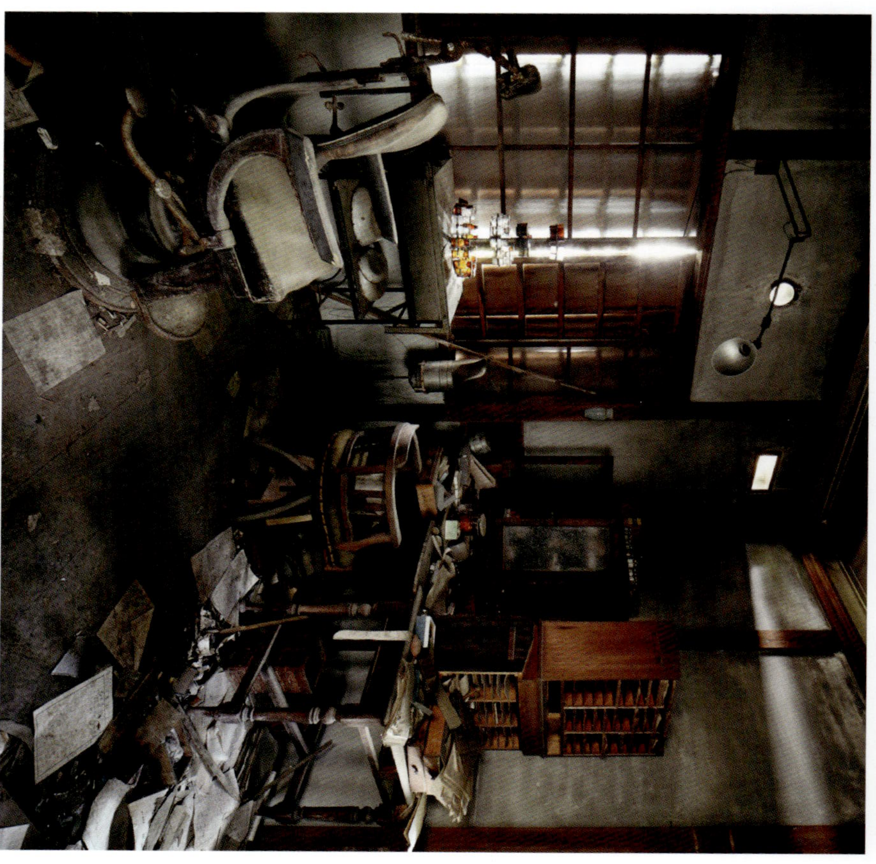

 △ Ghost Clinic, Japan, 2012 ▽ Dentist's Chair - Broderick Tower, Detroit, USA, 2010

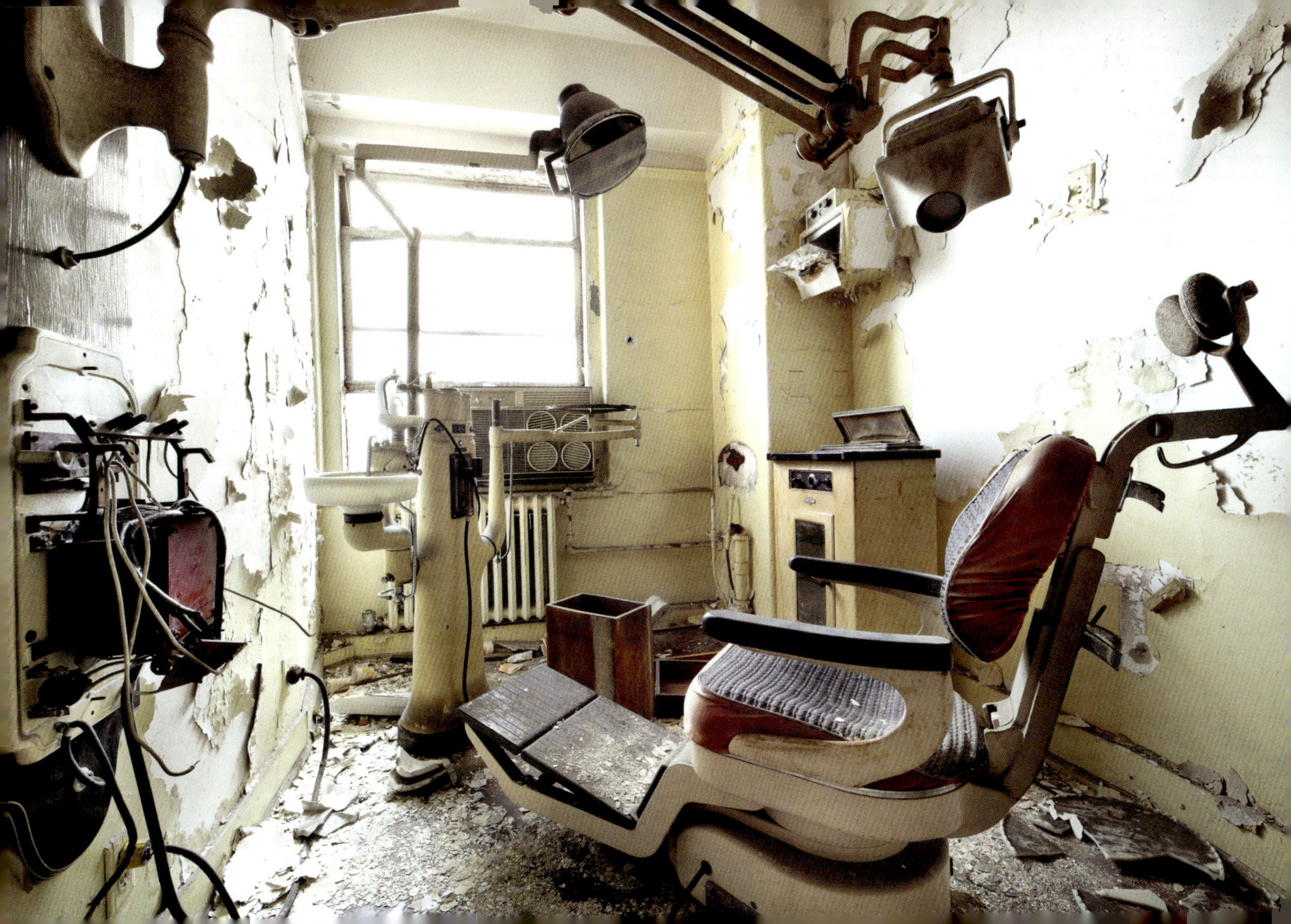

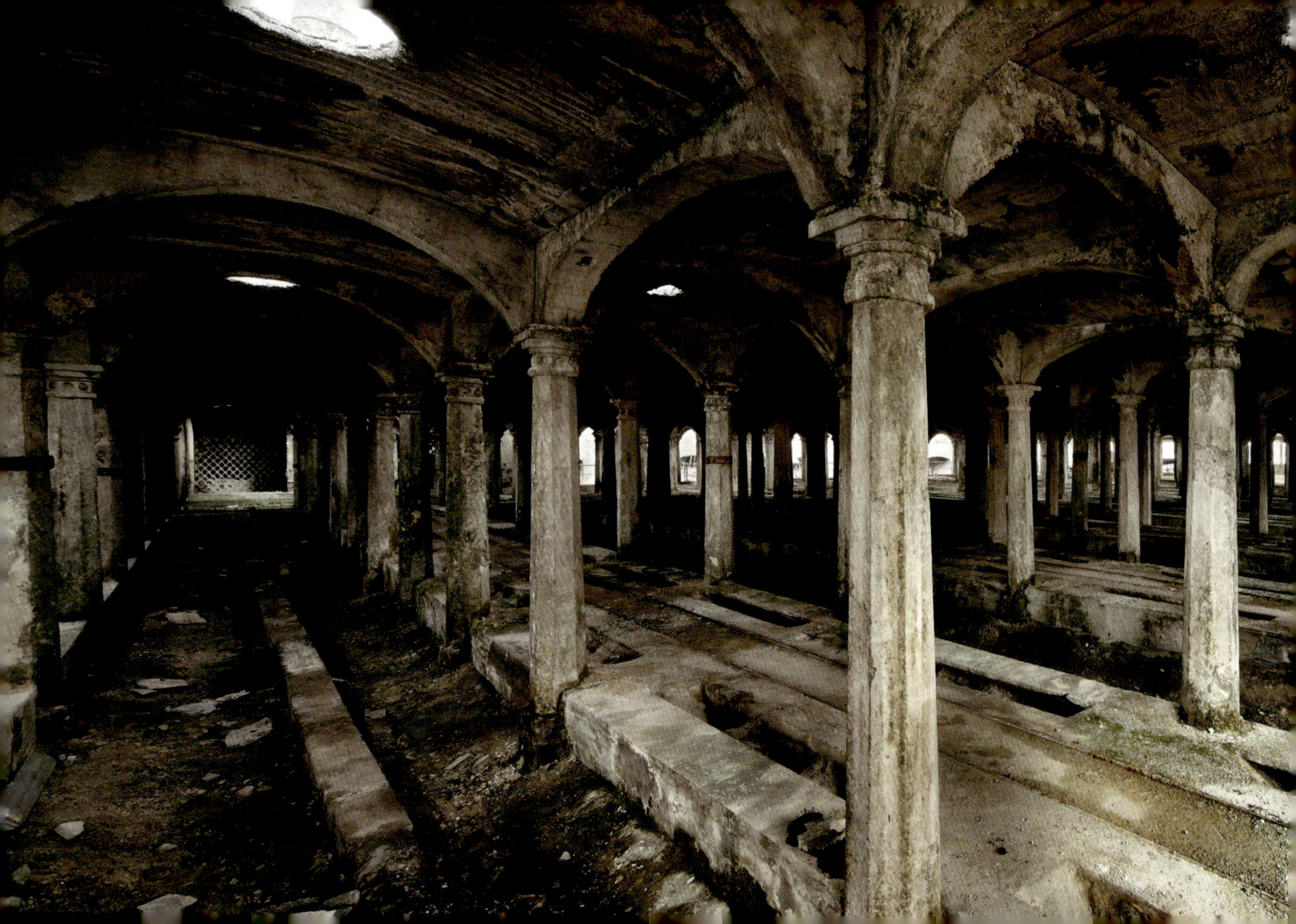

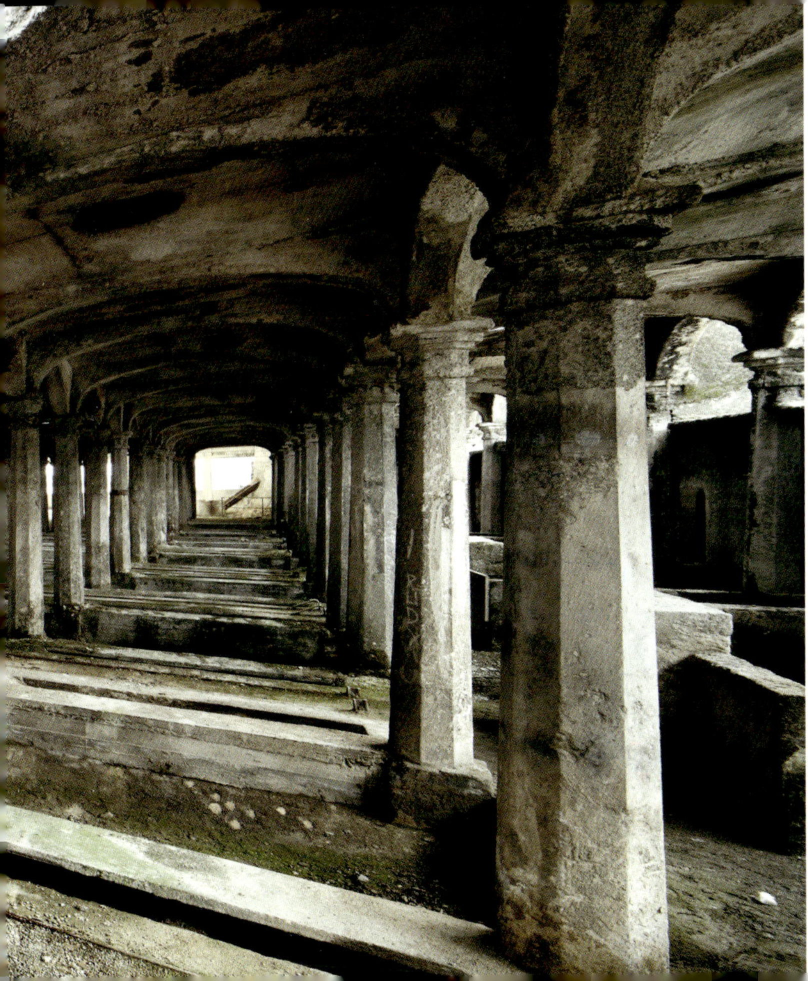

◁ MAGNIFICEMENT
ITALY, 2011

What genius dreamed up this mega cement factory? As monumental as a Greek temple, dark corridors like those leading to the tomb chambers of an Egyptian pyramid. And then that unmistakable copy of the Basilica Cistern in Istanbul.

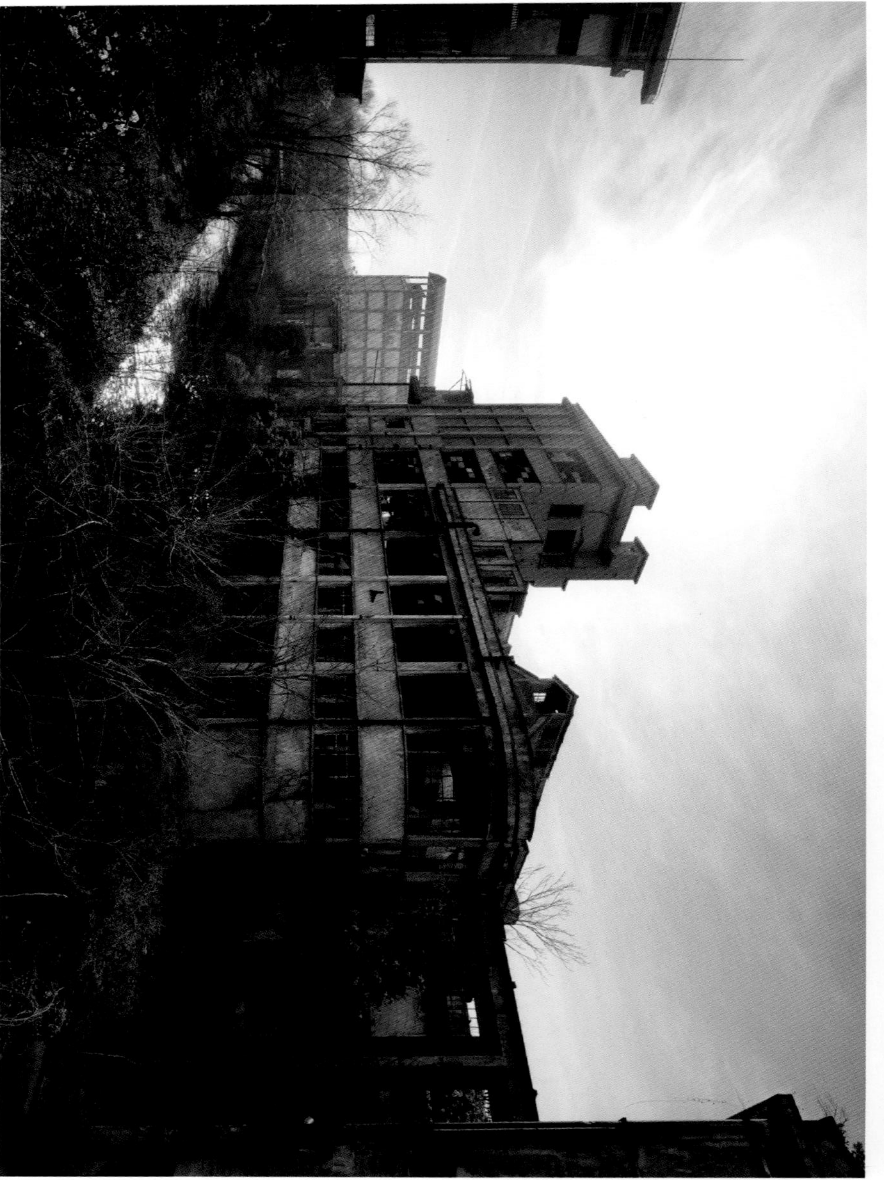

 Vita Mayer, Italy, 2011

 Vercelli Mosquito Theatre, Italy, 2011

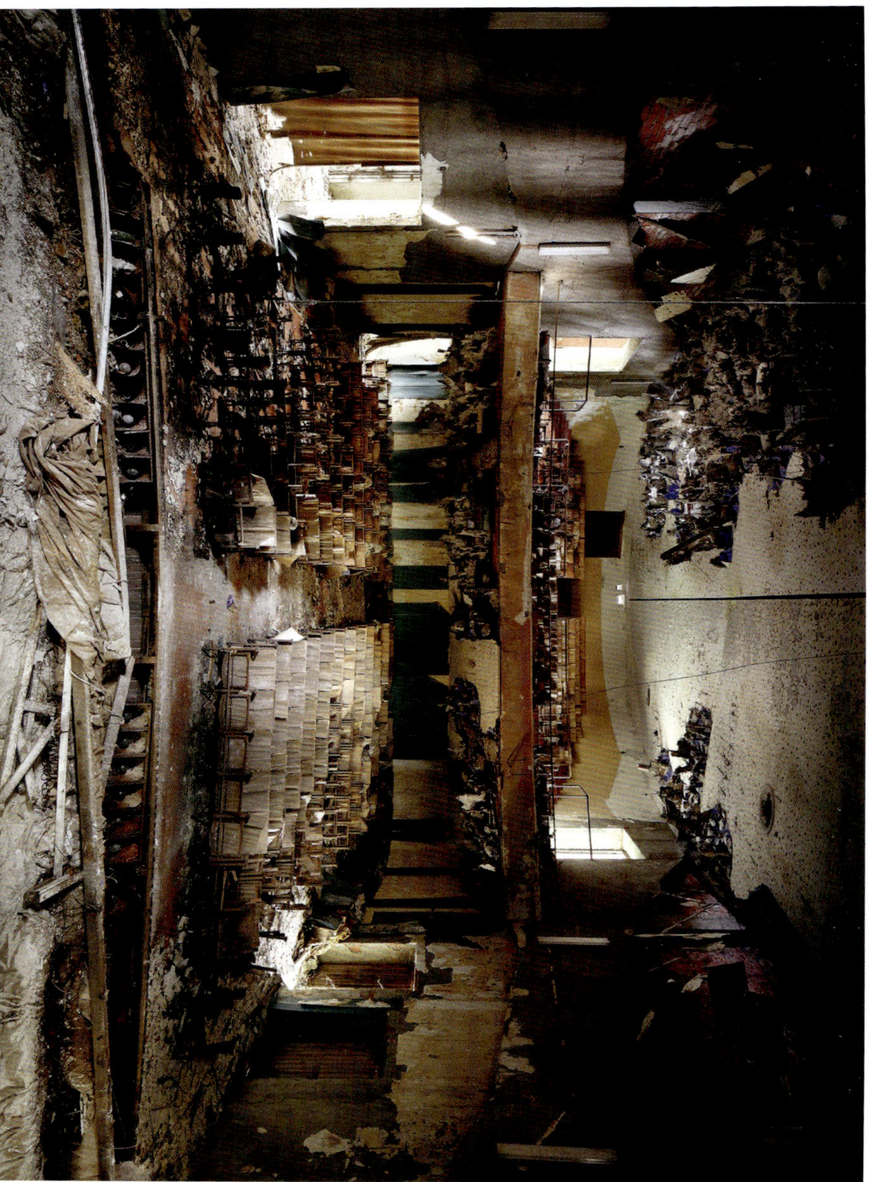

 Cardump Chatillon, Belgium, 2008

Cardump Chatillon, Belgium, 2008

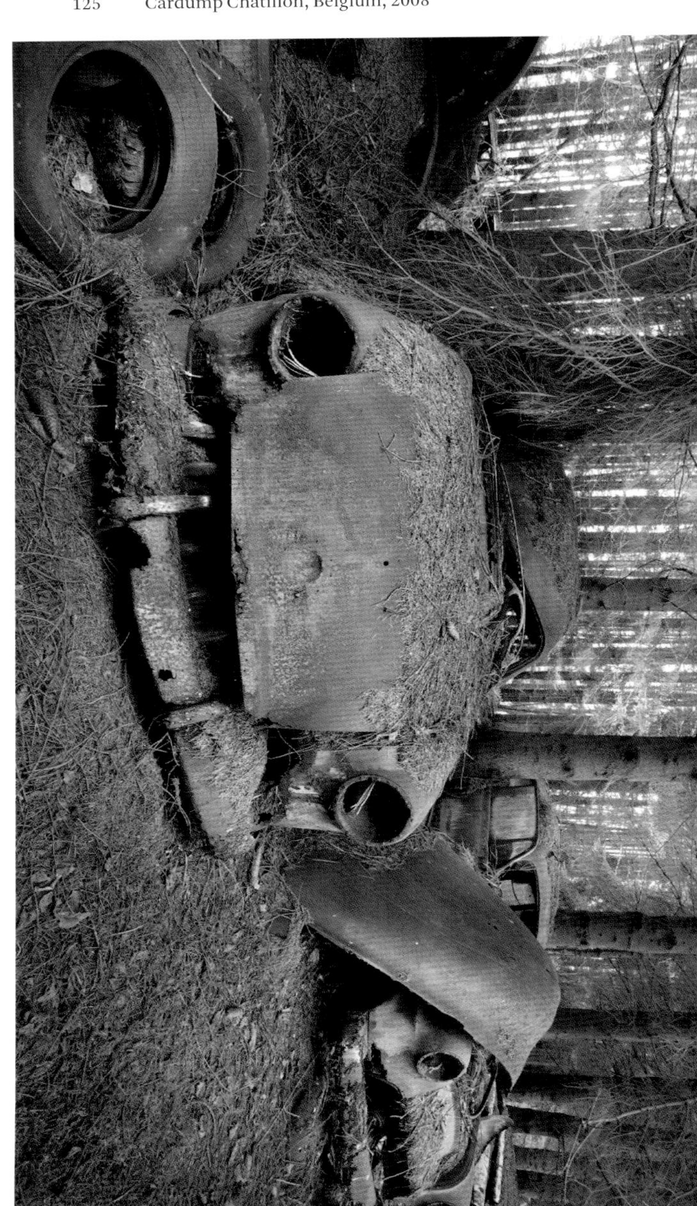

YUBARI DRIVING SCHOOL ▹
JAPAN, 2014

During my last visit in Japan, I was busy photographing in an abandoned amusement park. It was located at the edge of a deep ravine with a decorative bridge over a wild river deep below. Beautiful surroundings. I parked my car by the bridge and walked over it.

I had been photographing less than an hour when to my surprise a policeman waved at me frantically. Hiding quickly was not an option. I dreaded a difficult discussion, which would result from not knowing each other's language. The only thing the man asked was: 'Car bridge, you?' He was visibly relieved when I confirmed that. We walked together to the exit where his colleague waited, just as happy to see us. The explanation for their joy was: 'People park car bridge ... then suicide'.

They stayed till I drove away. ◆

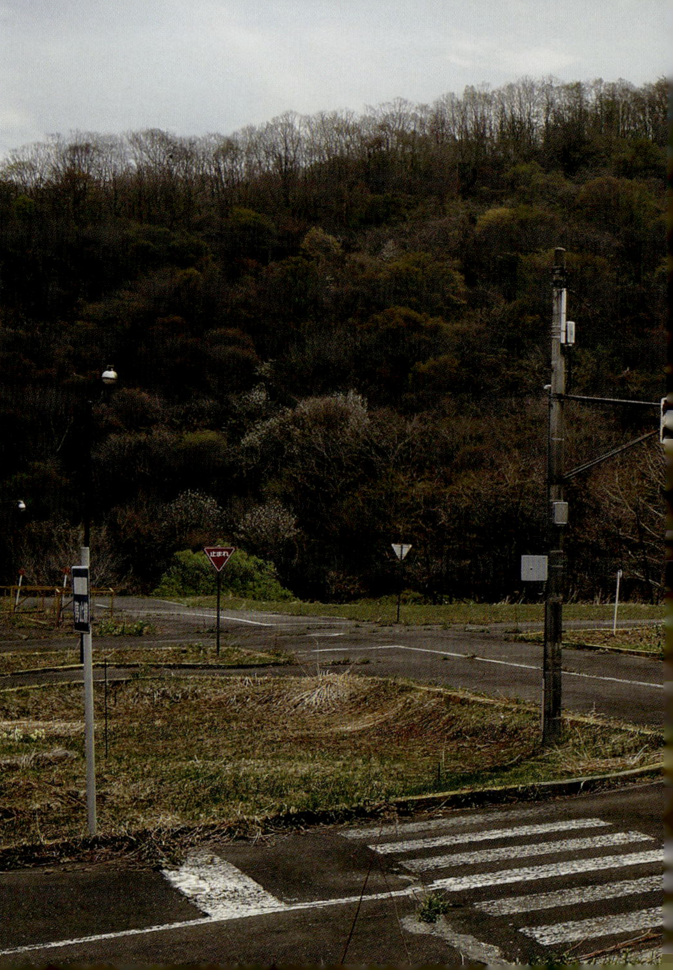

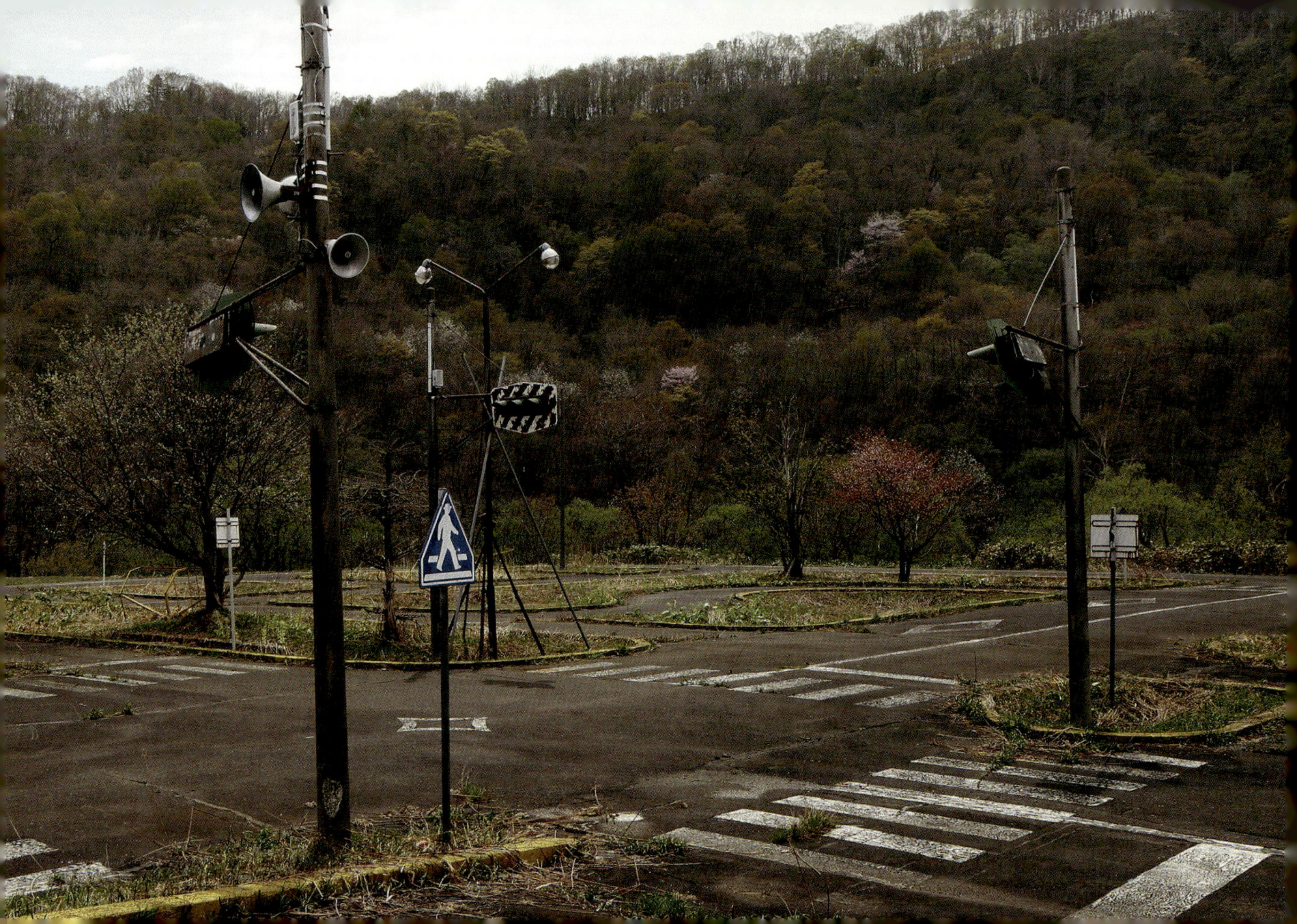

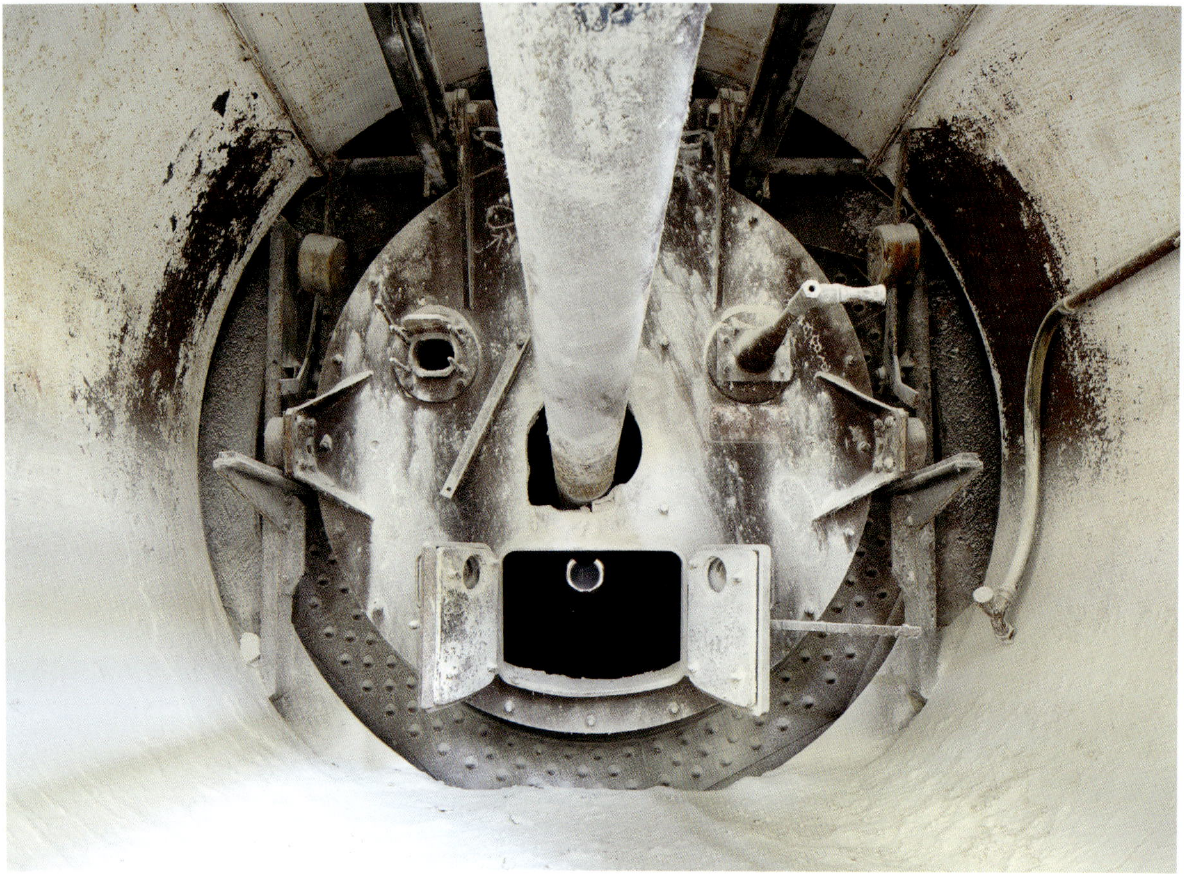

Pinoccio, Belgium, 2013

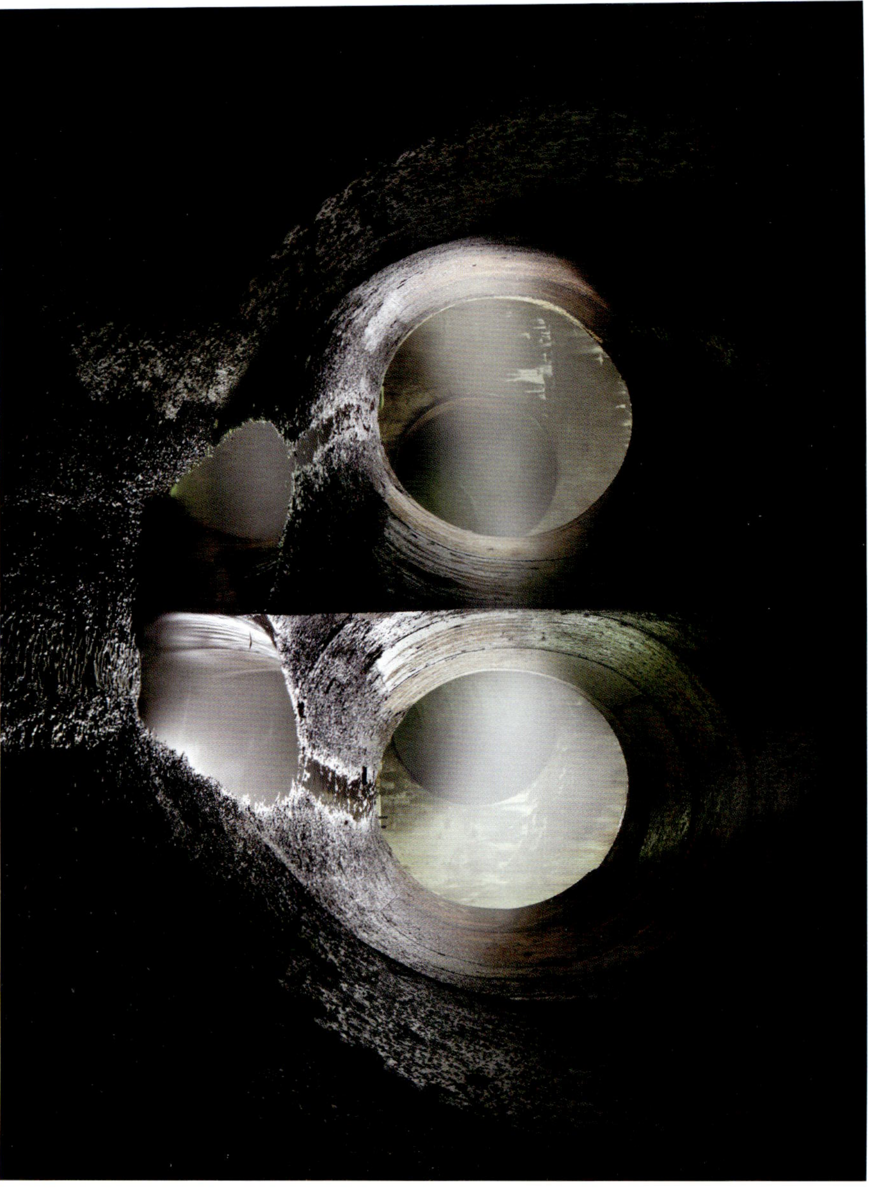

Wagakawa Power Plant, Japan, 2013

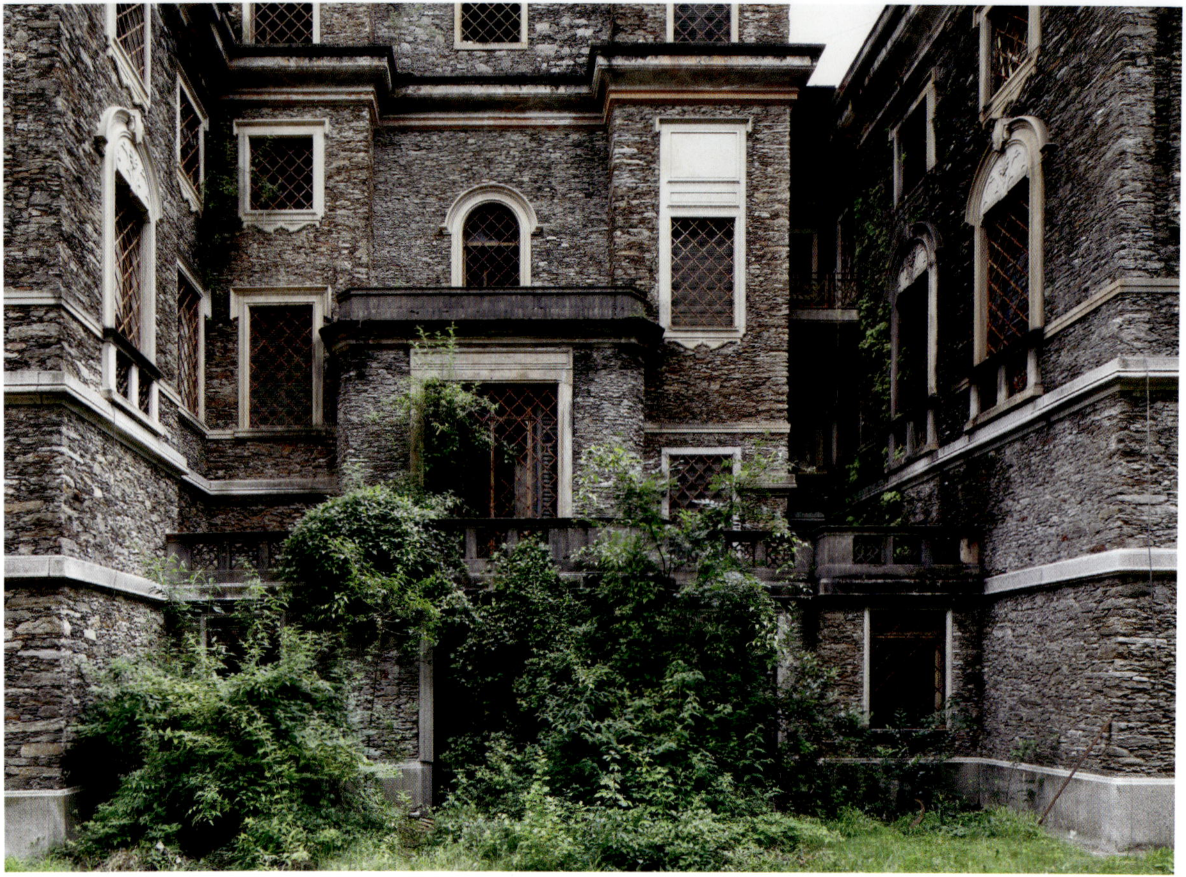

Facade - Villa Decadimento, Italy, 2011

Mitsui Bibai, Japan, 2014

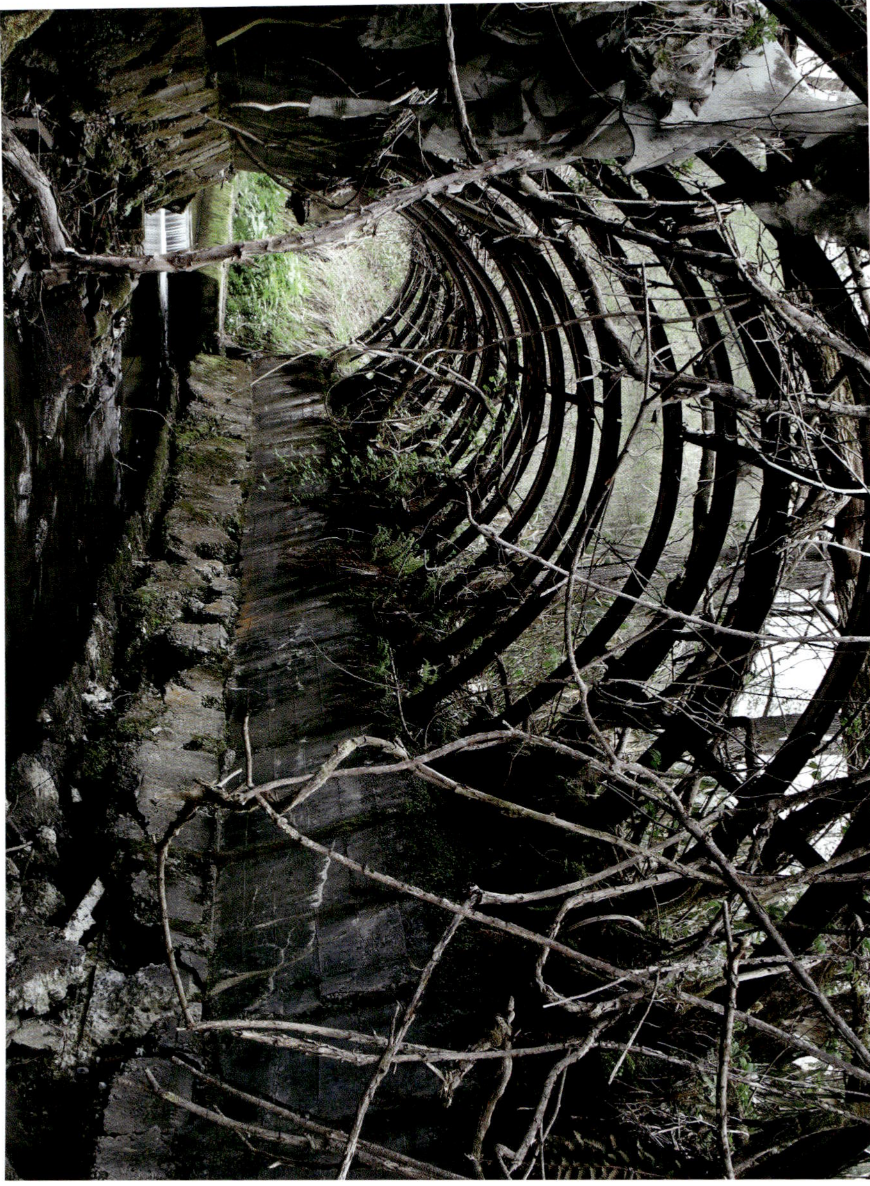

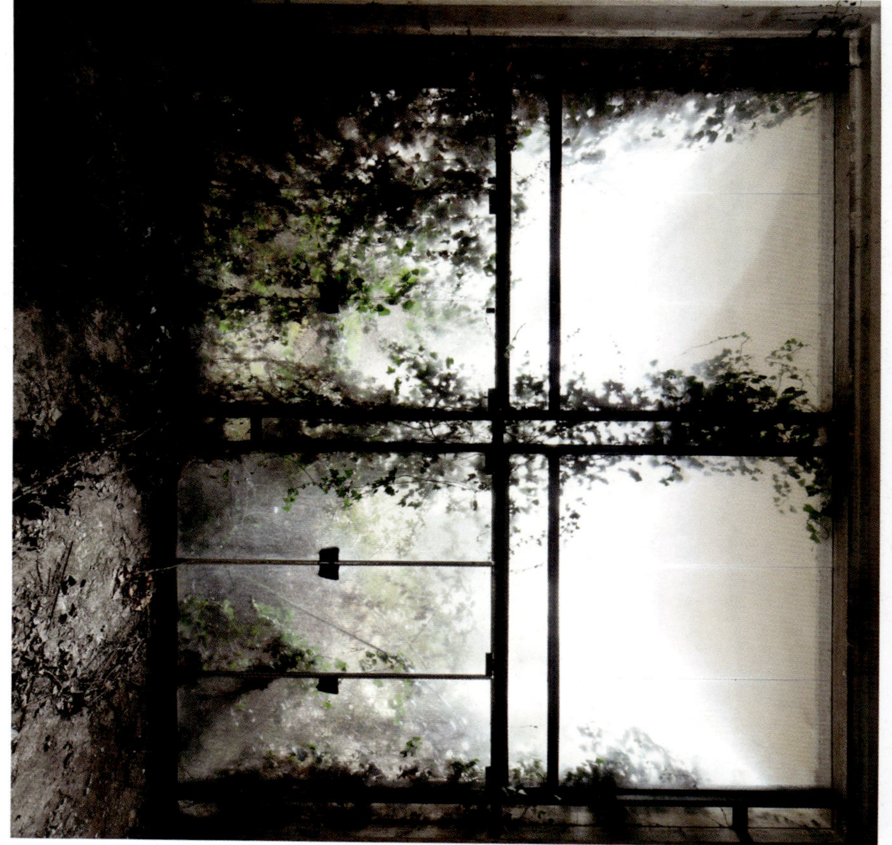

△ Let nature in!, Italy, 2011

▽ Ivy corridor, Belgium, 2009

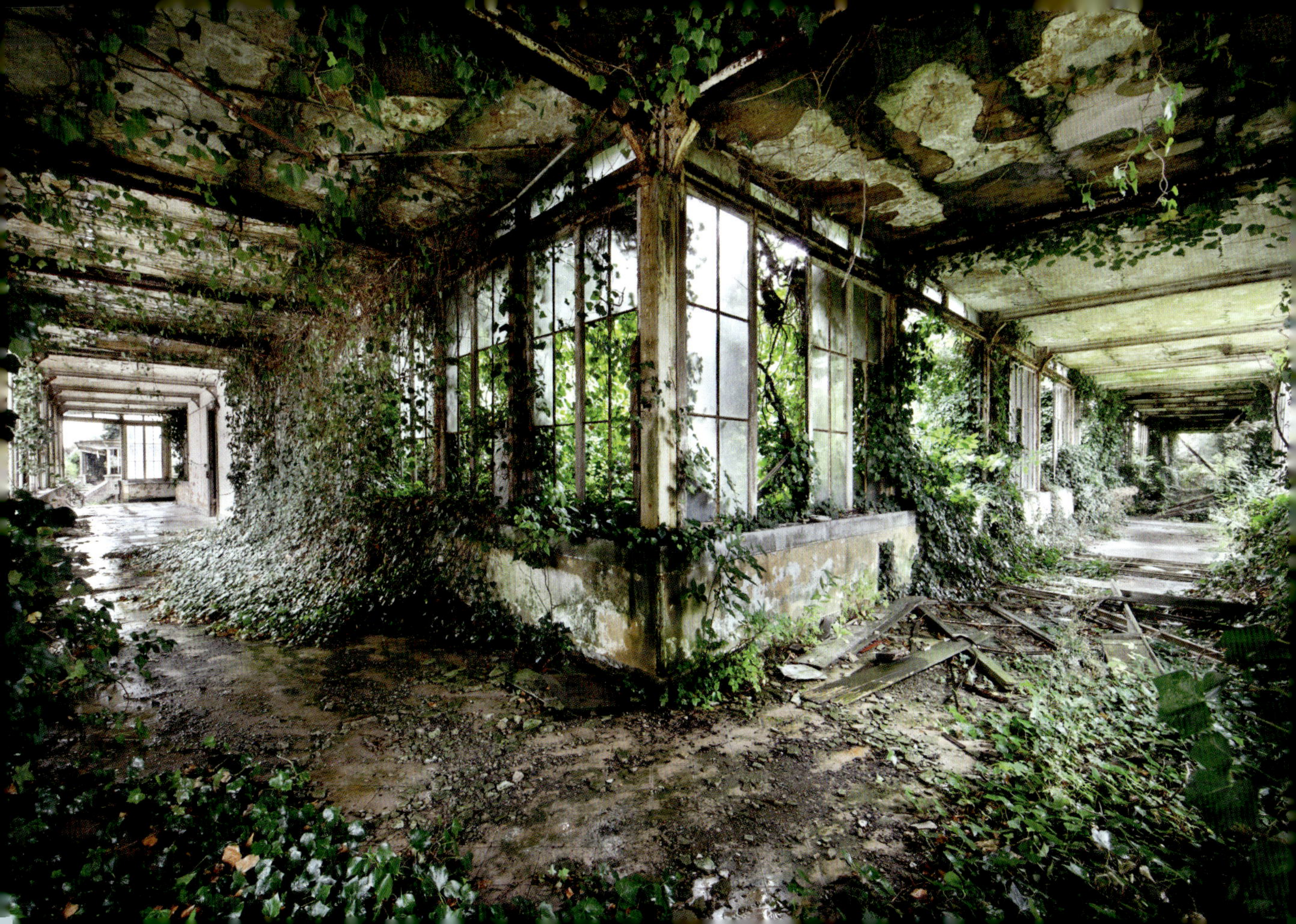

HAPPINESS ISLAND ▹
JAPAN, 2014

The old man addressed me in poor English. He had a small translation computer the size of a calculator. The conversation progressed slowly, but we had the time.

He told me that he was born on the island, but not his ancestors. His grandfather had a high position in the administration of the capital city. When his boss was found guilty of a mistake, his grandfather was banished to the island together with his young family.

The old man told me that he worked his entire life as a bus driver in the capital city on the mainland. He was married and had a family, but he spent a few months a year on the island of his youth without his wife, because she couldn't stand the plainness of the island life. ◆

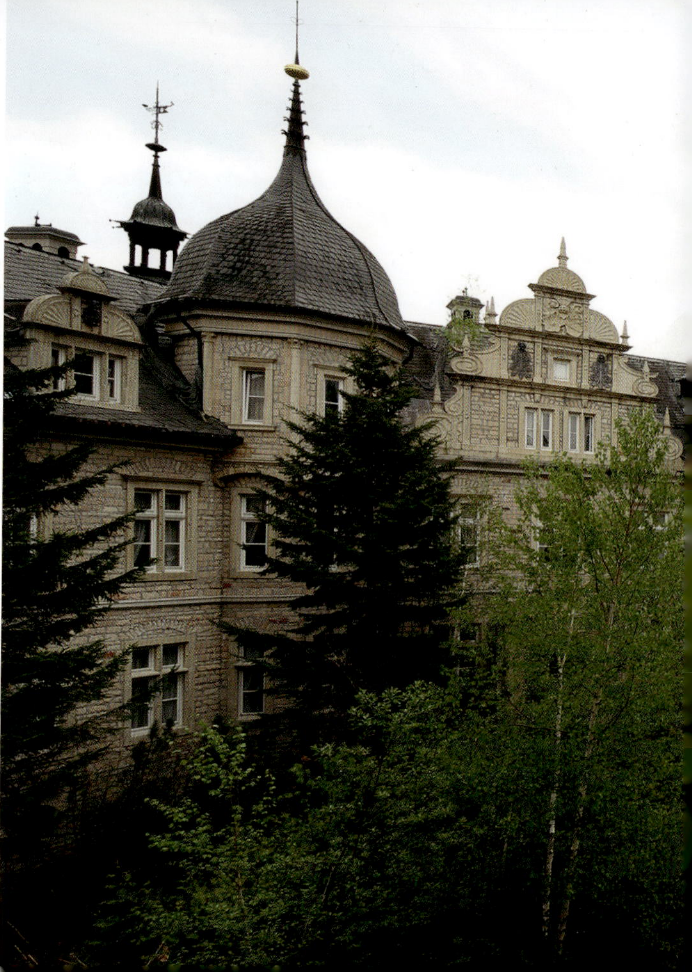

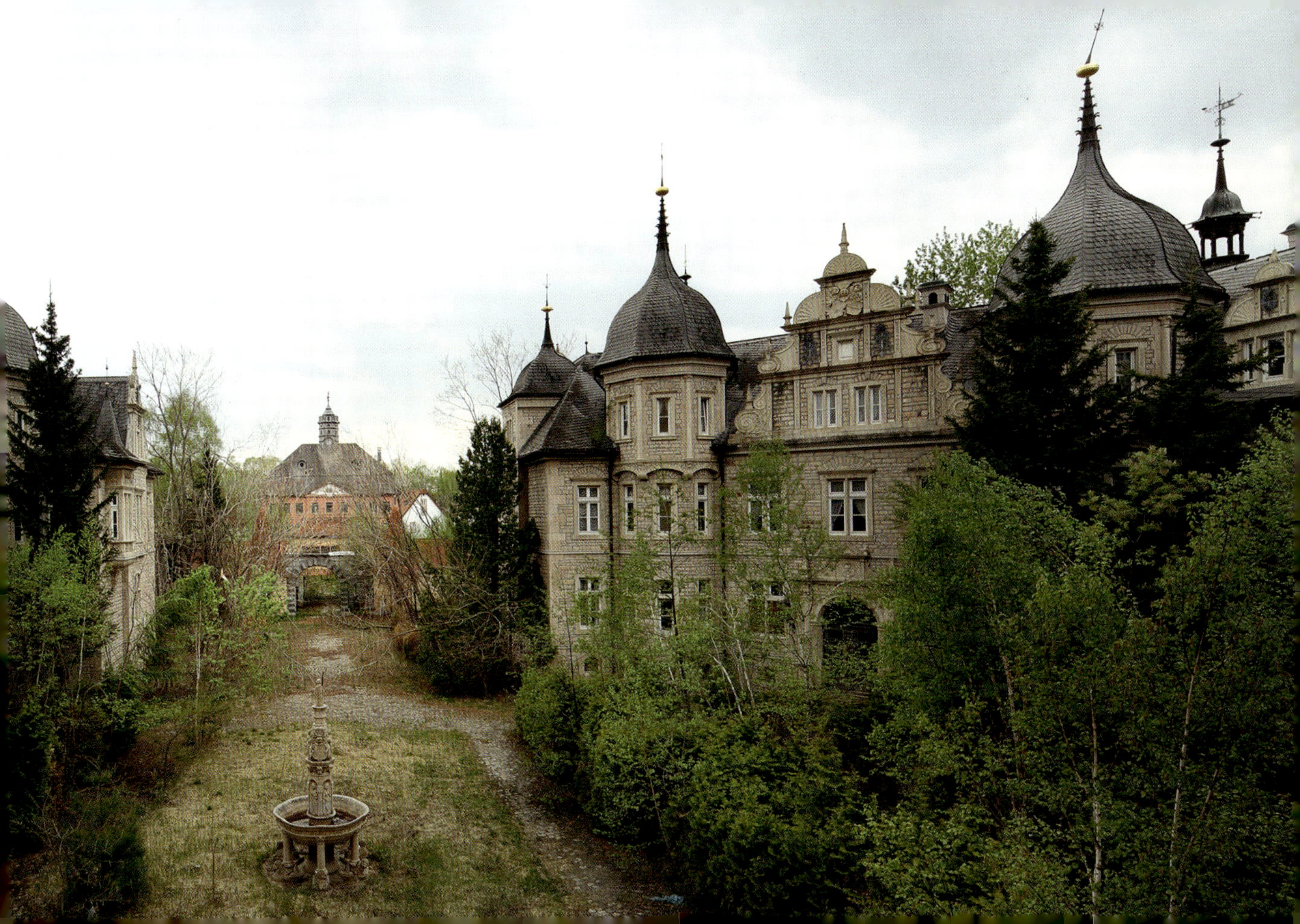

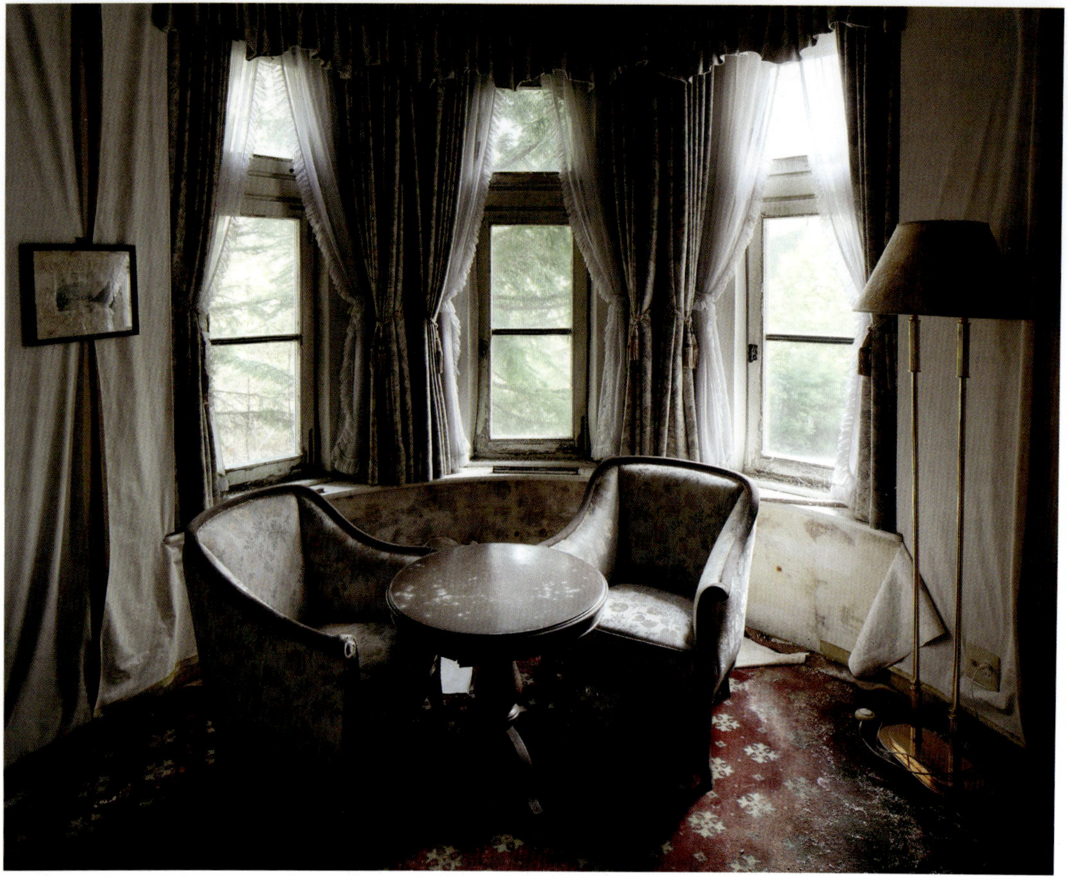

△▽ Hotel Happiness, Japan, 2014

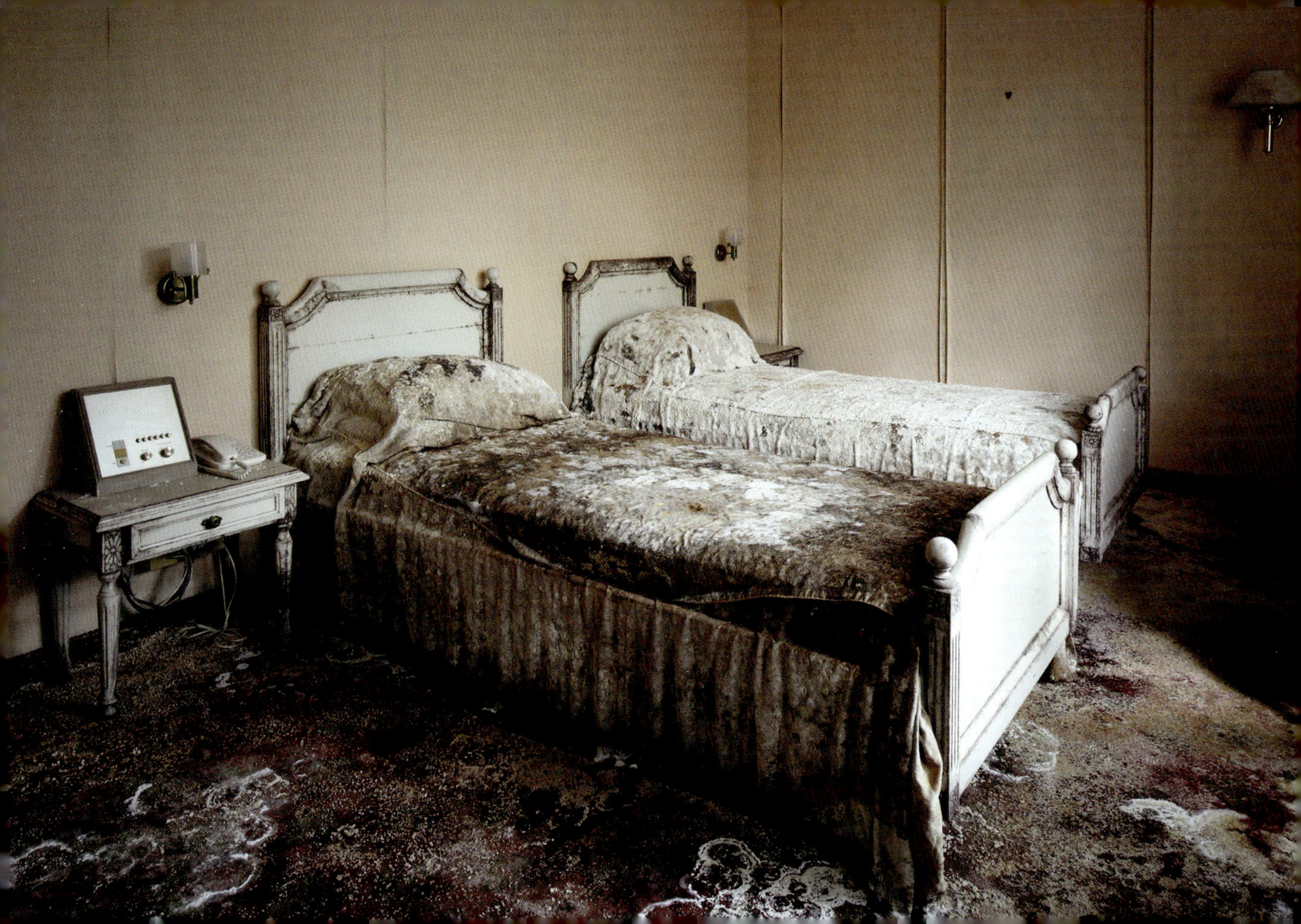

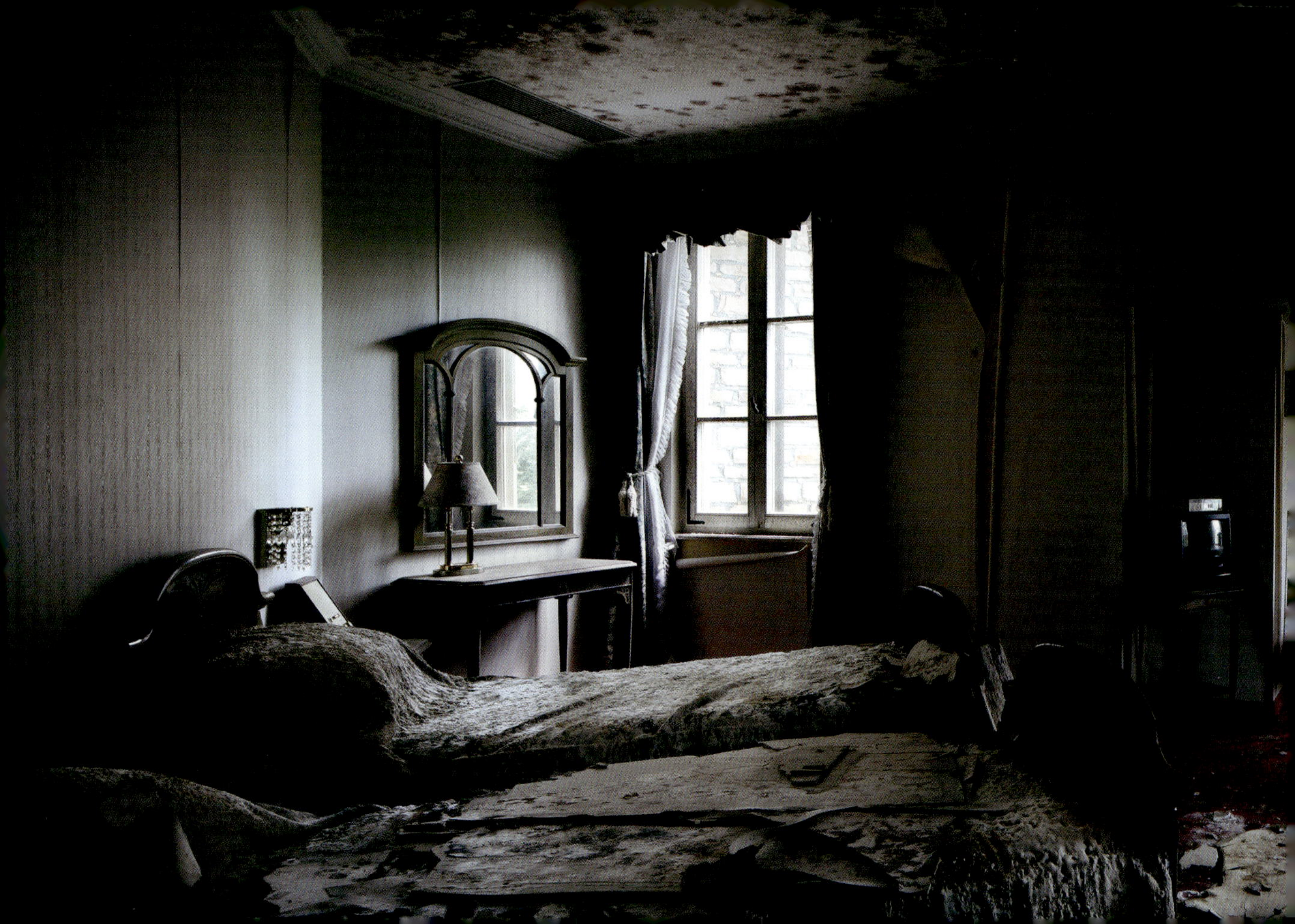

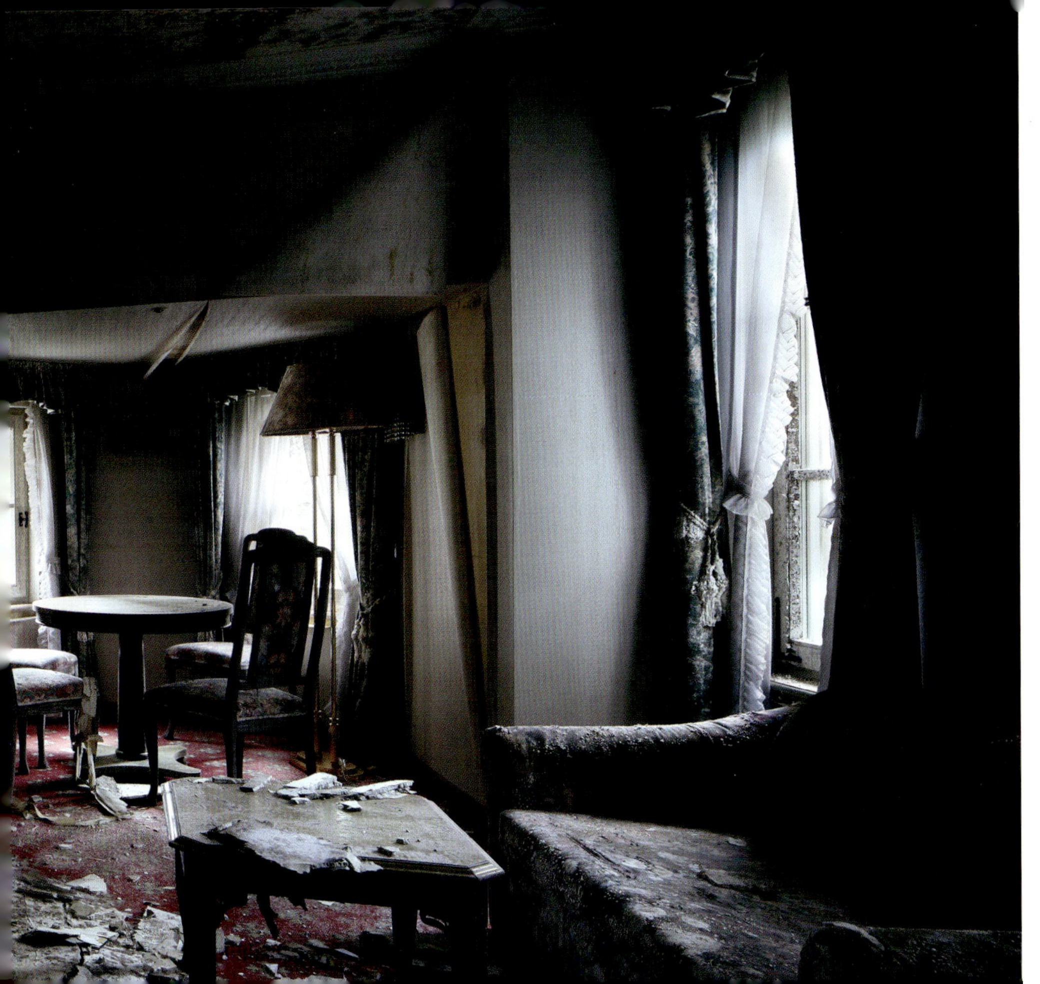

Hotel Happiness, Japan, 2014

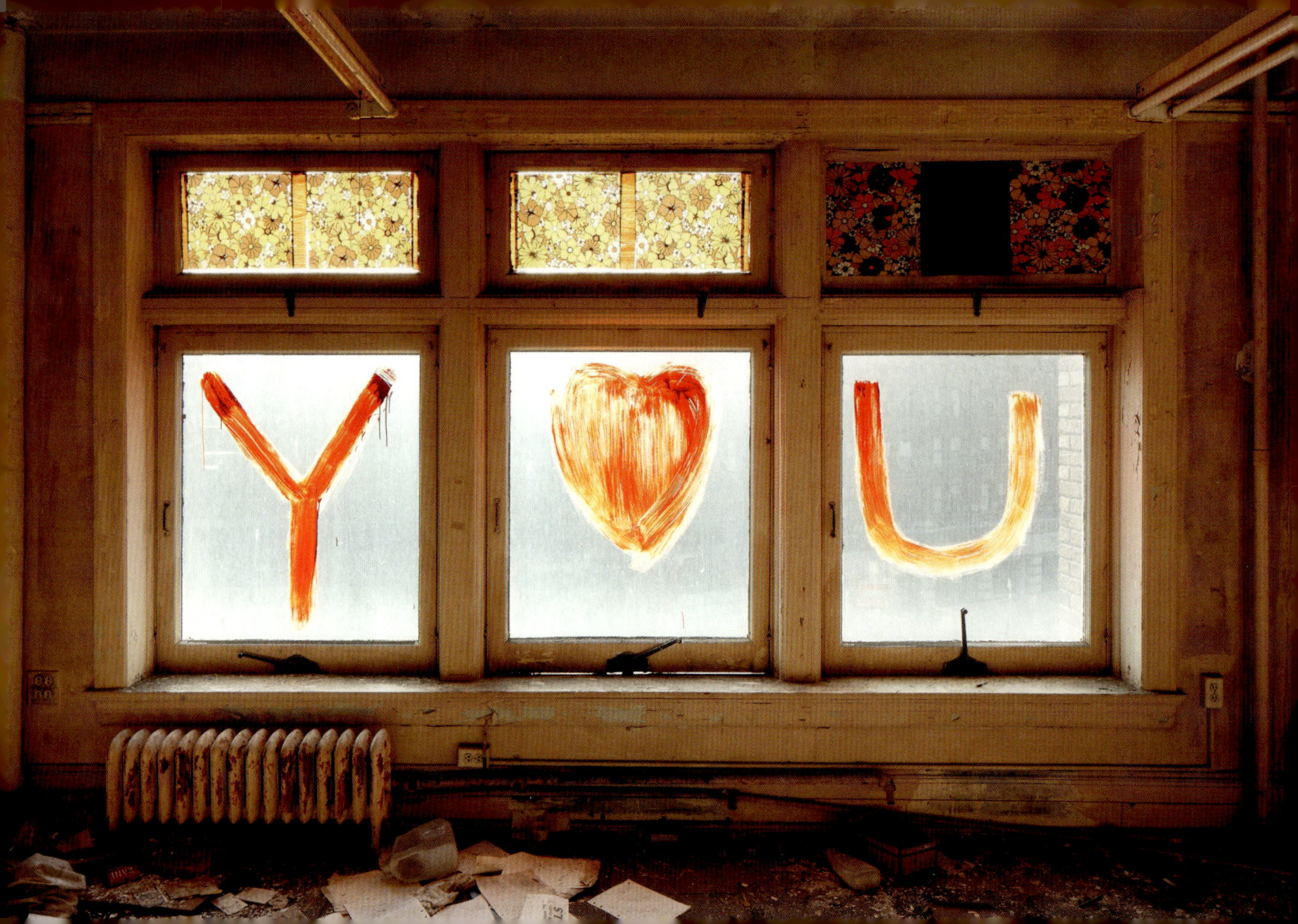
Y ♥ U

△ You, Farwell Building, Detroit, USA, 2012

▽ Sunshine Villa, Belgium, 2013

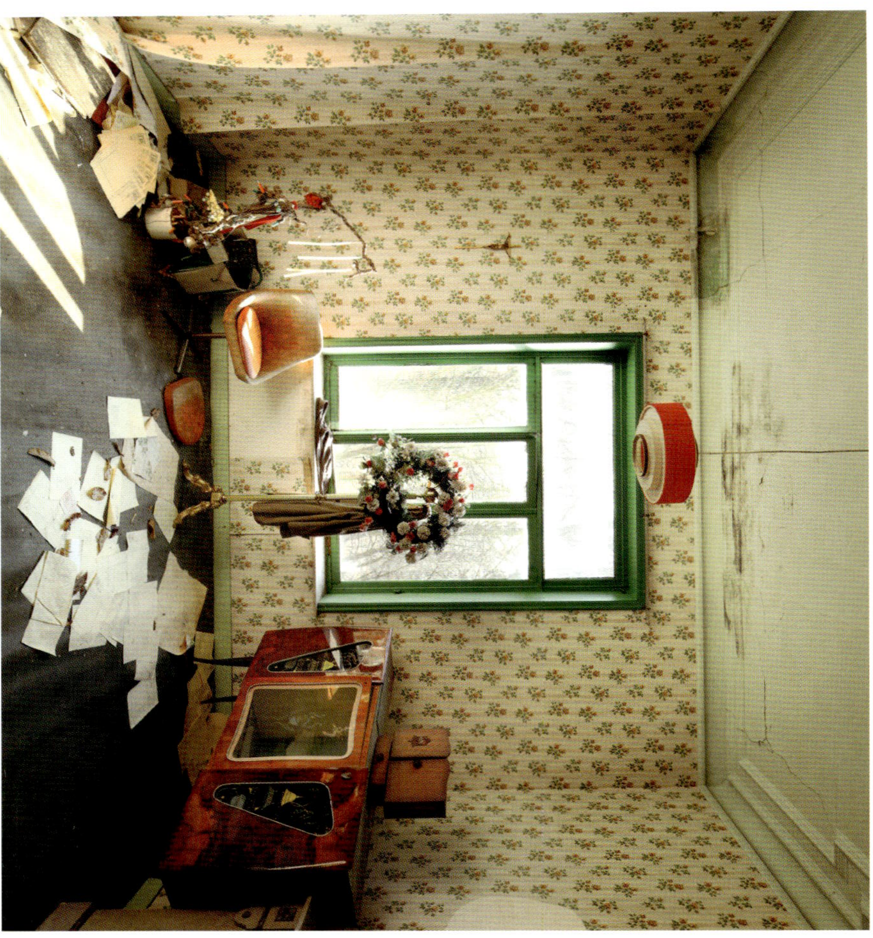

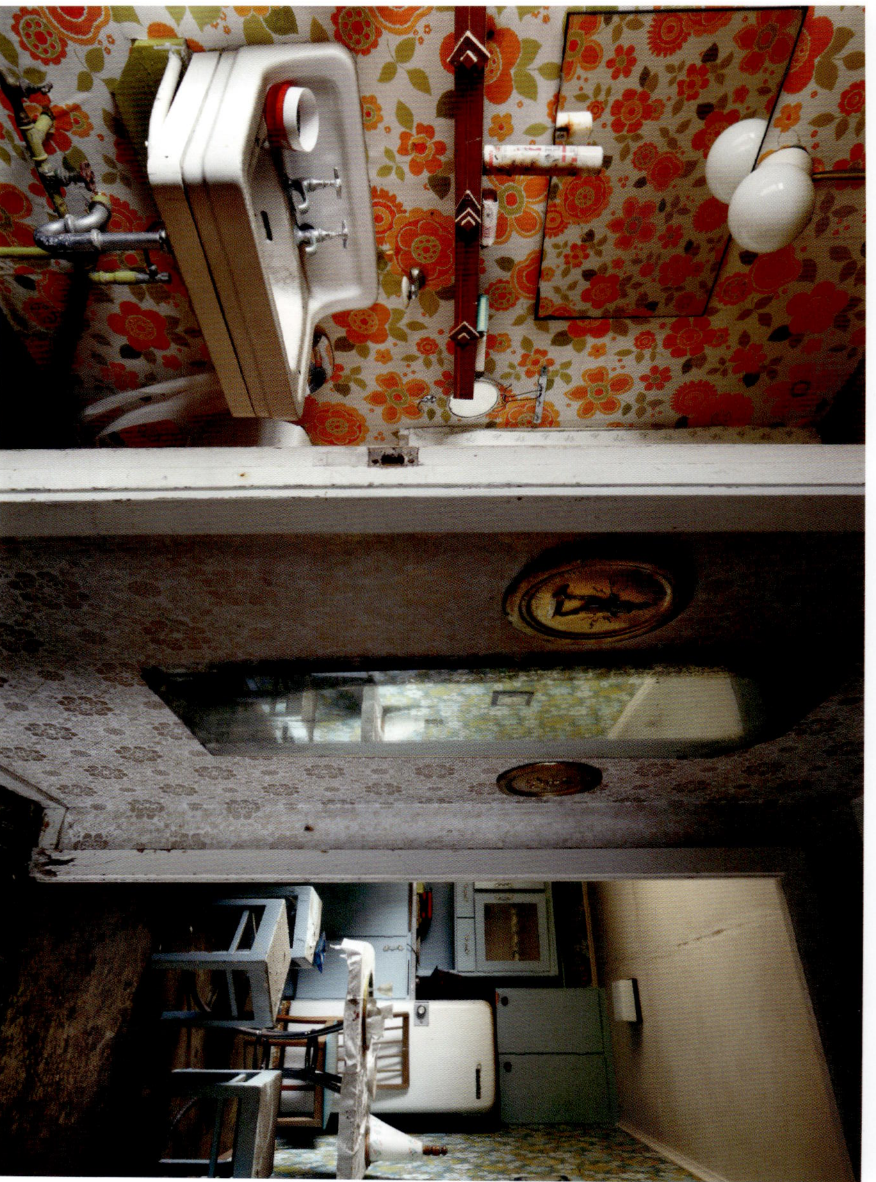

 Vik, Iceland, 2011

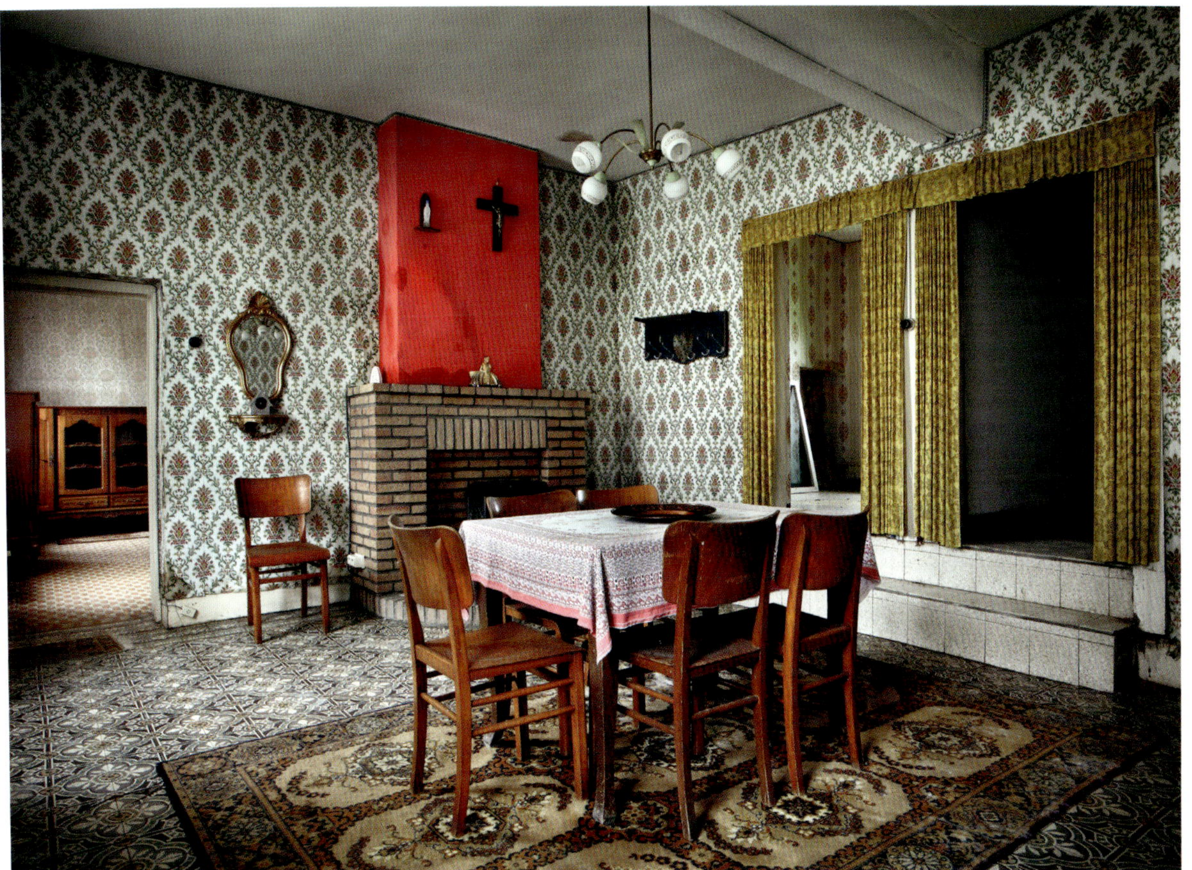

Apple Factory, Belgium, 2007

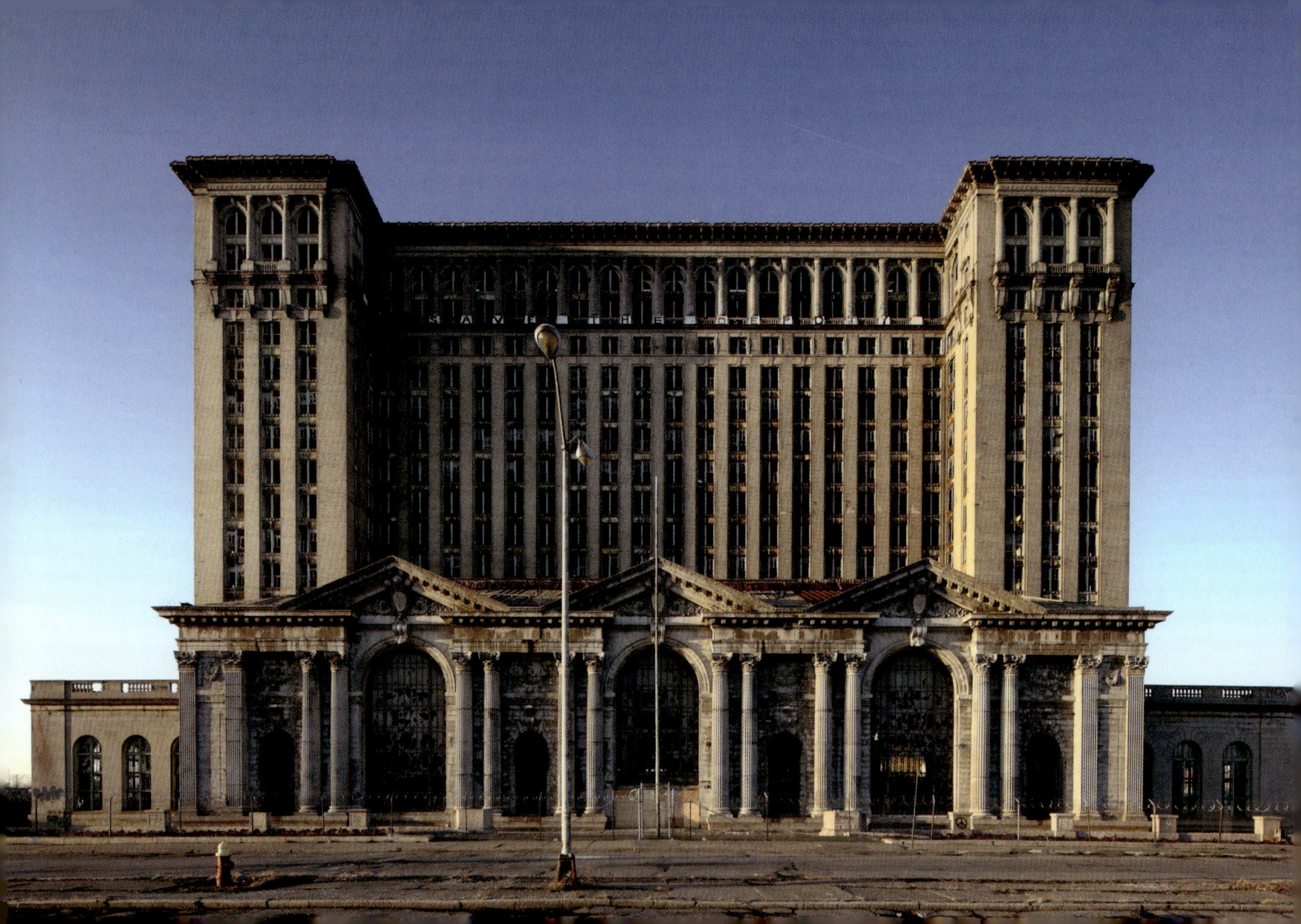
SAVE THE

◁ MICHIGAN CENTRAL STATION
DETROIT, USA, 2010

Detroit. The view through the broken windows from the top floor of the Broderick Tower is both breathtaking and uncanny. There is something strange about this city. There were hardly any cars driving on the wide, six-lane roads. Three cars were parked in the parking lot and the woman by the barrier was staring absently into space. On the pavement, a homeless person was wandering around aimlessly. The other skyscrapers around me stared at me with hollow eyes: most of the buildings are empty above the first floor, and you can sometimes see a curtain flapping out through an open window.

Is this the image of a metropolis after the Apocalypse? There is almost no one living in the city center and the surrounding districts any more. Many of the houses have been burnt out or look totally dilapidated. Over a third of the surface area is waste ground and nature is eagerly re-asserting itself.

In the distance, we saw the proud Michigan Central Station. Later on, I would be walking with Brett through its dark cellars, watching out for the Latino gangs that are rumored to hang around there doing shady deals (but in fact we encountered no one and had the monumental, graffiti-clad arrivals hall to ourselves).

Standing in the draughty corridors of the Packard Plant, in the basement swimming pool of Highland Park, or in Cass Tec High School's dining hall, I tried to comprehend the forces that had been at work here. The causes of Detroit's phenomenal rise and fall are well-known and well-documented, but observing it first hand is a different matter. ◆

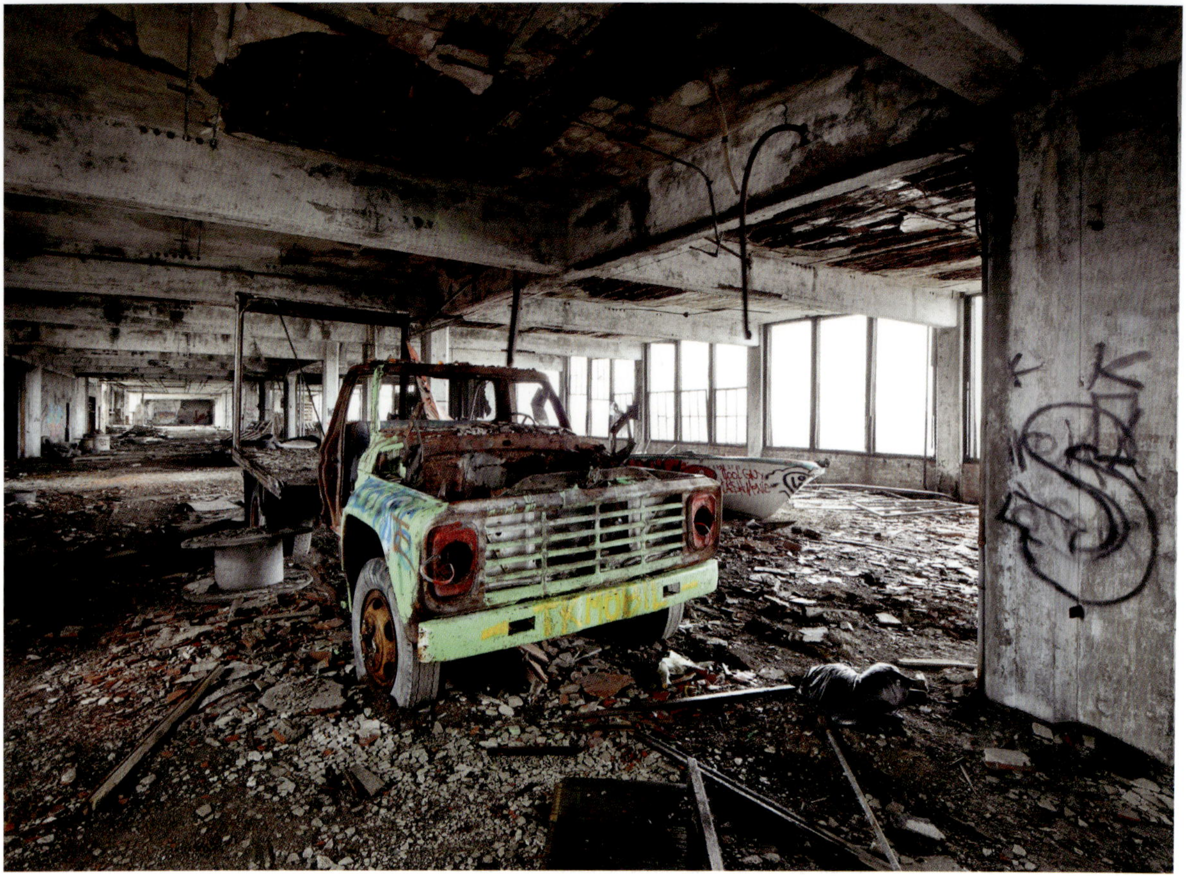

Packard Plant, Detroit, USA, 2010

Packard Plant, Detroit, USA, 2015

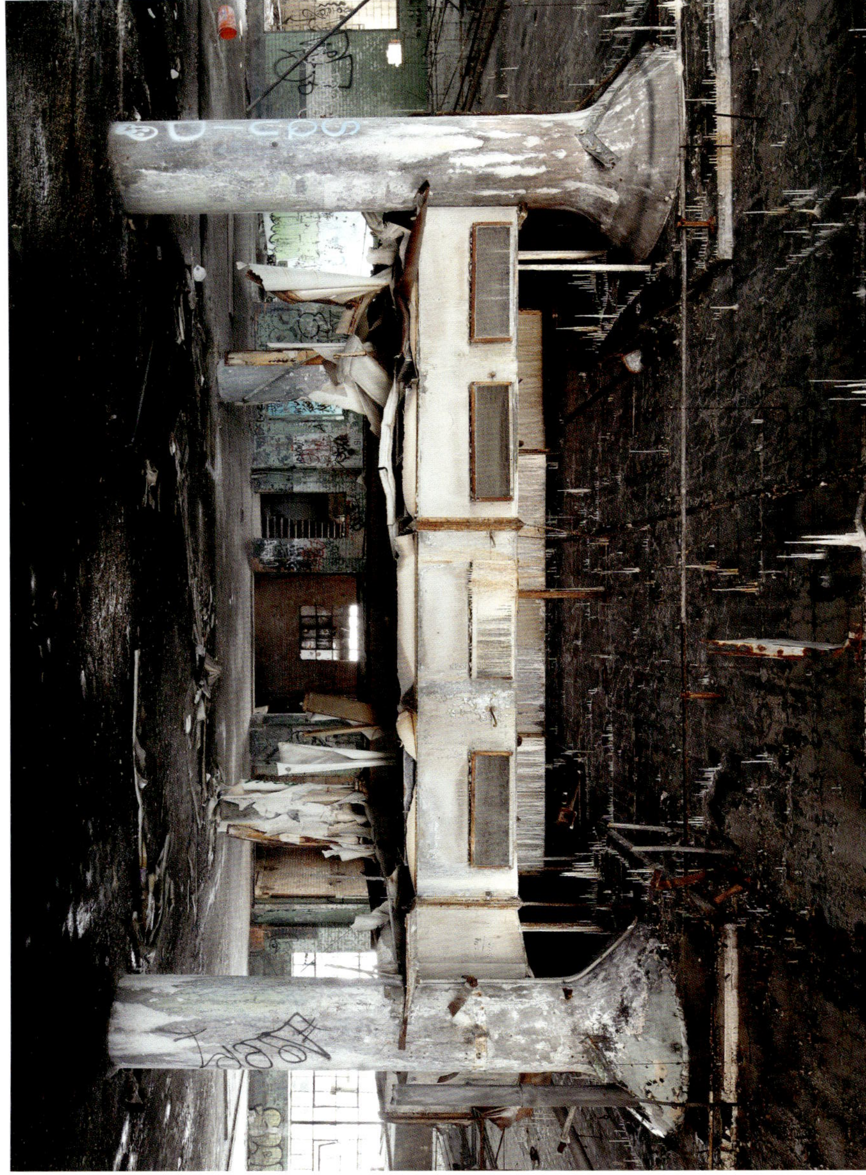

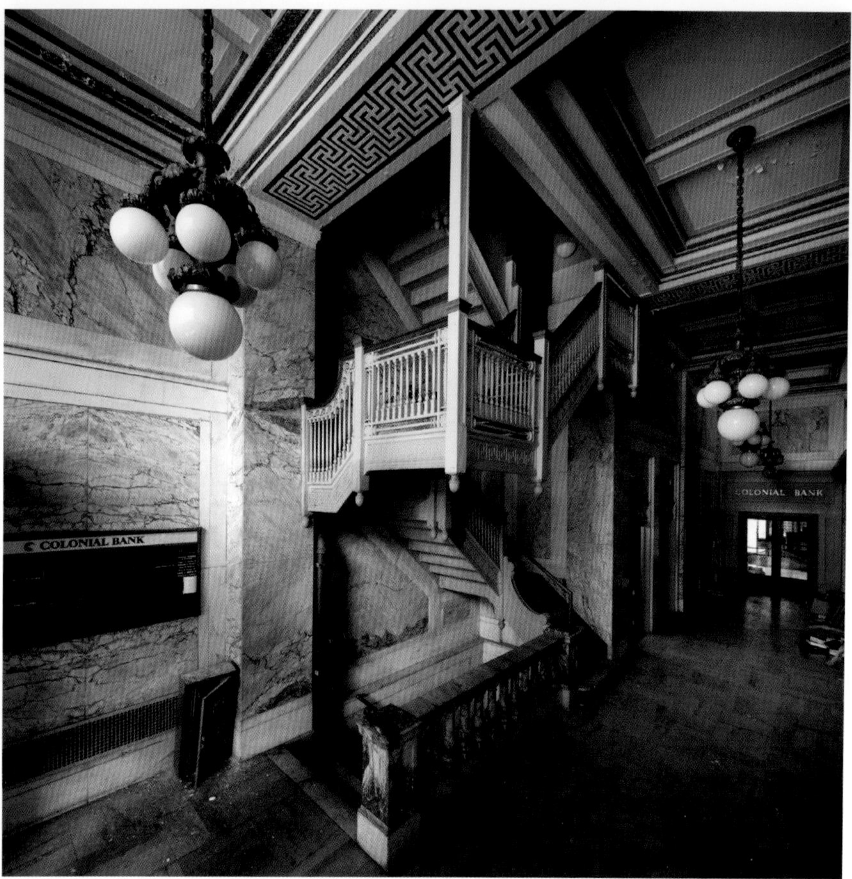

Colonial Bank, Alabama, USA, 2012

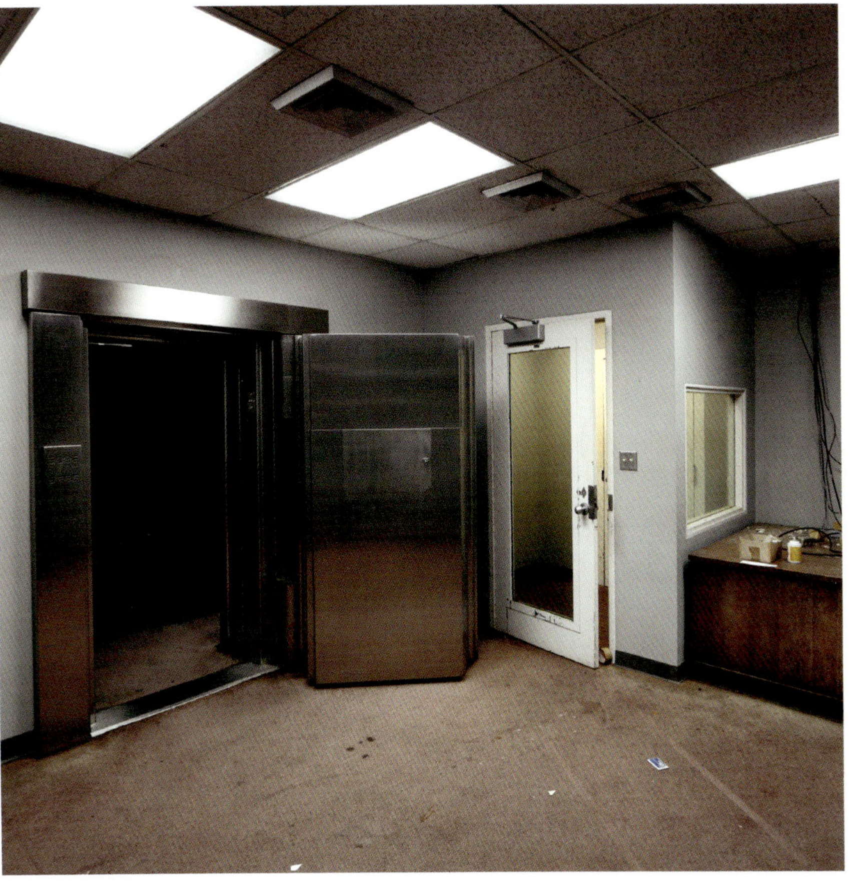

Colonial Bank, Alabama, USA, 2012

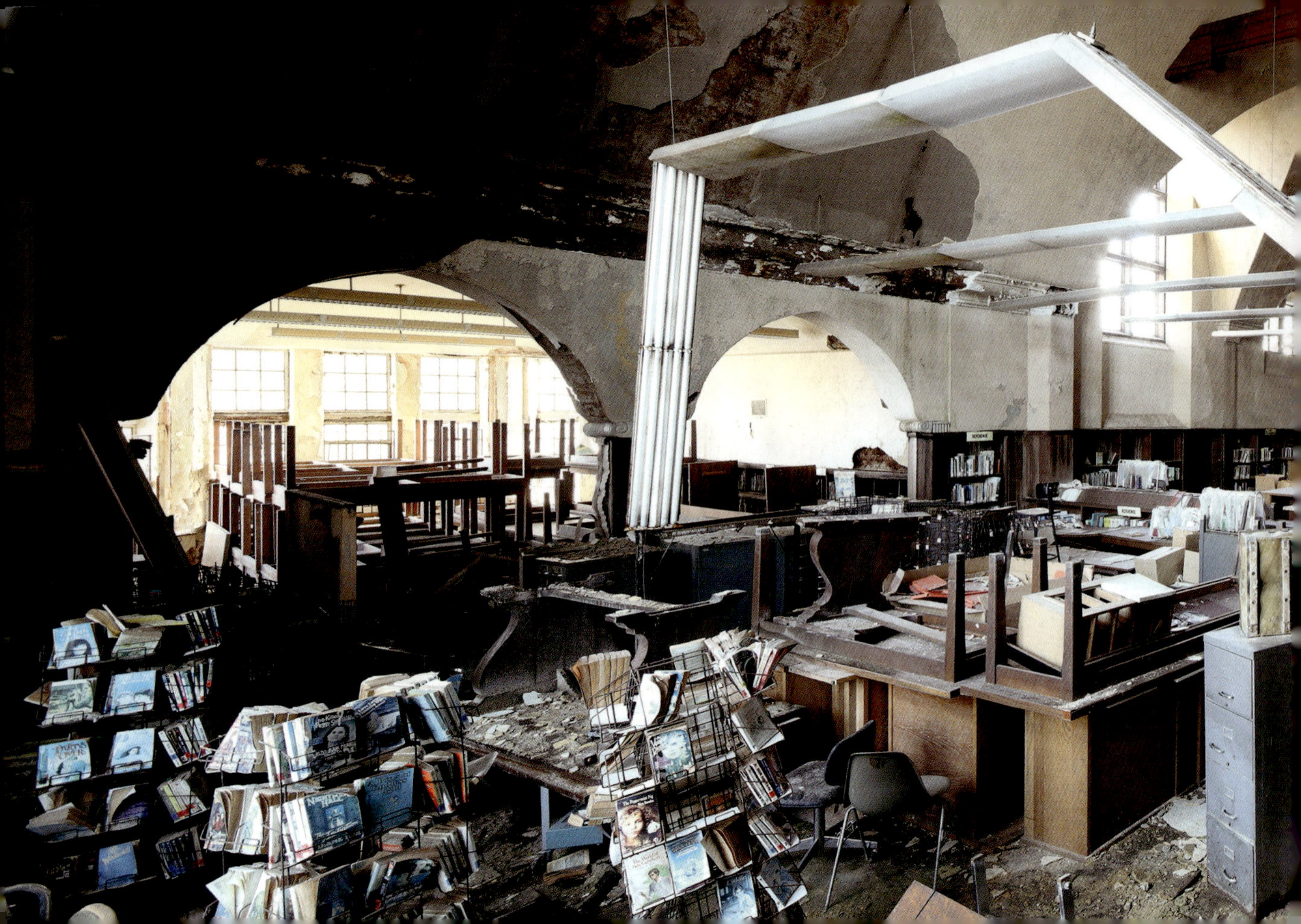

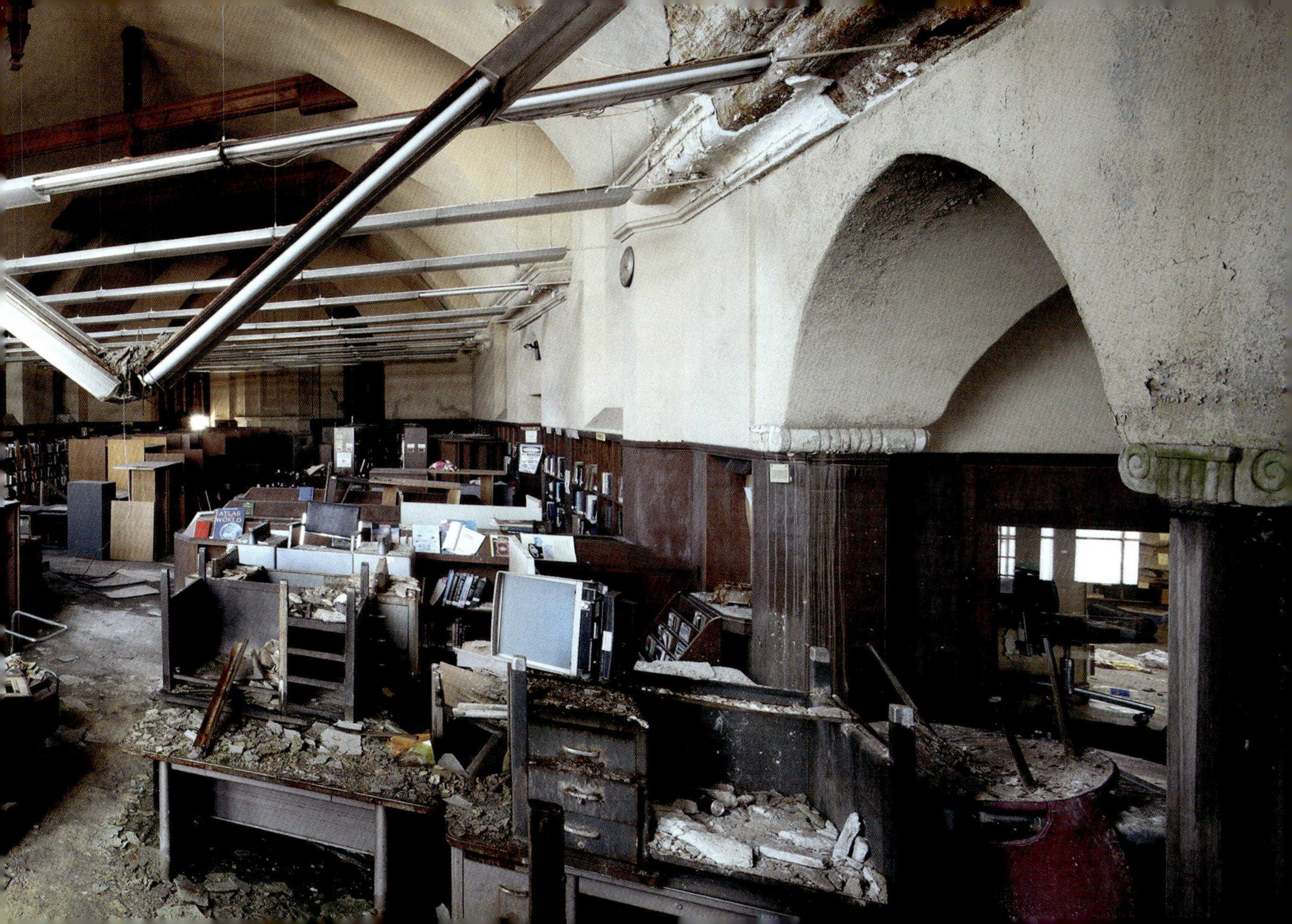
ATLAS
WORLD

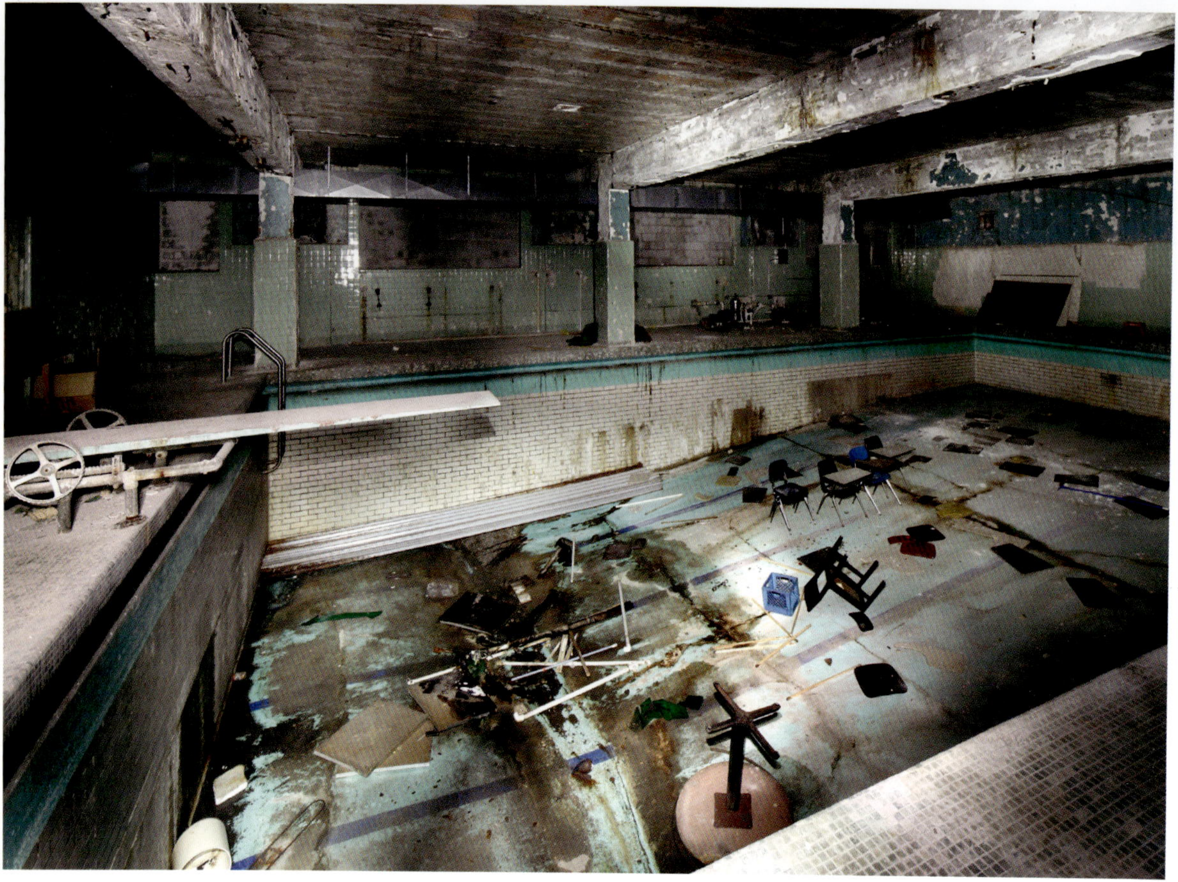

Highland Park, Detroit, USA, 2012

P150–151: Marc Twain Library, Detroit, USA, 2010

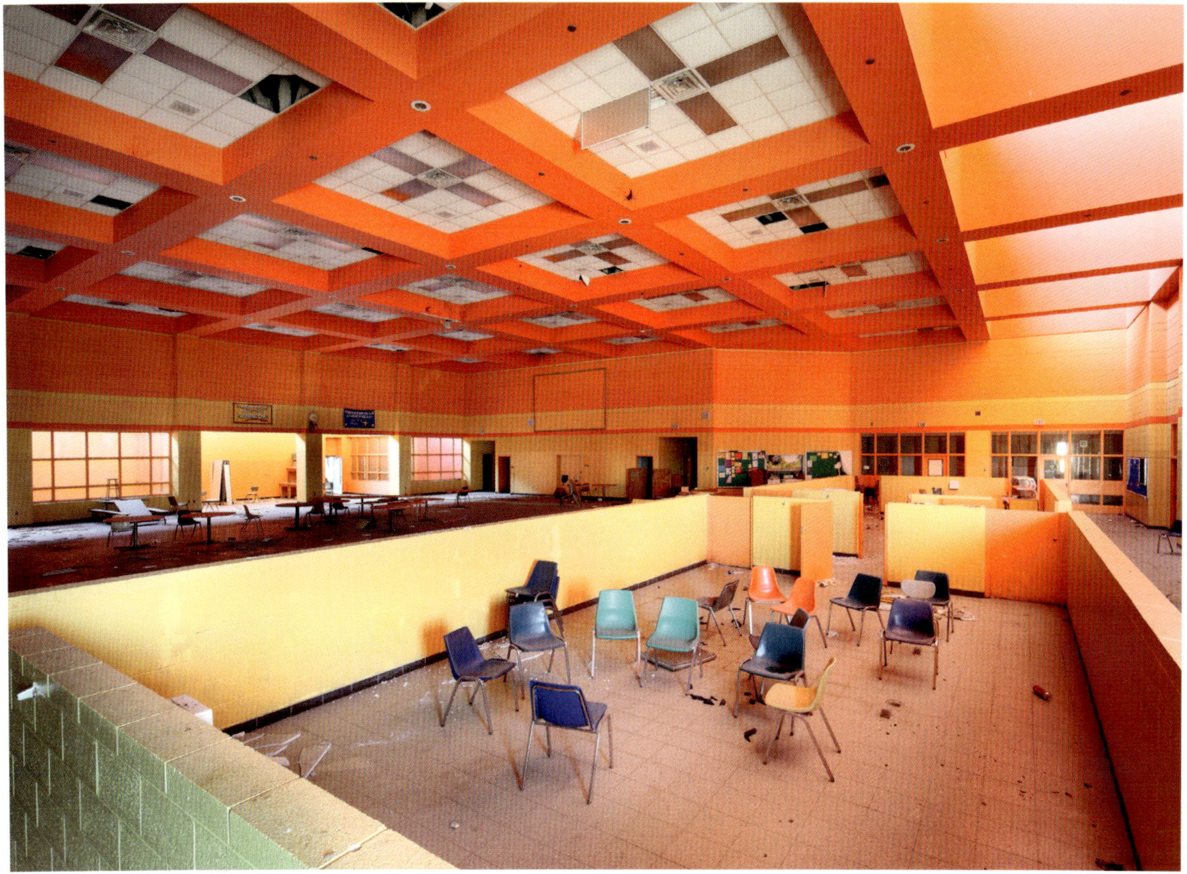

Cass Tech High School, Detroit, USA, 2010

St. David School, Detroit, 2015

 DDR Basketball - Krampnitz, Germany, 2013

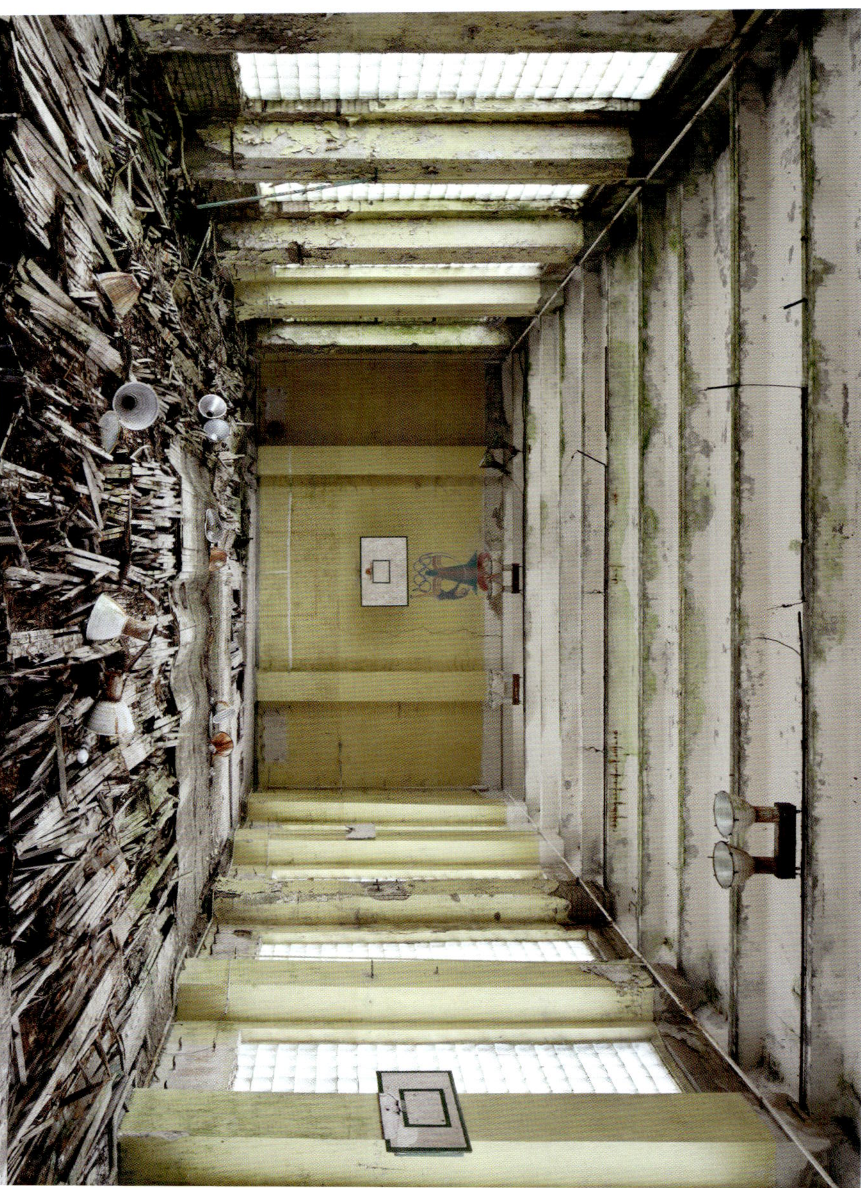

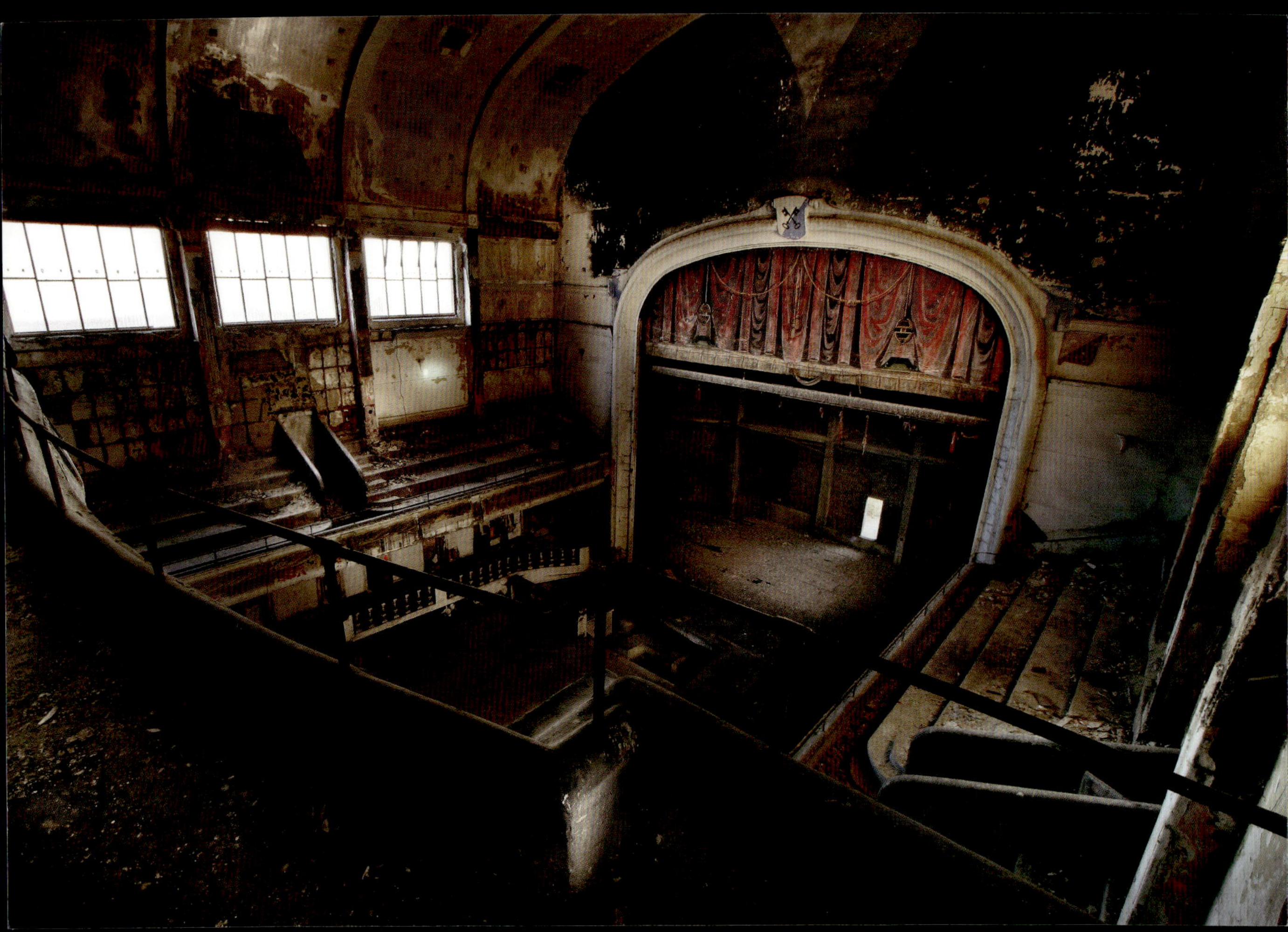

157 Cinevaria, Belgium, 2006

EPILOGUE

It is an enormous privilege to visit an abandoned building. Each time it feels like being invited. I come as a guest, with respect for these buildings that show their most sensitive side. Each has its story to tell. Some stories are short and concise, others long and hard to follow. But I never leave before hearing them. Occasionally, I have to search hard, but I always finally catch on. The silence says more than all the noise that was ever there.

Abandoned places touch a sensitive nerve. We are curious to know why these buildings were abandoned. Who lived there? What happened there? – the questions one asks when investigating a vanished civilization. My photos show our own forgotten civilization and what we have left behind. I observe our own crime scene. Not as a policeman but as a photographer. Not to establish the facts, but to reproduce the emotions of the moment. My photos, always detailed and seemingly objective, are open to interpretation and imagination. Ultimately, it is the spectator who rewrites the story of what took place: observation and imagination waken the buildings back to life.

What we see is often impressive, sometimes funny or endearing, recognizable or incomprehensible. Every visit is instructive, occasionally dangerous and always exciting! ◆

WWW.HENKVANRENSBERGEN.COM
WWW.ABANDONED-PLACES.COM

WWW.LANNOO.COM
Register on our website for our newsletter with new publications as well as exclusive offers.

TEXTS AND PHOTOGRAPHY:
Henk van Rensbergen

TRANSLATION: Bracha de Man
COPY-EDITING: Melanie Shapiro
BOOK DESIGN: Jelle Maréchal

If you have any questions or remarks, please contact our editorial team: redactiekunstenstijl@lannoo.com.

D/2016/45/98 – NUR 653
ISBN: 9789401434775